Stock Options Trading

For

Financial Freedom

In Just 3 Hours Per Week

Earn Weekly Income From The Low Risk,
High Profit Stock Market Options
Strategies That Really Work

MCNAE, MARLIN & MACKEN3IE
BOOK AND PERIODICAL PUBLISHERS
GLASGOW • NEW YORK • LOS ANGELES
QUEENS ROAD, GLASGOW, LANARKSHIRE G42 8OO SCOTLAND

Copyright © 2025 by McNae, Marlin and MacKenzie Publishers, Ltd., all rights reserved. Printed in the United States of America and in the United Kingdom. Let it be known that copyright shall be protected and defended against infringement by the Publisher.

Except as permitted by the United States Copyright Act of 1976, and the UK Copyright, Designs and Patents Act of 1988, no part of this publication may be reproduced, stored in a retrieval system or transmitted, in any form or by any means, electronic, mechanical, photocopying, recording, or otherwise without the prior written permission of the Author or the Publisher.
www.m3publishers.com

ISBN-979-8-89704-123-7

Front Cover Photo Art – Cottonbro Studio / Andrew Candelaria
Author Photo by Jordan Forbes

Third Printing 2025

Chapter on MoneyTreeVISIONS Copyright 2024 by Tommy Brown. References to VISIONS software is published with permission from Ronald Groenke.

Books by Brian Forbes

Entertainment Licensing and Merchandising
Stock Options Trading for Financial Freedom
Advanced Stock Options Trading for Financial Freedom
Stock Market Options Trading for Small Accounts
Investing and Income Strategies for The Entertainment Industry

Please contact the Author at forbesoptions@yahoo.com

www.highprobabilityoptions.com

If you give a man a fish, he will have a meal for a day.

If you teach him how to fish, he can learn to feed himself for life.

If you teach a man how to trade Options, he can have lobster tails with drawn butter sauce and caviar anytime and let someone else do the fishing.

Many years ago, I asked Producer, Director, Writer Rod Serling for some tips on crafting short fiction. He told me, "Learn how to fish." For a long time I thought he was using a metaphor and that his message was for me to learn some basic survival skills in the event writing didn't pan out. Turns out his daughter told me that he really meant it literally. He loved to fish and would spend the week in Hollywood dictating Twilight Zone scripts and then fly back for the weekends to his cabin on Lake Cayuga where he would take his dog and daughters and de-stress by fishing.

Coincidentally, I am writing this book in the very garage where Rod Serling set up his garage / office of the home he rented when he first came to Hollywood.

If you really want to fish, then it should be to relax on a lake or a river near a shaded forest – not because you have to for your next meal.

The opportunity for true financial freedom should be available to everyone. I wrote this book as a guide to an approach that has helped me, my family and friends for more than 35 years.

I confess the title of this book is misleading. The time I actually spend researching stocks and trading each week is less than 3 hours, usually less than 2. But if I had written 1 or 2 hours in the title it would have made this book seem much less credible.

There are no upsells here. I am not selling larger courses or subscriptions to stock tips that cost many hundreds or thousands of dollars. You need your money to build up your account and learn to make money on your own money. The main resources I talk about in this book may cost something, but with them the returns are well worth the cost. I also list many resources that cost little or nothing such as Youtube Videos that I've selected for you or other publications. In this book are all of the resources you need to become a successful trader of Stock Options and earn extra income over time, hopefully a short time.

The resources I introduce you to are not paying sponsors. They are longtime friends and fellow traders who have developed remarkable systems I have used myself and who like me, make themselves available personally to other traders to help them achieve their goals. I am truly honored to know them and recommend their products and services. When you start trading you have the opportunity to meet other traders and share information and techniques. Over time you'll become like extended family members and your trading can improve through trust. In this book you will meet a few of the people I trust and have built relationships with over years.

I wrote this with my heartfelt desire to help the many people in my life and the millions of people I don't know but would love to. There's no reason for anyone to be struggling financially.

I have made thousands of free copies of this book available to high school and college students, and to fellow workers in the entertainment industry who have been affected by the recent guild strikes.

My goal in writing this book is to teach the basics of Options Trading in a simple, really easy to understand language, using examples from everyday life. I want to present only those Options strategies that are low risk. If you use these strategies, you're not likely to lose money on the Options Trades themselves because all of them are protected by collateral, either with accompanying Stock Shares, or additional Protective Options. It is possible however, that stock prices may turn down or go up while you have these Options in play but no matter what happens, you'll still have your collateral, and you'll continue to be able to make money.

There is a trade off in writing this book because, while I want to present safe, profitable trading strategies, most require capital and many of the people reading this book have little savings or small accounts and need to build them up in order to make money with money in their account.

The fellow traders who I list as resources have alternative ways to build up small accounts. Both Ernie Zerenner and Tommy Brown can show you ways to keep risk at a minimum and still successfully build up a trading account. Ernie Varitimos has a system that, while it is a bit more complex, can be entered sometimes for as little as $20 or $30 a trade and possibly return 10 or more times that investment in a few hours in a single day.

I'm updating my book on Building Small Accounts, giving you the advice and guidance of 12 of the most experienced and successful Options Traders on their favorite methods of building up small accounts. I'm offering a number of free copies to those who sign up (free) on my website, which also has offers, updates, and helpful resources

www.highprobabilityoptions.com

How To Use This Book

Many people reading this book are hoping to learn to make money and become more financially independent in a relatively short period of time. Good News / Not-so-Good News: The not-so-good news is that successful trading takes time to learn. It can be a short time, that's up to you. But you need time enough to roll up your sleeves and get your hands dirty in the actual market trading. You can learn the basics from a book but it takes a little time in the field, in the trenches of the active Stock Market to learn where to place your trades (Strike Prices) and when, as well as which Stocks to pick and how to read all of the data that is affecting your Stock in the market. The sooner you get your account open and place a few trades, the faster you'll be proficient.

The Good News is that the strategies of trading Stock Options I have presented in this book are the easiest strategies to learn and the safest. I've also included a list of Youtube videos and other publications in the Additional Resources section at the very end of this book to help you come up to speed faster. AND in this book along with a good tutorial on trading Stock Options are the 3 really successful resources that I've found in my 35 years of trading Commodities and Stock Options that I already touched upon above. They are services run by fellow traders and personal friends that I hope you will consider making use of once you learn trading techniques. 2 of the 3 have trading picks either weekly or some daily and the 3rd trades the S&P 50 Index (SPX) daily on a Discord channel so you can communicate and trade live with other traders and exchange information with them.

You could put this book down right now and call them on the phone, tell them you're reading my book and you want a free trial on one of their advisory services. Assuming you've opened a trading account you could read their advisory and have a good chance of making a successful trade. They do have customers who just invest according to the information presented in the advisory information. It's a lot like the difference between driving your own car and calling an Uber or a Lyft. You can let somebody else do the driving and not even look out of the window, or you can drive a really nice sports convertible that you bought yourself after successfully learning Trading techniques and take it along the coast with your favorite music and the wind going through your hair. Your choice. My hope is that you'll want your own car and drive it with pleasure anywhere you want.

Ok, enough about fish and cars. You're reading this to learn about trading Stock Options and more importantly, how to make money and become more financially independent. For the most part, the low-risk, profitable strategies of Stock Options trading that I am presenting in this book are not going to necessarily rely on a thorough knowledge of all of the definitions and technical analysis that fill these almost 350 pages. BUT, the more you learn about all of the factors that affect Stock Options trading and the Stock Market as a whole the more your understanding will become second nature and help you to become a much more successful trader. By reading this book entirely, you'll also be better prepared to safely trade more advanced and more profitable strategies.

As always, I wish you much success and feel to drop me a line and let me know if you have any questions or concerns. I always enjoy meeting fellow traders.

Contents

Introduction	11
Disclaimer	20
Little Known Facts about the Stock Market	21
The Randomness of the Stock Market	43
What are Options?	51
The Options Contract	54
Time Value and Time Decay	59
The Meaning of Options Contracts	62
Volatility and Implied Volatility	67
Understanding Delta	76
ATM; OTM; ITM	82
Weekly or Monthly Options Contracts?	83
The Strike Price of Option	85
The Option Chain	93
Rolling an Option	103
Assignment	105
Options and Risk	113
Setting Up Your Trading Account	117
How Do You Buy or Sell an Option	119
How to use Scented and Unscented Candles	122
Support and Resistance	125
The Winning Strategies	129
The Covered Call	129
The Cash-Secured Put	141
The Wheel Strategy	145
The Married Put Collar	151
Protecting the Risks	156
Standard Deviation	159
The Expected Move	161
Technical Analysis	187
Moving Averages	190
Stochastics and RSI	201
Bollinger Bands	207
Fibonacci Retracements	211
Probability of Expiring Cones	220

TTM Squeeze Indicator	224
Advanced Option Spreads	227
Debit Spreads	230
Credit Spreads	237
The Iron Condor	241
Three Greatest Resources	247
1. MoneyTree Visions	249
2. PowerOptions	263
3. 0-DTE with the S&P 500	285
How to Avoid the Day Trading Rule for 0-DTE	305
Trading and Building Up Small Accounts	309
How To Find the Best Stocks to Trade	313
The Best S&P 500 Stocks to Trade	331
The Best S&P 500 Stocks for Small Accounts	333
A Final Word	339
Additional Resources	**340**

Introduction

Okay! I know what you're thinking and you're right. The Stock Market is not exciting, it's not fun, and it's not erotic, unless you consider Trading Naked (selling an Options Contract without collateral) or trading with your legs spread wide (the distance between two Options Contracts in a multi-contract strategy) or even that the first Stock Ticker Machine in 1867 was the first vibrator (it was bullet shaped and vibrated when the telegraph signals came through the wire).

That machine brought ecstatic pleasure to bankers and investors who were closed up in their offices all over the World, pulling the ticker tape out of the machine with sweaty palms, as their glassy eyes got wide. Yes, making money can be sexy and there is nothing like a surprising win in the Stock Market to make your eyes go white and curl your toes with pleasure.

My aim in writing this book is to show you how to have these wins. More importantly, my aim is to show you how to make money, by yourself independently in good economic times as well as bad economic times, whether the Stock Market is up, down or even staying steady in place. The techniques in this book can make money for you in any condition of the Stock Market or the economy.

With so much uncertainty in the World today who knows what economic opportunities are going to be available to young people coming out of universities and to those who are finding that their jobs are becoming more obsolete with growing technology, with increased competition, and with younger people replacing career professionals so corporations can save money and cut retirement.

Many people feel out of control in the midst of change and economic uncertainty feel lost and disillusioned and become subconsciously frozen with fear. Celebrated teacher and academic administrator Joesph Martinez has said that self-victimization is an epidemic in this country today and that self-empowerment starting at the elementary school level is vital for society to flourish.

Studies have found that trading in the Stock Market empowers individuals and also helps them learn to accept responsibility for their decisions.

The Stock Market is the perfect model of truly Free Enterprise. There are Exchanges and Brokers, but the Market itself is a gathering of buyers and sellers of securities (stocks, Options, index funds, etc.) and the process of transferring stocks is an auction.

Anytime you go to look at a stock chart you will see 3 prices listed. The Ask Price is what the current owner of the stock is asking for. Then next to it there is the Bid Price. This is the Bid Price that the buyers are trying to offer for the stock. Usually what you will see as a larger price is the Mark, or the Mid Point Price (between the Ask and the Bid Prices). This is the price that is a fair settlement price for the Stock. If you offer to buy the stock, you will put in your own Bid Price and hope that the

Seller accepts your Bid and your order fills. Throughout a normal trading day, the supply and demand for the stock will vary and this affects the price.

In this book I am presenting to you 5 basic, safe-to-trade Stock Options strategies that have extremely low risk. In fact, you probably aren't going to lose money on the Options themselves. Any loss you might have will be probably temporary and come from owning stock which might go down in value during your trade. Even if this happens, you still own the stock and most of the time your Stock will recover in a short time.

Stock Option trading came naturally to me as I hope it will to you. My actual profession for more than 45 years is Entertainment Marketing, Promotion, Merchandising and Licensing.

I was a student in the USC Business school when I started to intern at Paramount Studios in the late 70's. My interest was in Entertainment Marketing, Promotion and Publicity although it wasn't long before I added Merchandising and Licensing to my repertoire. At the time I started at Paramount, Gulf and Western was the conglomerate that owned Paramount along with other companies including Simon and Schuster Publishing, Catalina Swimwear, Bostonian Shoes and among others, Brach's Candies.

On the studio lot we used to call Gulf and Western, Engulf and Devour but I'll never forget meeting CEO Charlie Bluhdorn for the first time. He said that Paramount may be a single company housing motion picture, television and music entertainment, but unlike any other company in Gulf and Western, each motion picture produced, and each television show created were individual products that had to be marketed completely differently. Swimwear or shoes, or even auto parts, which is what Bluhdorn had started with all had solid well-planned marketing plans. Entertainment products were different. Each movie or TV Series had their own Producers and Directors, and each their own target market. Some would make money; some would lose money. But each entertainment project had to be marketed as a new and separate product.

I gained experience in treating each production as a new product and having to research everything behind it from cast and crew to the storyline and studying the target markets and promotional outlets for the best geographic distribution placement (which theaters to premiere and how long to book). This experience and mindset worked very well for both Commodities and the Stock Market as each of tens of thousands of stocks available each day are unique. Yes, you hear from time to time on the news that the stock markets have surged or that they've fallen. But each individual stock within the market as a whole has its own personality that you can see if you compare the charts.

I also found that my experience in negotiating licensing and merchandising agreements was not that different from the thought process and calculations of Commodity and Stock Options. Many of the variables are very similar.

While not romantic or outwardly as exciting as working in the entertainment industry, there are some real advantages to learning to trade Stock Options.

As long as you have a device and an Internet connection, you have a business of your own that you can operate anywhere in the World. When I'm travelling, I just take my phone and iPad, sometimes my laptop and I can complete or manage a trade wherever I go for as long as I like without worrying about whether I'll have a job when I come back.

Usually, trades don't take very much time to research and complete. I have the advantage of living on the West Coast so, while the Stock Market opens at 9:30am in New York, for me it's 6:30am and I usually complete my trades by 7:30 or 8:00am. And I'm not working on stocks during that time. Since a lot of activity happens over the weekend, I usually like to wait for 45 minutes to an hour after the market opens for the dust to settle and see where stock pricing is. Then I enter my trades in a matter of a few minutes and outside of a couple of quick check-ins during the week. I'm done until market close on Friday.

You don't need an office to trade Stock Options. Most of the time when I make my trades on Monday morning, I'm still in bed in my pajamas with my tablet. I was originally thinking of titling this book, How to Have Weekly Income Without Getting Out of Bed, but nobody would believe it, although it's true.

You don't have to have special education, formal training, a college degree or a license to buy and sell Stocks and Stock Options. Unlike other businesses there is no barrier to entry as long as you are old enough to open a trading account and have the minimum amount to deposit.

There are Global Stock Exchanges all over the World. If you are not trading on the U.S. Stock Exchanges there are European Markets, Asian Markets, etc.

You can trade Stocks by yourself, so you don't have an employer or a company overseeing you. The time you spend is your own. You set your schedule and make your own time commitment. And you don't have to be popular.

because if you are trading Stock Options you don't have to be popular, or brilliant, or ambitious. You can truly be yourself and with some patience and tenacity, you can succeed.

I wrote earlier that you can become financially independent, but others can help you. One big secret of your success in the is the Community that you will have the opportunity to become a part of. When I started trading I met other traders and you start to share information. Veteran traders are more than happy to help each other because Stock Trading is not competitive. There are plenty of opportunities for everybody to share and make money, so nobody guards secrets.

Many of the Traders you meet may become friends as well. I've made a lot of friends in the trading community and we not only share trading advice and information, but we talk about our pets, our children we share vacation experiences, recipes, etc. I believe that not only in the trading community, but in every aspect of life, being part of community is often an enormous but often overlooked factor in success.

Chuck Collins, author of *Born on Third Base* wrote, "If we don't see the "commonwealth" or commons, that is the primary source of wealth and well-being, then we succumb to the myth that wealth is entirely the result of individual actions."

In this book I introduce you to 3 of many such close friends I've met through trading. You'll meet 2 Ernie's and a Tommy. I included them here because for the goal of this book, I trust them. Their methods of trading I know will be best to help you get started and become successful. And as importantly, they are accessible and love to help people like you find success in trading.

I grew up in suburban Detroit. My dad was a mob attorney who handled business affairs for among others, Jimmy Hoffa and his brother Bill. On Friday nights it was normal to see Tony Giacalone and members of his family when we went to have dinner with my grandparents. To me these were all normal people and they were a normal part of my life growing up.

Ultimately though it was a Cosa Nostra enforcer who taught me two of the most important life lessons which were hard lessons to learn but they're in every part of my life.

"Know what you know, but also know what you don't know" he told me. "Know what you're good at and be honest with yourself about what you're no good at". You leave that to somebody else" Then he pulled out a deck of cards and taught me an even bigger life lesson.

"When a deal isn't going your way, get out. Cut your losses. Come back again another day even stronger." He shuffled and asked me to cut the deck. Then he taught me how to play Gin Rummy. Gin Rummy was the most popular card game in the U.S. through most of the 20th century until Poker became more popular in the 1980's.

"You get good at this game," he said, "and you're going to do ok. Because like life, this game is not about winning. It's about surviving. It's about knowing when to stop a hand and take a few points. And you keep doing that. And you keep building up the few points you get." He looked down at the table as he finished dealing the cards.

"The longer you stay in the game the more open you are to get taken down by somebody else. Remember, there's always somebody else. Always some wise guy out there. So we're not just talking cards here. right?" He looked at me and I nodded. And we played Gin and he kicked my ass over and over again until I got better at knocking (finishing a hand early and trying to take points). I didn't Gin very often (a perfect hand) but I managed at least to keep him from winning. The longer you are in the game the greater the chance of an opponent stopping the game and grabbing your points.

Then later I was living in Beachwood Canyon in the Hollywood Hills underneath the Hollywood Sign, and my next-door neighbor by coincidence was also one of my favorite character actors, Eddie Jones. Eddie was from New York and played cards for serious money, both Poker and Gin.

Unfortunately for him he was an insomniac and we had an arrangement. If he couldn't sleep he would put his back porch light on, and if I was up (and I frequently was a late-night worker) I would come next door and we would play some hands of Gin, and only Gin because I was never bright enough to remember the rules of Poker. But as we played hand after hand, the lessons I had learned from the Enforcer kept coming to mind and they seemed to always fit whatever business or personal situation I was dealing with at the time.

Eddie Jones, Actor, Card-Player.

It's better to close out your trade when you have some profit than wait for a possible reversal of the stock price against you. If you are buying an Option and you have some profit halfway through your Contract toward expiration, consider closing out and selling your Contract back. You can always open a new one right away. If you are selling an Option Contract and the underlying Stock Price is moving against you, coming too close to your Strike Price, you might consider buying your contract back, or rolling it out, up or down, taking your small loss and go out and sell another contract.

So why this book? Back in the Summer of 2020 we were well into the COVID Pandemic and my then teenage daughters had previous hopes of getting Summer jobs. Well, that didn't happen, and while I was still moderately busy with licensing work, I didn't know how long this stay-at-home situation was going to last. I was doing my Stock Option trading on the side anyway although I did a lot more of it during the Pandemic.

But one day one of my daughters asked me what the stock chart was that was on screen of my laptop. As I started to explain the activity I realized that this could be a great way for my daughters to have some of their own income over the Summer as well as learn a skill that could help them if they needed to work during college or even after. Trading Stock Options is a great skill for young people in school.

The hard part was trying to explain Stock and Stock Option concepts in a language and with examples that they could understand. But I was able to do it. Soon their friends were asking questions about trading and then parents of my daughters' friends were asking and I realized that I had a great opportunity to help others with my knowledge and experience. So, I put this book together.

Then the motion picture industry strikes paralyzed the industry and I could see friends and coworkers struggling as productions shut down. I happily agreed to get free copies of the book to members of the movie and TV industries who were affected by the strikes.

Now I have revised this guide again. My honest and true ambitions have always been to proudly represent and promote things I enjoy and want others to have a chance to experience and enjoy. I've been lucky to have been a part of such a creative industry,

DISCLAIMER

Important notice

There is a risk of loss in trading stocks and stock Options and therefore it is not suitable for all investors. Past performance is not necessarily indicative of future results. Brian Forbes, the author is only providing educational services in this publication. Any materials contained herein are for informational purposes only and represent the opinions of the author and other contributors. Nothing contained herein shall be construed as a solicitation to buy or an offer to sell any securities or other investments. Any investment is inherently, risky, and not suitable for all persons. The author of this book and the publisher of this book are not registered in any capacity and does not provide investment advice, nor does the author recommend the purchase or sale of any investment.

Margin disclosure statement

The author is furnishing this document to you to provide some basic facts about purchasing securities on margin, and to alert you to the risks involved with trading securities in a margin account. Before trading stocks and stock Options in a margin account, you should carefully review the margin agreement provided by your brokerage firm. Consult your firm regarding any questions or concerns you may have with your margin accounts. When you purchase securities you may pay for the securities in full. or you may borrow part of the purchase price from your brokerage firm. If you choose to borrow funds from your brokerage firm, you will open a margin account with them. The securities purchased are the firm's collateral for the loan to you.

The author does not, will not and can not guarantee any specific outcome or profit. All traders and investors must be aware of the real risk of loss in following any strategy or investment discussed in this publication. The author does not know, nor can they take into account the particular investment objectives, financial situation or needs of any trader or investor using any investment strategy. None of the investment strategies presented in this book are ever intended as recommendations appropriate for any single investor. All investors must make independent decisions regarding investments or strategies mentioned in this book and should seek independent financial advice from a qualified individual or institution specializing in financial advice and knowledgeable about securities trading.

Little Known Facts About The Stock Market

The Stock Market got its name from the fish and meat market in London in the 14th century. The original stock market was also the site where stocks were placed, as in the punishment devices used for crimes. Later when a mansion was built it was the site of the beginning of the securities exchange.

But the real beginnings of the stock market go all the way back to the 1600's in Amsterdam. Back then in The New World, trading by the Dutch East India Company was big business and sending bigger ships for growing world trade required increasing amounts of capital. The company started allowing businessmen in Amsterdam to invest in individual voyages at first. Successful voyages would bring investors a nice profit, but not all voyages produced the same income from trade. Needing more and more capital, the Dutch East India Company started to sell shares in the company itself, allowing investors to share in profits of all voyages for as long as they held the paper shares, which they could trade or sell. The news of equity share investment spread throughout Spain, Portugal and eventually London.

By the late 1600's in London, shares of company stock were traded in coffee houses, where merchants, business owners, venture capitalists and ship owners would meet to trade. One such coffee house was owned by Edward Lloyd. Besides stock trading, merchants would find venture capitalists to fund shipping voyages to the Americas. The venture capitalists would find people who wanted to be colonists in the New World and they would provide provisions for the trips. In exchange, the colonists would send back goods from America. At first the venture capitalists were eager to finance these trips because they thought there was gold and precious metals on American land. Even though they weren't able to find much of the metals, they discovered the American soils were rich to grow tobacco, which was a very valuable commodity at the time.

Edward Lloyd wanted to get in on the action of the trades and started to underwrite (insure) the shipping voyages against weather related damage to the ships, spoilage of the goods on board and of course piracy. Many of the venture capitalists were also interested in underwriting the voyages. Insuring and underwriting these ventures became so popular that Edward Lloyd started his company, Lloyd's of London within his coffee house. Both commodity and equity investing as well as underwriting and insuring became big businesses.

This history helps to understand the counter-intuitive nature of Options buying and selling strategies by knowing how your deals parallel history.

If you are buying Options, you are following the steps of venture capitalists who financed the voyages for trade in the New World. And if you are selling Options you are taking on the role of the insurance underwriters of those same voyages.

You are buying Options in the hope that the underlying stock will go in your desired direction (up or down) and go further past your strike price for a profit.

You are selling Options as an insurance premium against the underlying stock moving toward your Strike Price.

In America in 1624 the Dutch had founded New Amsterdam, which is now known as New York. They constructed a large cement blockade wall from what is now Broadway, all the way to the East River. Today this is known as Wall Street which was the birth of the financial markets in the US. In 1792 24 stock brokers came together during the first financial panic of the new United States and formed the Buttonwood Agreement to serve as guidelines and regulation to ensure public confidence in the financial markets. The Buttonwood Agreement marked the actual beginnings of the New York Stock Exchange, although the New York Stock Exchange formally opened in 1817.

A New York Stock Exchange Floor Trader on Break

What most people don't realize is that when you buy a stock of a company, you are not buying it directly from the company itself. The Stock Exchange is an auction. When you look at the latest price of a stock, you are seeing what the stock is selling for on the open stock market based on a compromise between the Bid price (what the stock buyer is offering for the stock) and the Ask price (what the seller is hoping to sell for). The stock usually closes at a midpoint between the two.

Whenever you go through your platform or broker to buy a stock you may put in the price you are hoping to pay. Your order may or may not fill at the bid price you are offering, but the closer you get to the midpoint between the Bid and the Ask, the better your chances of owning the stock.

The two major Stock Exchanges in the U.S. are the NYSE (New York Stock Exchange, and the NASDAQ Stock Exchange (short for the National Association of Securities Dealers Automated Quotations) which was started in 1971 as the first Electronic Stock Market giving electronic quotations and in 1998 became the first Online Stock Exchange.

In 1860 Henry Varnum Poor, a financial statistician published a book called, *History of Railroads and Canals in the United States*, which listed the financial and operational status of the railroad companies. In 1906 the Standard Statistics Bureau was formed which published financial information on non-railroad companies and in addition created a Stock Index tracking 233 companies weekly. In 1941 the Standard Statistics Bureau merged with Poor's Publishing and became Standard and Poor's Publishing. The S&P became the benchmark of company financial information and credit ratings and in 1957 the S&P 500 appeared which was an Index of the top 500 publicly traded companies.

Meanwhile in the same multiverse in 1896, Charles Dow the founder of The Wall Street Journal started a Stock Index called the Dow Industrial Average which weighed 30 large publicly traded companies. By 2011

Today we take for granted the up-to-the-minute stock exchange information that we get at a second's notice through our devices. But there was a time when stock market information was not as quick to be delivered. Before the 1860's those investors who could have an office closest to the stock exchange had a clear advantage to buy and sell stocks. There were information errand boys who would take the latest stock information and run to deliver it down the street to various offices. The closer you were to the exchange the faster you had your information, the more accurate and up to date it was, and the faster your order could be placed.

It all changed in 1867 when Edward A. Calahan, an employee of the American Telegraph Company invented his Stock Ticker Device. This was a machine that could receive stock information from the stock exchange transmitted along telegraph wires to these devices anywhere. The signals were converted and printed out on a long spool of ticker tape, to be read. At first the information was sent as Morse code as in any communications of the day. Then in 1869 Thomas Edison improved on the Stock Ticker by using alpha-numeric symbols in place of the Morse code. This was the first time that financial information could be sent near real time as the actual stock prices changed.

Investopedia

The original information that was printed on the Ticker Tape was the Company's Symbol (the shortened name of the company as it appears on the Stock Exchange) and the Volume of Shares being traded during the session, as well as the price of the stock and an arrow showing whether the price is up or down from the previous closing price and the percentage of change.

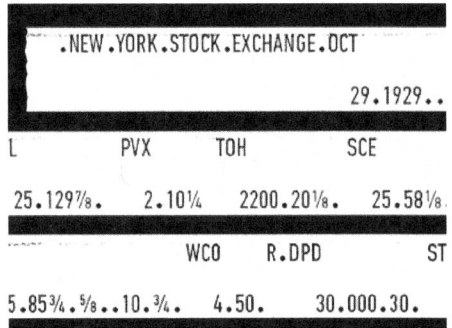 

Women at the Waldorf Astoria Posting Ticker Information.

For more than 100 years traders used Volume of shares as the major indicator of where the concentration of price action in the Stock Market was. Although there are a number of major indicators and technical analysis methods, most institutional traders and many veteran retail traders still prefer to rely on Volume Profile, an enhancement of the same simple information that was valuable to traders through ticker tapes for the last 150 years. Volume Profile today shows the Volume of stocks sold at various price levels. Stock price tends to then move toward the heaviest Volume Levels. But this is covered in my section on 0-DTE later in this book

There are 60 global Stock Exchanges and in the U.S. alone there are over 10,000 different listed stocks available through the New York Stock Exchange (NYSE), the National Association of Securities Dealers Automated Quotations

(NASDAQ) and Over the Counter stocks (OTC), not including Indexes, Futures, ETF's and other traded securities.

Over the Counter Stocks (OTC) are often smaller companies that want to sell stock but can't meet the often-expensive requirements of being a listed stock through the major exchanges like the Newy York Stock Exchange or the NASDAQ. They are still regulated by the Securities Exchange Commission (SEC) but because they are smaller, there tends to be lower volume and higher volatility.

You might think that the U.S. leads with the number of securities investors, but according to Michael Chaudhuri with Techno Sales analysts in Calcutta, India for example has over 160 million investors between their two largest Stock Exchanges, The Bombay Stock Exchange and the National Stock Exchange.

Market Sectors

Stocks are often organized by Market Sector

Stocks that are similar are organized by Market Sectors. There are 11 main Sectors

1. Energy
2. Materials
3. Industrials
4. Utilities
5. Healthcare
6. Financials
7. Consumer Discretionary
8. Consumer Staples
9. Information Technology
10. Communication Services
11. Real Estate

Knowing which Sector a stock is in helps in research because sometimes if a stock suddenly drops in value or gains in value the movement may be related to an event to another company in the same Sector. Sometimes an entire Market Sector can be experiencing gains or losses depending on economic or political factors. Many traders will try to diversify their stocks and Options to lower overall risk.

What is a Market Index?

An Index is a numeric score that measures the performance of a basket of stocks. Some of the major indices include the S&P 500; The Dow Jones Industrial Average; the NYSE Composite, and the NASDAQ Composite.

The S&P 500 are the 500 top public companies by Market Capitalization. So, the S&P 500 index measures the overall performance of stocks within the basket.

The Dow Jones Industrial Average is an Index of 30 large public corporations.

The NYSE Composite is an Index of 20 Blue Chip Stocks that trade on the New York Stock Exchange.

The NASDAQ Composite is an index of almost all of the stocks traded on the NASDAQ Stock Exchange. The Information Technology Sector carries most of the weight of the index. The NADAQ 100 includes the top 100 non-financial companies on the exchange and accounts for about 80% of the index weighting of the Composite.

You can trade an Index in the Stock Market but you can't actually buy or sell a share since an Index is really just a measurement based on underlying stocks. If you trade the actual S&P 500 Index (SPX) it can be expensive. As of today the SPX is trading at $5,997.00. But there are ways to trade the

S&P 500 Index. One very affordable way is with Options on either the Index itself (SPX), and the other is through the ETF (Exchange Traded Fund) with SPDR S&P 500 ETF Trust (SPY)

Mutual Funds

A Mutual Fund pools investors' monies to create a managed portfolio of diversified stocks and bonds and other securities that are managed by money managers. The largest Mutual Funds invest in S&P 500 and other Indexed stocks. Because these Funds are professionally managed and widely diversified, they tend to provide lower risk and consistent profits.

ETF's (Exchange Traded Funds)

ETF's are similar to Mutual Funds in that they are a basket of stocks creating a single Fund. But ETF's don't have professional management for the Fund and like stocks, an ETF can be traded just like an individual share of stock and throughout the day. The first Exchange Traded Fund was the SPDR S&P 500 ETF Trust (SPY) which tracks the S&P 500 Index. But there are many ETF's which cover stocks in specific sectors or even commodities. For example if you want to avoid stock market uncertainties and invest in Gold without having to buy actual Gold Bullion, there are 4 Gold Exchange Traded Funds. The best performer of these this last year with over 30% return was FGDL (Franklin Responsibly Sourced Gold ETF). But other specialty ETF's include stocks in healthcare; home construction; renewable energy, etc.

Bonds and Bond Yields

The U.S. Government is loaned money through the sales of Treasury Bonds. Treasury Bonds are a much safer investment than the Stock Market because they are backed by the U.S. Government. But often Investors can make more money in the

Stock Market. When Stock Prices fall investors sell their stocks during an economic downturn and buy the much safer Treasury Bonds instead. When there is growth in the economy and Investors want better money making opportunities, they sell Bonds and buy Stock in the Stock market in the hopes of higher profits.

The Bond market is generally inverse to the Stock Market, meaning that when Bond Prices move up and Bond Yields come down, it means the Stock Market is moving down and selling off stocks to buy Bonds as a more secure investment. When Bond Prices come down and the Bond Yields move up, the Stock market is moving up and investors are buying stocks in the Stock Market. Watching the daily Bond Prices and Bond Yields on the U.S Treasury Bonds can give you a good indication of what is happening in the Stock market.

Should You be Trading Your Favorite Company?

There are really two questions here. The first is, are the companies you are interested in publicly traded companies so that you can buy stock and Options?

The second is, should you be trading your favorite companies or is it better to trade stocks in high performing companies that you may be less familiar with?

Once a company has its IPO (Initial Public Offering) of stock there is a set number of shares released at an agreed upon initial price for sale per share. From here the market itself determines the value of the stock from day to day depending upon public investor demand.

A good example might be Rivian Motors. I was on my trading platform the moment that Rivian stock was offered for sale on November 10, 2021, but I didn't purchase stock immediately. The stock was introduced at $78.00 per share but quickly dropped. I purchased 100 shares of Rivian for $38.00 per share. I always purchase stock in 100 share blocks so that I can make money selling Options using the stock as collateral.

Although the stock is currently selling for $14.00 per share, I have more than made up for any losses on the stock price by consistently selling stock Options on Rivian over the past several years. I've sold various types of Vertical Credit Spreads; Iron Condors; Calendar Spreads, and of course Covered Calls. The Option premiums I have received from Rivian have made it a profitable stock for me. And this is what I hope to teach you to be able to do in this book.

Over the years there have been successful public companies that are looking for more capital than their initial stock sales brought. In these cases, a company can split its stock over time. For example the Coca Cola Company (K NYSE) has split its stock more than a dozen times since it went public in 1919 and Apple (AAPL NASDAQ) has more than five times. When a stock splits, as an investor you receive more shares, but the total value remains the same to start. In other words, If you own 100 shares of Apple at $100.00 per share and there is a 2 to 1 stock split, you now own 200 shares of Apple with a value of $50.00 pr share. A company doesn't have to do a 2 to 1 split.

Recently Chipotle Mexican Grill (CMG NYSE) offered a 50 to 1 stock split. So, if you had 100 shares of Chipotle at $100.00 per share, you would have 5,000 shares at $2.00 per share after the split. The purpose of splits is to make stock that is popular more available to a wider range of investors in the hope that the new shares will increase in value as capitalization increases and make the stock more attractive to investors.

Companies may be privately held or publicly traded. A privately held company is usually owned entirely by an individual, partners or even family members. There may not even be shares issued, but ownership is private and therefore so are financial records and most company information. There aren't the same types of strong regulations and scrutiny about what the company does and its financial information. And most importantly, a privately held company has total control of its business decisions. They don't have to take the direction or advice of their investors.

A publicly held company is owned by investors such as yourself who buy stock. Because publicly traded companies are under tremendous scrutiny of the government, all financial information as well as company information becomes public knowledge. There are very stiff regulations for a privately held company to become a publicly traded company and they have to adhere to these.

Often Family Companies Want to Stay Privately Held

Some companies want to be privately held and stay within ownership of partners and perhaps family members. A good example is the Bissell Floorcare Products Company.

In 1876 Melville Bissell and his wife Anna had a crockery shop in Grand Rapids, Michigan. They were tired of trying to clean sawdust and particles from the carpets in their shop and so Melville designed, invented and patented a one-of-a-kind carpet sweeper.

People coming into the shop were more interested in the carpet sweeper than the crockery, and so their business in floorcare products began. In 1889 Melville passed away and Anna became the first female CEO in the United States. The Bissell carpet sweeper became so popular that England's Queen Victoria insisted on having them in her palaces.

Today, generations later, the Bissell Floorcare Company is still located in Grand Rapids, Michigan and is owned by family members as a privately held company

Sometimes Privately Held Companies Have Proprietary Information

And then there is the case of Badalament Bananas. While you may not have heard of Badalament Bananas they were a formidable competitor to Chiquita, Dole and Del Monte, but they were privately held since 1903.

According to Thomas Badalament, the design and idea of a sticker on fruit and specifically bananas started with Badalament. Long after Badalament Bananas had their label, Chiquita came to Badalament in the early 1960's and asked if they'd mind if Chiquita slapped a label on their fruit as well. All other companies followed suit.

But what made Badalament Bananas such a special and formidable company was their outstanding service and their willingness to design solutions for their customers, some of the largest grocery chains in the country. This included the development of mobile ripening facilities designed to replace the large footprint, expensive fruit ripening rooms used by other fruit distributors. Badalament had designed and patented a unique air flow system to be used in reefer truck trailers that took the heat away from the fruit as they lay in trays and aerated them more evenly to help them ripen more quickly and efficiently. At one point, in addition to their hundreds of transport trailers, they had over 500 of the mobile ripening reefers in use for fruit distributors.

The design and construction of the ripening systems were proprietary and patented. Keeping the company privately held could have been a better way to keep the competitive edge.

Going Public Doesn't Always Mean a Company has to Reveal Proprietary Information

Most of the time, when a company goes public, they are giving up rights to private information about the company and its products and services. A good example is the Coca-Cola Company (K NYSE).

In 1886 a pharmacist in Atlanta, GA named John Stith Pemberton was intending to market a temperance drink and a patent medicine. He had injuries sustained during the Civil War and wanted to create a medicine that would help his chronic pain. Since cocaine was legal back then, he wanted to create a tonic with cocaine from the extract of coca leaves and caffeine from the kola nut. He created a cola flavored syrup and took a jug of it to the local Jacobs' Pharmacy to try. The first glass was mixed with soda water, and the proprietors loved it. They sold the cola as a refreshing soda fountain drink for 5 cents a glass. The first-year sales averaged 9 glasses a day. Pemberton's partner and bookkeeper, Frank M. Robinson suggested more advertising, and came up with the name

Coca Cola from two of the drink's main ingredients from the coca leaves and the Kola nuts. Robinson created ads with the name written in his fancy handwriting.

The success of the drink grew, but Permberton became ill and just before he died in 1888, he sold rights to an entrepreneur named Asa G. Candler who then incorporated Coca Cola in 1892. Candler was a master at both marketing and sales and distribution. By 1900 Coca Cola was available in pharmacies and soda fountains in every state in America.

In 1899 two lawyers from Chattanooga, TN approached Candler about bottling Coca Cola, thus taking the drink outside of the four walls of soda fountains. A contract was signed and by 1920 over 1,200 Coca Cola bottling franchises were active throughout the United States.

By the time Candler took over Coca Cola, cocaine was being outlawed without a prescription and so additional sugar and caffeine were introduced to replace the small amount of cocaine.

The wide distribution network Candler set up and the bottling franchises helped catapult Coca Cola to become an international brand quickly throughout the 20th Century. But back in 1919 Asa G. Candler couldn't have predicted the success of Coca Cola well into the 21st Century and there were a lot of competitors producing copy-cat products and even using similar names and script for their bottles and advertising. In 1915 Candler had bids put out for a new bottle design in attempts to differentiate the original Coca Cola from copy-cat competitors and the Root Glass Company of Terre Haute, Indiana submitted samples of what is now the distinctive, curved and ribbed Coke bottle. The design was sketched by Earl Dean of the Root Company to look like the ribbed, elongated shape of the cocoa bean. Design patents were filed which protected the distinctive bottle for a number of years, but ultimately the patent ran out. The Coca Cola Company petitioned the U.S. Patent and Trademark Office to allow the bottle design to be officially trademarked which would provide continued legal protection. The trademark was ultimately granted.

In 1919 Candler decided to sell Coca Cola to a businessman named Ernest Woodruff for $25 Million who took the company public that same year. In its initial public offering on the New York Stock Exchange, a share of Coca Cola sold for $40.00. Today the market capitalization of Coca Cola is well over $180 Billion, and a single share purchased in 1919 (with dividends reinvested) would be worth more than $12,748,802.

If Coca Cola is a publicly traded company, then why isn't the secret formula available to the public? Just because a company goes public, it doesn't mean that they can't keep some proprietary information from investors. If you buy a share of Coca-Cola, it doesn't give you the right as an investor to get your hands on the secret formula for the cola drink.

But in this day and age with high technology any food chemist can crack the secret formula of Coca Cola, and in fact it has been done. Even if you were able to get all of the ingredients and proportions to make Coca Cola it would be virtually impossible for you to compete with the well-established, wide distribution and marketing network Coke has. Additionally, there is only one plant that has been issued a permit from the DEA to process decocainized essence from the coca leaf and they aren't going to sell it to you.

Here is the original formula for Coca Cola –

- Citrate Caffeine, 1 oz.
- Ext. Vanilla, 1 oz.
- Flavoring, 2.5 oz.
- F.E. (Fluid Extract) Coca, 4 oz.
- Citric Acid, 3 oz.
- Lime Juice, 1 Qt.
- Sugar, 30 lbs.
- Water, 2.5 Gal.
- Caramel sufficient

Mix Caffeine Acid and Lime Juice in 1 Qt Boiling water add vanilla and flavoring when cool.

- <u>Flavoring</u>
    - Oil Orange, 80
    - Oil Lemon, 120
    - Oil Nutmeg, 40
    - Oil Cinnamon, 40
    - Oil Coriander, 40
    - Oil Neroli, 40
    - Alcohol, 1 Qt.

Let stand 24 hours.

When Ernest Woodruff decided to take Coca Cola public in 1919 he did it to help finance the growth of distribution networks and worldwide marketing. He wasn't concerned about investors interfering with the expansion of the product.

Disney Never Wanted to go Public

There are cases where a company will go public out of necessity of survival, not because the owners want to. Such is the case of Walt Disney.

In 1921 Walt Disney and Ub Iwerks in Kansas City, MO formed the Laugh-O-Gram Cartoon Studio making cartoons for the new animation industry. Film was in its infancy and although there were silent feature movies being produced at the newly created studios in New York and Hollywood, animation could easily be done with little equipment almost anywhere. Although their cartoons were reasonably successful in Kansas City, it wasn't enough to keep their studio afloat. In 1923 Walt closed their carton studio in Kansas City and moved to Los Angeles to join his brother Roy who was out west recovering from Tuberculosis.

Disney and Iwerks had made a short, animated pilot cartoon called Alice back in Kansas City and in 1923 brought it with them to Los Angeles where they were able to sell it to a distributor. They opened a small shop called The Disney Brothers Cartoon Studio. Soon friend and animator artist Ub Iwerks followed them to Los Angeles and joined their small company. Through a producer they were able to get a contract with Universal to produce cartoons with the character Oswald the Rabbit.

At the time Walt and Roy didn't know a lot about rights and their distributor / producer went behind their backs and even hired some of their animators away from Disney to get a bigger cut from Universal. Then to make matters worse, the Disneys found out that they didn't own the rights to Oswald the Rabbit. Instead of giving up, and with the help of their friend Ub Iwerks, Walt and Roy created a new character called Mickey the Mouse. Their first released pilot of Mickey in 1928 was set with synchronized sound called Steamboat Willie. The cartoon was so successful the brothers moved to a larger workshop and the Disneys were able to secure contracts with other studios. The Disney Brothers Cartoon Studio became the Walt Disney Studio.

In 1930 a man in New York offered Walt $300 for the rights to put Mickey Mouse on writing tablets and thus Disney's merchandising (and all character merchandising) was born. At the same time, an advertising executive named Herman Kamen, also from Kansas City, MO contacted the Disneys with a proposal to take over and develop their merchandising. Within two years Kamen had more than $35 million in merchandising revenue which greatly surpassed the revenue made from the cartoons. One of the most successful merchandized items, the Mickey Mouse wrist watch sold so many that it saved the company from bankruptcy during the years of the great depression.

With the merchandising money and revenue from the cartoons Walt decided to make the first feature length animated feature in 1937. Snow White took three years to produce and although its original budget was $150,000 it went more than 10 times over budget, costing $1.5 million. He borrowed extensively to build his new studio in Burbank and to hire animators and crew to produce the film. Although the film was a major but unexpected success, Disney was finding it difficult to pay his debts particularly to Bank of America and was facing the loss of his Studios. It was Roy who convinced Walt to take the company public and issue stock over the counter to raise money to continue their success.

One day Walt was taking his daughters to Griffith Park to ride the carousel and had an idea to create an amusement park where both parents and children could have fun together. At first he was going to build his Disneyland on 3.2 acres in Burbank near his own studios, but soon realized that he would need much more land to realize his dream and he formed the

WED Enterprises (now Walt Disney Imagineering) company to design and build Disneyland and bought 160 acres of orange groves in Anaheim, CA. To help realize his dream of the Disneyland Park, Walt and Roy hired concept artists; architects, and engineers. Kenneth Strickfaden who had designed and built all of the electrical effects machinery for the Universal Frankenstein movie sets was hired to coordinate the sound with the movements of a duck puppet and created the first audio-animatronics figure.

At the same time television was in its infancy and he wanted to take advantage by producing television series content through yet another Disney company.

Walt and Roy combined all of the Walt Disney related enterprises and did an initial public offering of stock on the New York Stock Exchange in 1957 as Walt Disney Productions at $13.88 per share. The stock is currently trading at $141.00 per share, but, if you had invested $1,000 in 1957 in Disney stock that would have been about 70 shares. The stock has split eight times since then, so you would now have more than 28,000 shares at a value of over $3.9 million not including a hefty sum of cash dividends.

While Walt always preferred to keep his business enterprises privately held, the financing offered by having public investors has provided enough capital over the years to help make Disney the most powerful media company in the world today.

The Randomness of the Stock Market

Being exposed to the stock market is a lot like watching a dark, classic film noir like Laura, *Double Indemnity*, *The Maltese Falcon* or *Witness for the Prosecution*. Its personality is erratic and you never know when you wake up in the morning which way market sentiment will go, or for how long. One day a jobs report comes in and there is conflicting data, leading the market to have doubts about future interest rate cuts by the Federal Reserve. The markets plunge and the media reports the worst day in so and so days or so and so months, and the prospect is of nothing but darkness ahead and doom and gloom. Then literally two trading days later for no apparent reason, maybe a corporate deal going through, or some individual media analyst speculating on a successful outlook in a sector, or another economic report comes in signaling better news from the Federal Reserve and the bond rate goes down, so the stock market is suddenly soaring.

This is what the market is like day after day, week in and week out. The trick is not to get too emotionally involved. The stock market seems almost completely irrational, but you don't have to be. Make a plan and stick to it. Remember that the markets are super sensitive and react disproportionately but usually these reactions are temporary. One minute a company misses earnings expectations and their stock sinks. The next day a corporate executive on Wall Street announces that his toddler is finally potty trained and stocks surge.

Several years ago, then Federal Reserve Chairman Alan Greenspan was speaking at an economic society dinner. He used to write his speeches while sitting in the bathtub smoking a cigar. He came up with a term "Irrational Exuberance" referring to the possibility of over-inflated equity prices and though his words were not meant to be anything serious or prophetic, his speech was televised. During the speech the Tokyo stock market opened and as a result of his mention of "Irrational Exuberance" the Tokyo stock market crashed, followed by the crash of markets worldwide.

There is a lesson to be learned from Alan Greenspan. Out of High School Greenspan was a saxophone and clarinet player. He then studied music at one of the most renowned schools of music, Julliard. He played with the Henry Jerome band and then played with jazz great Stan Getz. Somehow in the two years he studied at Juilliard he decided that music wasn't going to be his calling and so he changed his educational focus to economics. Another fellow student Larry Harmon played with the Woody Herman Band while Greenspan was playing with Henry Jerome. But the two knew each other. Eventually Alan Greenspan had become a famous economist and Leonard Garment had gone to law school and became personal counsel to President Nixon. On day Nixon, who was a very talented piano player was tickling the ivories to release some stress and Leonard Garment reflected on his days at Julliard, and then he mentioned that Nixon should meet Greenspan. The rest is history, as Alan Greenspan become personal economic advisor to Nixon and then went on to be the longest running Chairman of the Federal Reserve Bank.

So, what are the lessons here? Firstly, knowing that the Stock Market can be volatile and reacts to many types of events from political announcements to analysts' reports to a myriad of data and reports on inflation; consumer consumption; and employment. And then there are the meetings of the Federal Reserve. But there are also seemingly insignificant events which frequently can provide highly profitable money-making opportunities, not only with Stocks but especially with Stock Options, since they are so leveraged. If you can learn to select the right underlying stocks and the right Options you can take advantage of highly leveraged profits every week or every month no matter what direction the market is turning and even if it doesn't move at all.

It seems almost every week a new report or indicator comes out which affects prices in the Stock Market. Here is a list of the major ones investors pay attention to – I'm not at all suggesting that you read or study the actual reports themselves. But you should just be aware that when they are released, the information contained in them does usually have at least a temporary effect on Stock market Pricing. I keep a trading journal and I always mark in the calendar when these crucial reports are to be released.

Gross Domestic Product (GDP)
Gross Domestic Product is a measurement of all of the country's goods and services for a specific period of time. It is one of the most influential indicators because it reflects the general state of the economy.

Measures of Employment
Both the Unemployment Rate and the Monthly Report from the U.S. Bureau of Labor Statistics (BLS) are key influencers on the Stock Market because investors know that solid employment translates into good retail sales and a healthy economy. The first Friday of every month the BLS releases the Nonfarm Payroll Figure and the same day the Unemployment Rate is also released.

Price Indexes that Measure inflation

There are several reports that are released monthly, the Consumer Price Index (CPI), the Producer Price Index (PPI) and the Personal Consumption Expenditures Price Index (PCE) which measure price changes on various goods and services from month to month. Changes in prices indicate a level of inflation and since Consumer Spending makes up more than two thirds of the Gross Domestic Product (GDP) these numbers , especially the PCE which is the preferred measure of the Federal Reserve are watched very carefully, as they have a direct effect on whether or not the Federal Reserve is going to increase or cut interest rates in order to control inflation. When the Federal Reserve increases interest rates it makes it harder for people to buy products, especially those that rely on financing, as financing becomes more expensive for consumers. This puts a damper on retail spending which ultimately cools inflation, but higher interest rates also slow growth in the Stock Market. The opposite is also true though. When the Federal Reserve cuts interest rates it makes it easier for consumers to finance products and spurs economic growth as well as the Stock Market.

Consumer Sentiment
The Conference Board releases the Consumer Confidence Index on the last Tuesday of each month, and the University of Michigan Has it own Consumer Sentiment index which is also released monthly.

Durable Goods
The Department of Commerce Census Bureau publishes its Durable Goods Report near the end of each month.

Retail Sales Reports
Retail Sales Reports give a direct and clear indication of the health of the economy

Purchasing Managers Index
The Purchasing Managers' Index (PMI) is a survey that goes out to many executives in industry covering many topics crucial to business growth.

Industrial Production
The Industrial Production Index is a report released by the Federal Reserve which measures factory output.

Earnings Reports
Quarterly Earnings Reports are public and mandatory for all publicly traded companies. Investors in the Stock Market watch very carefully during earnings season not just to see how the individual companies they have invested in are doing, but Stock Prices for companies in the same Market Sector are affected by competitors' earnings performance.

Individual Analyst Ratings
There are hundreds of Financial Analysts with major financial institutions that track and rate companies' performance on a regular basis. Unlike Quarterly Earnings Reports or scheduled financial reports, Analysts can rate a company's Stock Performance at any time. They always seem to come out of the blue and these ratings have a direct effect on the company's Stock Prices in the short term.

Political or Legislative Actions
Political announcements not just here in the U.S. but in countries where American products and services are sold or manufactured can have an effect on Stock Prices.

The Federal Reserve Bank
Although it's not an indicator, actions and announcements by the Federal Reserve can often have profound effects on Stock Market Prices. The Federal Open Market Committee (FOMC) is the monetary policy making body of the Federal Reserve Bank. They meet 8 times per year and over 2 days they make and announce decisions on the interest rate changes, if any.

Ina addition to the regularly scheduled meetings of the FOMC the minutes of their recent meetings are released typically 3 weeks later, and more detailed information within the minutes can stir the market as well.

MarketWatch has a weekly calendar available to let you know what information is coming down the line.

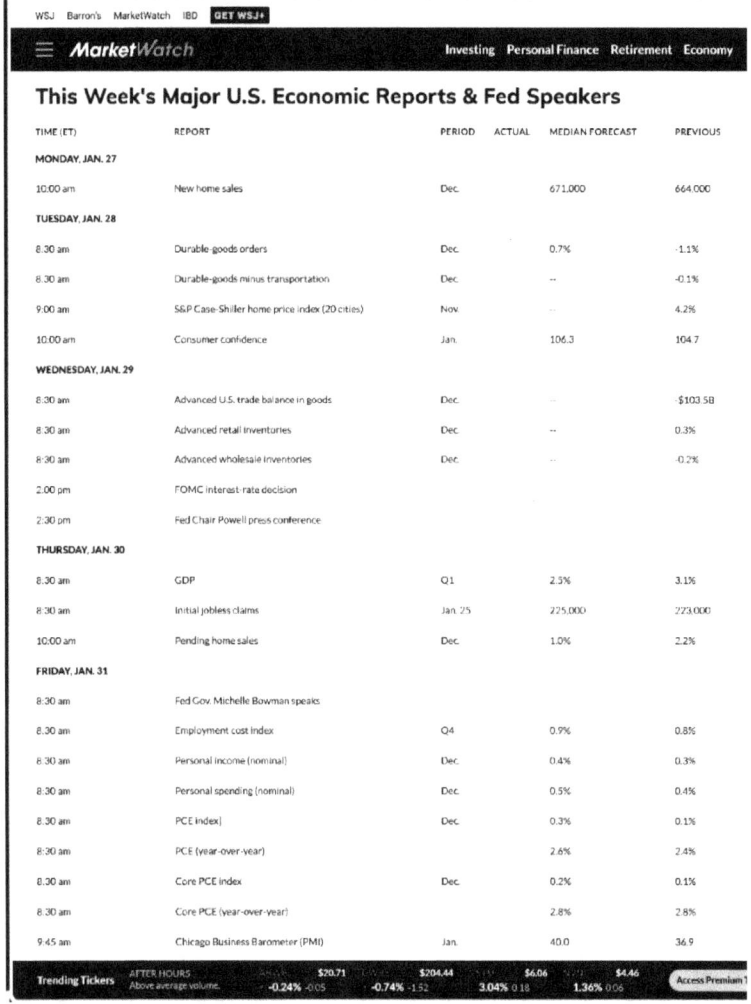

This is why it is best not to rely too heavily on Technical Analysis Indicators to try to predict price action in the Stock Market. I start the morning by going through top-line news stories from the Associated Press and Reuters and then I go through the Investor's Business Daily, Yahoo Finance and sometimes the Wall Street Journal and MarketWatch to get an idea of events that are influencing the Stock market for the day.. I also look at the list of companies that are leading in pre-market trading. Then I look at individual company information to determine stock health and after I have made some choices of which stocks I might want to sell Options on, I look at the individual Stock charts and examine some of the basic indicators. I never rely only on Technical Analysis to make my choices, just to affirm my choices.

There is no way to predict which stocks are going to move or which way. Be open to investing in companies and sectors that you might not normally be interested in. You don't want all of your stock in one company or one sector. Diversification can help prevent major losses. Be on top of major news and economic events and don't spend so much time with Technical Analysis at the expense of being on top of the news.

If you look at Yahoo Finance, or The Wall Street Journal on any given day, there is a list of stocks that are gaining and a list of stock that are losing for the day. Be open to learning about stocks and companies that you normally wouldn't know anything about. TESLA; APPLE; AMAZON; Nvidia and GOOGLE aren't the only companies in the S&P 500 or the Dow 30 or the NASDAQ 100. There are thousands of other winners out there. And always genuine opportunities to profit trading Stock Options with reasonable risk management and some basic strategies that form a plan.

Stocks move up, you can make money with Stock Options. Stocks move down, you can make money with Stock Options. Stocks consolidate (stay in a sideways range) you can make money with Stock Options. And there are a number of simple strategies in this book to help you succeed in any market condition.

There are hundreds of economists, so-called financial experts and analysts who are making predictions about the market. About half are Bullish on the markets (believe in the growth and prosperity) and about half are Bearish (believe there is going to be a correction or downturn in the market).

Just the other day there was a report on the lumber and home construction industry from woodcutter analyst Charles Milham (pronounced Mlm) in Shoreditch outside of London. He was reporting that although home repair and home construction is trying to rebound from the pandemic, it is possible with heavy tariffs the cost of lumber and other home renovation and construction items might see a rise in prices. That together with higher interest rates could affect the market sector hard.

What are Options?

Options in one form or another have probably been used for thousands of years. The first recorded use of something similar to our modern Options was recorded by Aristotle in Ancient Greece about 2500 years ago. He told a story of the philosopher Thales of Miletus (620ish BC – 540ish BC) who was also a great mathematician, astronomer and an amazingly accurate meteorologist.

Thales of Miletus

Thales was both criticized for choosing philosophy and science over making money, and challenged about predicting the weather over an entire season.

As olive oil was the top commodity of the day, supply had much to do with the weather and harvest numbers. Thales predicted an especially good harvest and he went to the owners of the olive oil presses offering them a reduced but non-refundable fee to control the rental of their oil presses over the next harvest season.

This was a gamble for him, as, if the olive harvest was minimal, there wouldn't be a lot of olives to press. If however the olive harvest was large and successful he would be able to rent out all of the time on the oil presses and make a substantial profit. Since the owners of the presses didn't know what the harvest would be like, they figured it was better to have some guaranteed money than take a chance on the weather for the harvest season and perhaps take a loss.

Thales had predicted the weather for the harvest correctly and he made quite a substantial profit .He was able to prove to skeptics 2 things. First that he was able to scientifically understand and predict the weather, and secondly that a philosopher could also become wealthy.

In this story, Thales basically bought an Option. He paid a guaranteed, non-refundable fee to control the use of the olive oil presses at a reduced rate for a specific period of time. In doing this, he contracted for the right but not obligation to use the presses for his own profit. Had the harvest been bad or good, he didn't have the obligation to use the presses but he had the right to do so during the upcoming season.

The sellers of the Option were the owners of the olive oil presses. They were happy to receive a guaranteed fee, not knowing if there would be a substantial harvest.

Here is a Greek inspired recipe for making you sit through the story of Thales of Miletus

saláta me eliés kai manitária
Greek Olive and Mushroom Appetizer

8 oz Greek green Chalkidiki olives, pitted
8 oz Greek black olives, pitted
8 oz button mushrooms

8oz sliced almonds
½ cup pale cream sherry
¼ cup unsalted butter
8 oz Stilton blue cheese
1 Loaf French bread
Toothpicks

Preheat oven to 350 degrees (F) 176.67 (C). Place sliced almonds on a lightly greased cookie sheet. Place almonds in heated oven for 15-20 minutes or until lightly brown and toasted.

With a small butter knife, stuff the olives with Stilton cheese.
In a skillet melt ¼ cup butter and stir in ½ cup sherry.
Place stuffed olives, button mushrooms and toasted almond slices in the butter sherry mixture and simmer for 25 minutes.
Place olives, almonds and mushrooms in a serving bowl with toothpicks.
Pour remaining butter sherry mixture in a dipping cup to serve with French bread.

Recipe courtesy of Graham Fothergille, Chef de cuisine to Royalty, and Descendent of Sir George Fothergille, General to Willam the Conqueror and the First Norman Baron of England.

One of the more famous examples of Options and Futures Contracts being used was in Amsterdam in the early 17th Century. tulips had become such a rare and coveted commodity that a single flower of a rare color variant could bring 1 million dollars in today's money.

Many normal colored variety tulips would go for 1 or 2 hundred thousand dollars or 150,000 pans of pom. According to Dutch historian Tony Moll, a single tulip bulb in 16 34 could get you a large mansion on the waterfront in Amsterdam. Soon seeing the enormous opportunity in trading, speculators became involved and offered Options and Futures Contracts on tulips. The tulip buyers would buy contracts to lock in prices for future delivery of tulips, and tulip sellers would sell the contracts (which by law were not enforceable). In 1637 when there was an over-abundance of tulips, the tulip market crashed and investors couldn't collect. -+

The Option Contract

By definition an Option is an agreement between a buyer and a seller to settle shares of Stock at a specified price by a certain date.

An Option is a contract tied to a specific underlying Stock or Index or ETF (Exchange Traded Fund).

1 Option Contract Always Equals 100 Shares of Stock

Unlike stock shares which you can buy a single share or many shares, A stock Option contract controls 100 shares of stock, no more, no less.

Expiration – The Time Limit of Options

With a stock Option there is a time limit. There are weekly Options, there are monthly Options. You can buy a monthly Option months in advance. You don't have to buy only the current month or week. Many Options are bought a year or two years down the road. If this is the first week in October, you might want to buy a January monthly Option or a March monthly Option. Or if you are buying weekly Options you may want to buy this week's or you may want to go out another week or a couple of weeks. But all Options have an expiration date.

An Option in some cases is like a lottery ticket and in some cases like an insurance policy. Whether you are buying lottery tickets or insurance, there is always a time limit.

Options Can Allow Profits in Both Directions of the Market

When you own stocks you only make money if the stock goes up in price. In the world of stock Options, you can make money if the stock price rises, you can make money if the stock price goes down, and you can make money if the stock stays the same price. You do have to specify when you order the Option contract which direction you are favoring. This isn't something you can decide after you purchase the Option.

In the world of the stock market the two animals that represent the sentiment of the market are the Bull and the Bear. If you are Bullish it means that you are optimistic and you think the market is going to go up. If you are Bearish it means that you think the market is going to go down. In a Bull Market, investors are optimistic and the markets tend to grow. In a Bear Market, investors are pessimistic and activity is slower.

But whether the market is Bullish or Bearish, with Options you can make money either way.

If you believe that stock prices are going to increase and you want to profit from the incr4ease, you would buy a Call Option. Call is the upward direction of the market.

If you believe that stock prices are going to go down and you want to profit from the decrease of stock prices then you could buy a Put Option. Put is the downward direction of the market.

Each Option contract controls exactly 100 shares of the underlying Stock.

An Options contract can be bought or sold on its own. You don't have to buy or own the underlying stock.

The Option contract is good for a specific time period. In other words, the Options contract has an expiration date.

Not every Company on the stock exchange offers Options but many are Optionable.

Some Options contracts have weekly expirations, some have monthly expirations and some have quarterly expirations. But you can buy or sell an Options contract with a weekly expiration date a week away or several weeks out if you want. You can also buy an Options contract with a monthly expiration for the next month or many months out. And if you want to stay in the Options market for a longer haul, you can buy or sell Quarterly Options

You make money on a Stock only if the price of the Stock goes up and you lose money if the price of the Stock goes down. When you buy or sell an Options contract you can choose a direction and you can profit if the Stock price goes up or down depending on the direction you choose.

If you are buying an Option hoping or expecting the price of the underlying Stock will go up you would buy a Call Option. If you are buying an Option hoping or expecting the price of the underlying stock will go down, you would buy a Put Option. Call is up and Put is down. (You can remember it because you would call somebody up or put somebody down.)

Call Up **Put Down**

Not everyone trading Options is buying them. On every Options trade there is a buyer and a seller. So who is selling Options and why?

Once you set up your trading account you will have the opportunity to buy an Option with the money in your account, or you can sell an Option. The question I get asked most often about selling Options is, How can I sell something I don't actually own? Don't I have to buy an Option first before I can sell it? After all, if I want to sell some Stocks, I have to first buy them. So how can I sell Options and receive payment (premium) right away without purchasing them first?

The answer is of course you can! Here is why. When you are selling an Option you are basically selling an insurance policy. Let's say that you decide you want to start a car insurance company in your own neighborhood. You could go to your neighbors and tell them that you will insure their car and they can pay you a monthly payment, an insurance premium in advance, to make sure they are insured. Each person who signs up starts paying you $100 per month premium and you insure them. In this case you sold them something you did not own first. When you sell a Stock Option, the buyer of that Option pays you a premium in advance and you are providing insurance.

Statistically more traders make money selling Options rather than buying them. Although Option selling carries greater risk than buying Options, there are also much greater opportunities for profit by selling Options. Most Options expire worthless, which means most buyers of Options aren't profiting and most Options profits are going to Option sellers. There is a much greater chance of making money by selling an Option rather than buying an Option.

When you buy an Option you need the underlying stock price to move in your direction to see any profit and to exceed your Strike Price to reach full profit potential. In other words you can only make money if the stock price moves significantly in your direction. If you are selling an Option you can money if the underlying stock price goes down, doesn't move at all, or even if the Stock Price moves up toward your Strike Price but doesn't exceed it. In other words you have so much more opportunity to make money by selling Options.

So why do people buy Options if there is less of a chance of profit? Because there is less and limited risk for a chance at making money. Why do people buy lottery tickets? Because for a small investment there is a possibility of making a lot of money. When you buy an Option your risk is capped. You can never lose more your initial investment. You may win you may lose, but you can never lose more than what you paid for the Option. You have rights but not obligations when you buy.

When you sell an Option, there is more risk depending on the strategy you use but there is also a greater chance of profit. If you are selling Options, as long as you attach the Option to collateral you can trade safely. All of the strategies that I recommend in this book are safe to trade in terms of the Options. You may have heard stories about how dangerous Options can be and how people have lost everything in their accounts from Options that have gone against them. This is because they were Trading Naked. Naked is the term used when Options are sold without protective collateral.

A Stock has the Value the Market gives it. You go to your trading platform or financial news and look up the price of the stock based on what the market is currently buying and selling it for. An Option is priced differently and has both Intrinsic Value and Extrinsic Value.

The Extrinsic Value of an Option derives its worth from the expected movement of the stock and the time value before expiration of the Option contract.

The Intrinsic Value of an Option is the actual value of the Option once it is ITM (In The Money) which means it's profitable beyond the Strike Price.

Time Value and Time Decay

So here is where I would expect most readers to throw the book down. Let me guess. It was enough to get the idea of Calls and Puts and it was ok until I started with the Extrinsic, Intrinsic Values and the ITM (In The Money), OTM (Out of The Money) and ATM (At The Money) stuff, right? And I haven't even gotten to the Strike Price yet!

It's going to be a lot easier if I take you on a mental road trip now. It's going to be kind of like one of my favorite movies, Love Actually, where there are several stories and they jump around and then tie together at the end.

My daughter really loves the music of Sabrina Carpenter and she wanted to see her in concert here where we live in Southern California. The concert date was 4 weeks away and the tickets went on sale online at midnight one night. She sat up with her computer and at exactly midnight she hit the keys on the keyboard and tried to get tickets. Within seconds the tickets were completely sold out and she wasn't able to get one. At the time the tickets were selling for a price official on the concert site for $600.

Over the next couple of weeks the tickets became available through individuals and ticket agencies and as the weeks wore on the price went up from the $600 to $700 and $750 to $800. 2 weeks before the concert I called my friend Eddie Espinosa at Eddie's Tickets in Studio City to see what he could get my daughter a ticket for. $1,200 was the going price at that time. I had to bow out. Interestingly I got a call back the week before the concert. The price had been lowered to $800.

The day before the concert I got another call. The tickets we now going for $600 again, the same price that they were originally offered for at the beginning. I didn't bother to pick up the ticket, but we heard from a friend that as people started lining up to go into the theater Saturday night, scalpers were offering tickets for $200 and finally $100 as the line started to move into the building. Once the concert started, the tickets were worthless. And Sunday morning, all of the unused Sabrina Carpenter concert tickets weren't worth the paper they were printed on, or should I say the QR Code configuration on the phones.

I am using this event to illustrate Time Value and Time Decay which are important concepts in Options Trading. The value of the concert tickets varied by Supply and Demand, but more importantly you can see how Time affected the price of the tickets. Like Options Contracts, the concert tickets had an expiration date, this being the date of the concert itself. And the concert tickets had an Intrinsic Value and an Extrinsic Value. The Intrinsic Value was the printed, official original price of the concert tickets, which was $600 on the Official Concert Site.

But in the first couple of weeks since there were a limited number of tickets and enough time to wait for people to become more interested in the concert as promotion was increased. So, there was Time Value which brought the ticket price at its highest to $1,200 as awareness and interest in the concert increased.

There was also Time Decay. As the concert came close to its playdate and time, the value of the ticket started to decline quickly. This is exactly what happens in an Options Contract. When you buy an Options Contract which has both Intrinsic and Extrinsic Value there is enough time for your contract to gain value (or lose value). When an Option Contract gets close to its expiration. The Decay of Time Value drops quickly and exponentially largely in the week just before expiration, until at the day of expiration they are often going for a penny.

Photo Amy Harris/Invision/AP
If Sabrina Carpenter appeared at the New York Stock Exchange she could sing "Nonsense" because it would be.

Weekly Options Contracts don't have as much Extrinsic Value since the expiration date is so close. For monthly contracts

Time value and Time Decay become important considerations and factors.

So, the overall value of the Option relates to the price of the Stock but not exactly from the stock price itself. The price of an Options contract tends to be responsive to the movement of the stock price, but it can move up or down on its own even if the underlying stock price doesn't move.

The Meaning of Options Contracts

I think the reason there is so much mystery surrounding Stock Options is that I don't know many Options traders who can explain simply what an Option is or what it does. This is probably because Options have different uses for different traders.

To somebody buying an Option it could be like a lottery ticket. To others buying or selling Options they could be an insurance policy to help minimize losses if the stock they own goes down in value or insurance against the stock moving against them. But anyway, an Options contract involves risk.

When you buy a lottery ticket you are risking the cost of the lottery ticket to gain a larger prize. If you are buying a stock Option you might be doing so for a similar reason. You might be betting on a stock going up or down in price and want to take advantage of the move by buying a Call Option (you thin the stock price will be going up) or a Put Option (you think the stock price will be going down).

Alternatively you might be buying a stock Option as insurance. Maybe you own shares of a stock and want the stock to increase in value, but also want to insure against the stock losing value. In this case you could buy a Put Option as insurance. If the stock you own goes down in price, the value of the Put Option increases, covering any loss of your stock.

If you are selling an Option instead of buying an Option it is as if you are selling the Option buyer an insurance policy. The buyer has bought an Option expecting a price change in the Stock. You are betting that there will not be any change in the Stock Price, or, that if there is a change it will not come up (or down) to your Strike Price.

An Options contract is a bet. When you buy or sell an Options contract you are assuming risk. Its just like being at a Casino in Las Vegas. If you are buying an Option you are a guest of the Casino, trying to make a big win. If you are selling an Option you are the owner of the Casino. You have the statistical edge of winning over time.

In reality an Options contract is a sort of insurance policy. As in the example of Thales and the olive growers, both side of the agreement had a risk factor involved. Thales risked the money he paid to the owners of the olive presses, and the Olive press owners also had risk. They were settling on a lower (but guaranteed) fee for the use of their presses than they would receive if all of the olive growers paid them directly in a good harvest year.

In the case of stock holders, both sides can be winners or losers. If you buy a stock at a low price in the hopes of watching the stock go up in price over time, you may have bought it from an investor who owned the stock long before you and bought it at a much lower price. In this case, you've both won. In the case of Option however, there is always a clear winner and a clear loser. The Options contract will expire and either the buyer or the seller will make money.

An Options contract controls 100 shares of stock. If you buy 1 Options contract and the price of the underlying stock goes up then you are controlling profit on 100 shares. Let's say that you want to invest in Tesla but each share of Tesla is going for

$300.00. And let's say that you have $1,000 to invest. You could buy 3 shares of Tesla- Or you could buy a $300.00 Call Option with an expiration 1 month out for a per share price of $10 (the total amount you'd pay is $1,000.00 because the contract is for 100 shares at $10.00 per share). Let's say that during the term of your Options contract (1 month) the price of Tesla goes up to $350 per share. If you owned 3 shares you'd have realized $150.00 from the profit of your 3 shares. If you had the Options contract you'd be in a position to buy 100 shares of Tesla at $300.00 even though the market price is $350.00. Your profit on the transaction would be 100 shares x a profit of $50.00 per share, or $5,000.00 (minus the Call).

Multi-Billionaire Investor Warren Buffet has made most of his tremendous profit by using one of the strategies that I am presenting to you in this book. He sells Cash-Secured Put Options. He only goes with a stock that he wants to own, but would rather acquire the shares at as much of a discount as he can get. So after selecting his favorite stock, he sells Cash-Secured Puts and in so doing collects Premium for selling the Options. Then if the Stock Price falls down past the Strike Price of his Put Options, Mr. Buffet is able to purchase stock he wants to own at discounted prices.

But most Options traders aren't interested in buying stocks at a discounted price and then owning them or selling them. The potential profits in trading Options come from the constant price changes throughout the day, every day of the Options contract. You can buy or sell an Options contract and within seconds see profit or loss. Many Options traders hold onto their Options contracts for a day or two, or a week or two, depending on the term of the contract. A general rule many Options traders follow is that once they've realized at least 50% of their potential profit, they close out their position and then look for a new contract to trade in.

How are prices of Options determined? There is a pricing model called the Black Shoals model which helps determine pricing of Options, but the pricing changes quickly and is affected by supply and demand and by Implied Volatility. In our example above, the $300.00 Call Option (Monthly) happened to be priced at $10.00 per share when I checked. But if there was an announcement the next day of potential legislation having to do with clean air or electric vehicles, or if Tesla's earnings report was coming up this would greatly affect Implied Volatility and there're the price of the Options contract increase dramatically.

So what is Implied Volatility? In the stock market world you will here about Volatility. Volatility is the tendency for a stock to make sharp moves up or down in a short period of time. If the market is volatile then stocks might drop one day and then soar the next. This is actual volatility, or what is called Historical Volatility.

But there is something called Implied Volatility which is an important measurement but is very different from actual or Historical Volatility. Implied means possible or expected. It isn't real and it hasn't happened, but Implied Volatility will affect prices of Options so it's an important concept to follow and understand.

In the example of owning a neighborhood insurance company and selling insurance to your neighbors, you were collecting a premium of $100.00 per month from each driver. But let's say one of your neighbors has an uncle coming to stay with them and he needs insurance but he has a reputation for drinking heavily and then getting behind the wheel. Are you going to charge him the same $100 per month for insurance? Probably not. Why not? Because there is a greater chance that he will either cause or be involved in an accident for which you will have to pay an insurance claim on. Now, you don't know for sure that he is going to have a problem, but there are indications that imply instability or volatility in your normal claims payout statistics. These indications are what we call the fear factor and in the stock market it is called Implied Volatility. Just before President Biden introduced legislation that would help clean air and promote electric vehicles, there was an expectation in the market that this legislation would affect the stocks of Tesla, Lucid, Rivin, Nio and others.

io and other companies. The Implied Volatility coming up to the date of the legislation announcement was very high, and so the Options prices on tesla and the others rose dramatically. Just before company earnings are reported the implied volatility of those companies' stock rise pushing up the prices of the Options.

This is why the measurement of Implied Volatility is worth checking. If you are buying an Option with high Implied Volatility you are paying a very expensive price for the Option. This is good if you are selling an Option, but just as in stocks, profits come from buying low and selling high. If you are buying an Option you want to look for low Implied Volatility and if you are selling an Option you want to sell for the highest price possible during high Implied Volatility.

Volatility and Implied Volatility

Cedar Point, the amusement park in Sandusky Ohio has some of the most notorious rollercoasters in the country. Some are the higher old creaky wooden coasters and some are the newer faster steel coasters.

Top Thrill 2 Roller Coaster at Cedar Point in Sandusky, Ohio reaches a height of 420 feet and speeds of 120 mph.

Let's say that you are in line to ride the Top Thrill 2 coaster at Cedar Point. The line you're standing in starts to move forward and you notice there is more adrenaline starting to go through your body. As you move further through the line and hear the screams your breathing rate become faster and as you get closer to the start of the ride, there is even more adrenaline pumping into your system. Just before you reach the platform you get a look at the height of the vertical track you are about to climb and your heart rate has increased. You reach the platform and step into one of the cars and the bar is pulled down to secure your body. Your fear and anticipation of what you are about to experience has reached a high point. Even though you haven't been on the ride itself yet, you have experienced the uncertainty and fear of anticipation while you were advancing in line.

This uncertainty and fear of what might happen in the future is what is known in the stock market as **Implied Volatility.** There be some upcoming event that causes uncertainty and fear in the market. Maybe there is a Federal Reserve meeting coming in the next days or weeks and there is concern about changes in the interest rates. Maybe there is a vote coming up in Congress that might affect regulations of technology or pharmaceutical stocks. Maybe there is an election or an anticipated Presidential speech that might have an effect on the economy or the climate which in turn could affect a sector of industry.

There are always events that affect the outlook of the stock market which is why the market is so unpredictable. But the presence of specific upcoming events may cause uncertainty and fear with traders, and an increase in Implied Volatility, and an increase in stock Options prices.

Remember in the beginning of COVID, when customers bought out all of the supplies of necessities like toilet paper, disinfecting cleaning products, macaroni and cheese boxes, etc.? When demand goes up supply goes down and prices increase. Think of stock Options as the toilet paper of the stock market. When uncertainty goes up, demand for stock Options goes up, supply goes down and the prices of stock Options go up.

Why do traders buy more stock Options when there is uncertainty and fear in the market? Because Options can be used to protect stock positions. If you are heavily invested in stocks, you might want to buy protective put Options. Others see the higher Implied Volatility as opportunity to sell Options at a higher inflated price believing that the Options prices will come back down. There are a number of reasons why traders buy more Options in volatile markets. But for whichever reason they choose, the increased demand in Options causes Options prices to increase, even though the actual stock prices may not move. It is the expected move that affect the increase in Option prices.

Let me repeat and clarify what I just wrote. Stock Options prices are not directly tied to the prices of underlying stock. Very often over time a stock's price may not move very far up or down, but because of Implied Volatility, (that is the market's fear and expectations of a larger move in the stock's prices) the Options prices may vary dramatically. In times of lower volatility, the Options prices are more responsive to the actual stock price movements.

Volatility is best defined as how far and how quickly stocks move. If stocks move up or down quickly then volatility might be high. Conversely if stocks aren't moving very far very fast then that probably represents low volatility.

One of the factors that increases both demand and Options prices in the Options markets is fear of something happening that will affect the market and therefore Option pricing. This fear is known as Implied Volatility. Implied volatility is different from actual or historical volatility because Implied Volatility is the market's sentiment of what might happen in the future.

If you're going to be trading Options, then the measures of Volatility and Implied Volatility become very important, because Volatility directly affects Options pricing. When volatility is high, it means there is more uncertainty in the market and Options traders are quick to buy more Options.

Many traders are going to try to buy Options In anticipation of large moves up or down. Other traders might buy Options to protect the stock they have from going down too quickly. As more Option traders buy Options, the price of the Options will rise due to increased demand and decreasing supply. Options sellers will sell Options to meet the rising demand and that means that the prices of Options are going to be higher. If you're buying Options, then this is bad. If you are selling Options though, higher volatility means higher premiums and that is how you make money selling Options.

Remember the idea in Options as in most areas of business is buy low and sell high. If you are buying Options you want to buy at the cheapest price you can find, and if you are selling Options you want to sell at the highest prices you can get and then buy them back when they are at their lowest price.

In general when there is a downtrend in the prices of the underlying stock, volatility will increase. Increasing volatility means that the chances are greater that there will be bigger moves of the underlying stock and this increases the probability that the Options will finish ITM (In The Money). Higher probability of an Option move means the delta will increase and the price of the Options will increase.

Remember that Options closer to the actual stock price are more expensive because they have higher probability of moving either up or down and expiring ITM (In The Money), meaning there is a greater probability that the stock price will move to meet the Options strike price before expiration. As the actual price of the stock moves farther away from the Option's strike price. The Option is less expensive. This is because the probability of the stock price reaching the Option's strike price before expiration decreases the farther away from the stock price the Option is.

So, how do you know when looking to buy or sell an Option whether volatility is high or low, or whether implied volatility is likely to be high or low in the future?

The CBOE (Chicago Board of Options Exchange) has a real time index called the Volatility Index (VIX) which measures Options trading activity of Options in the S and P 500 and extends the implied volatility information out 30 days. Basically, this measures the market sentiment of where traders think the market will be looking forward.

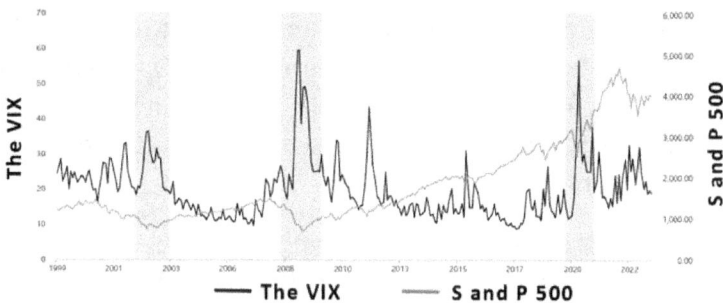

When the VIX is high, stock prices tend to drop. When the VIX is low, stock prices tend to rise.
At VIX levels of 25 and below the market sentiment is optimistic and this is a signal for traders to buy stocks
At VIX levels above 30 the market sentiment is cautious, and traders are beginning to sell off stocks.
Illustration courtesy of Sunlife Assurance.

This measurement index is also widely known as the Fear Index. When the VIX is high then stock prices are likely to fall, and when the VIX is low, stock prices are likely to rise.

Remember though that Implied Volatility changes, and if a feared influence or event doesn't happen the way the market feared they would, volatility can change in minutes.

Additionally, on many trading platforms, when you pull up an Options chain, the IV (Implied Volatility) will be listed as a percentage. IV percentages of 50% or over are considered to have high implied volatility whereas IV percentages of less than 20% are considered to have low implied volatility.

Be sure to look at the Delta of your Options because the current Delta gives a pretty good estimate of probability of the Option expiring ITM (In The Money).

How Can You Lose Money With Volatility

The Options trading Techniques in this book are less sensitive to volatility. But in some of the more advanced Options trading techniques that you might want to try, volatility will have a direct effect on whether you are profitable in a trade or lose money in a trade.

Here is an example. Let's say that Nike (NKE) is trading at $100.00 per share. And you believe that the stock will increase over the next month, so you buy a Nike 110 Call Option expiring in 30 days. This means that if Nike's stock price finishes above $110.00 at expiration your Option will be ITM (In The Money) and your Option's Delta will be 1.0 meaning that for every dollar rise in Nike stock above $110.00 per share your Option price will rise at $1.00 per share.

This great, but most traders who buy Options aren't interested in buying stock at expiration. They hope before expiration to make money selling the Options they've bought. Most successful Options traders who buy Options don't keep them until expiration. In fact they try to figure out what a reasonable profit will be and when they reach that amount they sell. Or they try to figure out the maximum profit they can make, and when they get to 50% of that maximum profit, they sell.

The logic behind selling Options early before expiration is simple. The longer traders wait after a profit has been realized, the greater the chance that the market might still have time to change and turn against them. You can make more money in the long run by grabbing some profit, closing your position and then buying into another stock Option. There are always more opportunities in the market, thousands of them at any given moment.

The problem is that if you purchased an Option when IV (Implied Volatility) was high (because you purchased the Option just a few days before Nike's earnings report and there was enough uncertainty to drive Option prices higher.) you paid $2.47 for the Call Option (2.47 x 100 shares = $247. But Nike's earnings were positive and the stock price rises slightly, The lack of uncertainty causes a decrease in IV (Implied Volatility) and the price of the Option decreases. Just before expiration you want to sell your Option for a profit but you find that the price of the Option is now .35 (.35 x 100 shares = $35.00).

Yes, the stock has increased in price, but you bought the Option at a high inflated price due to high Implied Volatility. Now the Option price has come down because of lower implied volatility. You bought high and are trying to sell low.

Bottom Line – If you are buying Options, you want to buy at the lowest price you can in the hopes of selling your Option at a higher price before expiration

How Can You Make Money With Volatility

The way most Options traders make money in the stock market is to sell Options. Think of it. If you are buying stock Options, you can only make money if the stock moves in your direction and it has to move far enough to create an increase in Options prices. But if you are selling Options you can make money if the stock moves in either direction and especially if the stock doesn't move at all. There is a lot more opportunity to profit by selling an Option.

Here's an example with Nike (NKE) again. Let's say that it is January and Nike stock is trading at 100 and you have bought a Nike Feb 110 Call. This Call Option is a monthly Option going out 30 days from today. If Nike stock goes down at expiration, you've lost the premium you paid for the Option. Of course, that's all you can lose so your loss is limited. But even still, you've lost the money the Option cost you. If Nike stock goes up in value to 110 at expiration, you've still lost money, because the Option can't turn a profit until it is higher than $110.00 per share, That is your strike price, and even more than that because you have to consider the cost you paid for the Option to begin with, you are not even at breakeven on your Option until Nike stock goes beyond $110.00 per share plus the amount you paid for the Option.

Now let's say that instead of buying the Nike Feb 110 Call, you decided to sell the Nike Feb 110 Call. Instead of paying the premium for the Option when you buy and open the contract you would be paid and receive the premium amount. The moment you sell the Option, the premium you are paid is deposited immediately into your account. If by expiration Nike hasn't gone higher than $110.00 per share, you keep the money. So in this case you have a greater chance of remaining profitable. If Nike stock goes down, you keep the money. If Nike stock stays at the same price, you keep the money. If Nike Stock increases in value you still make money as long as it doesn't exceed 110.00. Even if Nike stock does exceed $110.00 per share, you still may be able to make some money as long as the premium you received is more than the loss above 110. For example, let's say that you received a premium of $3.00 by selling the Option. You would have $300.00 deposited in your account ($3.00 x 100 = $300.00). If the Nike stock price closed at $111.00 per share, your loss on the Option would be the difference between the actual closing price at expiration minus the strike price of your contract. In other words $111.00 - $110.00 = $1.00. So your loss would be $100.00 ($1.00 x 100 = $100.00). Since you received a premium of $300.00, even though you have a partial loss you still are $250.00 profitable.

Understanding Delta

Why should you care about the measurement of Delta?

How does an increase or decrease in the price of the underlying stock affect the price of the Options contract? One of the commonly used Greek measurements is called Delta. Delta is the change of the Option's price in response to a $1.00 increase or decrease to the underlying stock.

The Delta measurement has a range between 1.0 and -1.0 (negative numbers refer to Put Options). The closer your OTM (Out of The Money) Option's Strike Price moves toward the Stock Price, the higher the Delta. When the Option's Strike Price is ATM (At The Money) or, equal to the Underlying Stock Price, the Delta would be .50. Why? Because at .50 there is a 50 / 50 chance that the Stock Price could move up beyond your Option Strike Price and then be ITM (In The Money). If the Underlying Stock Price rises above your Strike Price, the Delta will move toward 1.0 (for a Call Option), or -1.0 (for a Put Option) Delta also changes as the stock price changes because the probability of meeting the Strike Price changes as well.

Delta also has a different use. The Delta of the Options contract can also be used as a probability measurement.

Let's say that you're bullish on Tesla (TSLA NASDAQ). That means you believe that Tesla stock is going to rise over the next week and you have $1,000.00 to invest. Tesla is currently trading at 225.53 per share. You can buy 4 shares of TSLA and then have enough left to take your friends to Buco de Beppo to celebrate, or you could buy an ATM (At The Money) 225 weekly Call Option which is currently selling for $435.00 (4.35 x 100 = $435). Instead of owning 4 shares of Tesla you would now control 100 shares of Tesla.

Why wouldn't you want to spend more of the $1,000.00 and buy more Options or a more expensive deep ITM (In The Money) Option? Because remember that if you buy shares of Tesla stock and the stock doesn't increase in value or even goes down in value in the next week, you still own the stock and knowing Tesla, you'll be able to become profitable on the stock soon enough. But if you buy or sell Options, they will expire. So, if the stock price of Tesla doesn't go up in value past your strike price you've lost your investment.

For the sake of example, let's say that you've bought a weekly September 20, 2024 Call Option with a strike price of 225 which is ATM (At The Money). The Option cost you $435. Now let's say that overnight Tesla got some good news about foreign investment into one of their overseas plants and the stock increases in value. Well, one of the friends you took to Bucco de Beppo the other night wants to buy the same exact Call Option that you bought.

Now that Tesla stock price has increased do you think your friend is going to be able to buy the exact same Option for the same price you did a day before? Of course not. The probability that your trade has increased because the stock has gone up. If your friend wants to buy the exact same Option which is now ITM (In The Money), he will have to pay more for it. What does this mean for you? It means you don't have to wait for Option expiration, you can cash out, sell back your Option and take profits early. Prices of Options change from day to day and from moment to moment.

Many stock Options traders have no intention of keeping their Options contracts through expiration. They are looking to cash out and take their profits early because the stock could go down again the next day.

When you buy or sell an Options contract you pay the current price (or receive money if you are selling) of the Option which is tied to the price of the underlying stock. No matter which way the stock price moves during the term of your contract, the price of your Option will also move, but not at the same rate. The Delta is the sensitivity and change in price of the Option based on a one dollar change in price of the actual stock.

In other words for every dollar the stock price changes up or down, the value of the Option will also move up or down but not necessarily at the same rate. The Delta measurement is dynamic and changes according to time, volatility, as well as the actual price change of the Option. Since a movement of the stock itself will change the probability of the Option's Strike Price being met, this change in probability will also be reflected in the Delta measurement.

Generally speaking, stock prices that are ITM (In The Money) will have a Delta range of .51 – 1.00. This means that for a Call Option if your strike price is below the actual trading price of the stock and you are in profit (In The Money) your Option should be increasing at a minimum of .5 for every dollar increase in the stock and especially toward the Option's expiration the Option price will increase closer to 1.00 for every dollar increase in the actual stock price.

If the stock price is ATM (At The Money) which means that your Strike price is equal to the current value of the stock, the Delta should be at about .50. If the stock price is OTM (Out Of The Money) meaning that your Strike Price is above the actual current stock price, then the Delta measurement should be between .01 and .50. But again all of these numbers can change as the Option approaches expiration or if there is an increase in volatility.

This is the Tesla Option Chain Chart for the weekly Option expiring September 20, 2024, although it is September 11, 2024 today.

Let's take an example from Tesla. The above is a 20 day chart for Tesla stock.

Now let's go to the Options Chain for Tesla for a weekly Option that expires on September 20, 2024.

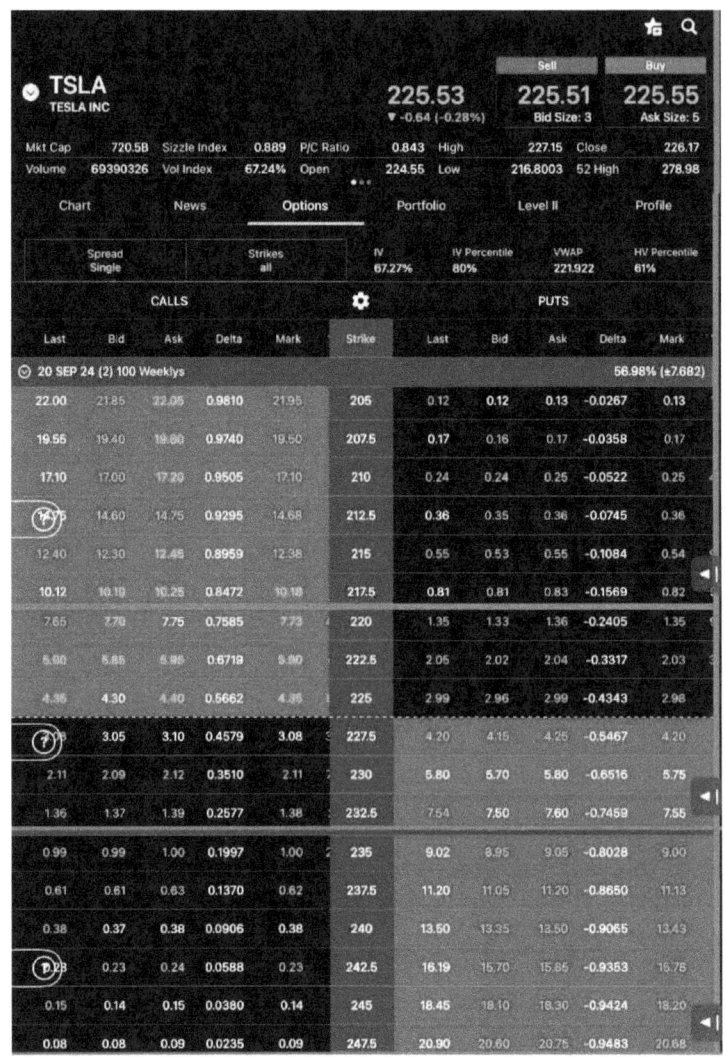

You can see on the above Option Chain chart that Tesla is currently trading at 225.53. The closest ATM (At The Money) Call Option has a Delta of .5662 and there is 10 days to go. The ITM (In The Money) Call Option with a Strike Price of 205 has a Delta measurement of .9810, and the Call Option with the Strike Price of 247.5 has a Delta measurement of .0235.

These Delta measurements mean several things. If the stock price of Tesla doesn't increase very much toward expiration of this contract in 10 days, then it makes sense that the probability of the price moving very far very fast in ither direction will be decreased. In this case if your Call Option Strike price is already ITM (In The Money) such as the 205 or anything much below the current stock price, the Delta measurement will increase. Conversely if your Call Option Strike Price is substantially OTM (Out Of The Money) the likelihood of the stock reaching your Strike Price is diminished and less likely, so the Delta measurement may decrease.

Not only does Delta show you how much your Option will increase in relation to a change in price of the actual stock, but Delta can be an accurate measure of the probability of the Option Strike Price expiring ITM (In The Money) or OTM (Out Of The Money).

If you are buying an Option you want your Option to expire ITM (in The Money) and if you are selling an Option you want your Option to expire OTM (Out Of The Money).

Had you purchased an ATM (At The Money) Tesla September 20 2024 Call Option with a Strike Price of 217.5 just 2 days ago. Then your Delta measurement now would be .8472 which indicates not only does your Option increase .8472 for every dollar Tesla stock price increases, but there is an almost 85% probability that your Call Option will finish ITM (In The Money) upon expiration (1.00 - .8472 = .1528). If you sold this Call Option it is not good news and you might want to get ready to take that chilled bottle of Absolut Red out of the freezer. It means that there is only a 15.28% chance of not having the Tesla stock price stay above the Strike Price at expiration.

You can look at the Put Options on the right side. If you bought the 247.5 Put Option, you are already well ITM (In The Money) and there is a .9483 probability that your Option will remain ITM (In The Money). If you sold this Put Option it is not good news and you are probably loading up the car to leave town. Note that for the Delta measurements on the Put side of the Options Chain table the measurements are listed as negative numbers. This doesn't change their value, it's just a notation that the number is referring to a Put Option. Even though the 247.5 Strike Put Option is listed on the chart as -0.9483 it still means that there is a .9483 probability that this Option will expire in ITM (In The Money).

The Concepts of ATM, ITM, OTM

What are the concepts of "At The Money". "Out of The Money". And "In The Money"?

Remember in Options trading you have 2 prices that you are watching. One is the actual price of the underlying stock. The other is your strike price. The price of the Options contract you have will change from moment to moment depending on variables. If you have a call Option it means you are hoping for the stock price to come up to your strike price and continue to rise further. If you have a put Option then the opposite is true. In this case you are hoping for the stock price to drop down to your strike price and continue to go down in price. In the case of a Call Option, your strike price is usually above the actual stock price and at this point you are out of the money – meaning the actual stock price hasn't yet come up to your strike price. When and if the stock price rises and meets your strike price at this moment you are ATM (At The Money). If the stock continues to rise above your strike price (which is what you hope for) you are now ITM (In The Money), you are in your highest profitable area.

In the case of a put Option, if the stock price is above your strike price, you are OTM (Out of The Money). If the stock price lowers to meet your strike price you are at the money and if the stock price continues to drop (which is what you are hoping for) then you are ITM (In The Money).

Which Options are Better to Trade?

Weekly or Monthly Options Contracts?

There are Traders of Options who trade the monthly contracts and there are Traders of Options who prefer to trade the weekly contracts. Which is better?

Neither is specifically better than the other. It depends on your style of trading and what your investment or income goals are.

The advantages of Monthly Options Contracts are that there is plenty of time until expiration for the underlying Stock Price to make a move in your favor. And because you have more time when trading a monthly Option, the Option Price is less sensitive to short term volatility. Weekly Options don't have a lot of time to make a large move. The premiums paid to you for selling a monthly contract are higher because there is a greater probability the Stock Price will move farther before expiration.

On the other hand, Weekly Options Contracts tend to have more volume so they are more liquid making it easier for you to get in and get out quickly at the price you want. Although the Premiums are higher on the monthly Options Contracts, you can sell more of them within the same time period as 1 monthly contract and so it is possible to have higher overall profits in the end.

I tend to prefer weekly Options Contracts because I like to make my trades first thing on Monday morning and then be out by expiration on the same Friday afternoon. This way I have the weekend to relax and regroup for my next trades on Monday morning, but I can relax the whole weekend and not worry about wild stock moves in afterhours Friday or premarket Monday morning.

There are times when it is an advantage strategically to have longer term monthly Options. For example in one strategy you'll learn in this book, the Married Put Collar, you buy a long term monthly Put Option Contract going out about 6 months for expiration and then sell weekly or monthly Call Option Contracts.

Another example of when you would want to sell a longer term Monthly Call Option is when you have stock that you've owned for a long time and the sale of which would result in long term capital gains. You might want to make money on the stock by selling Covered Call Options against it, but you absolutely don't want the stock to be assigned otherwise you'd have to pay long-term capital gains taxes. So the safest way to do it is to sell longer term Monthly Call Options so you have plenty of time to keep on eye on the movement of the Stock Price and plenty of time to buy back your Option Contract or Roll it Out if need be before expiration.

The Strike Price of an Option

When you buy (or sell) a stock you buy it (or sell it) at the current actual market price. When you buy or sell an Option you have to choose a Strike Price, which is a target price. If the stock price reaches this target or Strike Price, the Option can be exercised. But what does that mean? How does a Strike Price work?

Let's imagine for a moment that we are on a football field. Normally at the start of a game a coin is tossed at the 50 yard line, the center of the field. The winner of the toss has the opportunity to kick the ball as far as possible down the field to mark the location of the first play. But what if there was a different way to start the game? What if the winner of the toss could buy a position on the field as close to the other team's goal as they wanted.

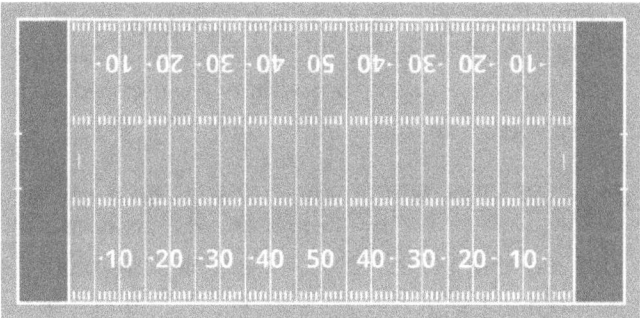

Let's say they would have to pay in points. They could have the ball placed as close as the 1 yard line but it would cost them 6 points. Since a Touchdown is worth 6 points and the extra point kick is worth 1 point, the team would be paying 6 points for the opportunity to be ahead 1 point. And there is still the possibility the defensive team might stop the touchdown. So, instead of buying a placement on the 1 yard line, the offensive team decides they could have the ball placed on the 10 yard line and it would cost them 4 points. At 10 yards there is still a good probability of gaining yardage and making a touchdown, in which case they would have paid 4 points for the opportunity to gain 3 points (6 points for the touchdown and 1 point for the extra point – the 4 points that the deal cost them = 3 points), assuming they made a touchdown and the extra point. But maybe they don't have 4 points to spare and they know that if they choose to have the ball placed further back at the 15 yard line it would cost them only 1 point. The probability of gaining enough yardage to get a touchdown is less, but they are within good field goal range for a kick. Here the further placement has cost them less and if they have good offense, they can still pull it off.

The different Yard choices are similar to Strike Prices in Options. If you buy or sell an Option at the exact same price of the underlying stock it is named ATM (At The Money). There is a very high probability of the stock price moving by the end of expiration of your Option. It could move up or it could move down, so there is a high probability you could gain or alternatively, you could lose.

Because of the high probability of stock price movement beyond your Strike Price, the Option could be very expensive to buy and you could also receive a very high premium if you sell it. But remember, if you are buying the Option, the stock price could move against you as well, and you might have lost a large chunk of money on an expensive Option.

Often Option traders will choose a Strike Price OTM (Out Of the Money) further out from the current actual stock price. The further away from the current stock price the less expensive the Option will cost because the probability is less that the stock price will move far enough to move beyond the Strike Price and reach maximum profitability.

When choosing a Strike Price for an Option it is a trade-off between the price of the Option and the probability of the stock price moving to meet or exceed your Strike Price.

When you are buying an Option, you usually want the underlying stock price to move toward your Strike Price, and to exceed it for maximum profit. When you are selling an Option you want to be as far away from the underlying stock price as possible and hope that the underlying stock price does not move enough toward your Strike Price and absolutely doesn't go beyond your Strike Price.

So, how does this work in the real world of Stock and Option trading? For example you can go to your trading platform, or Yahoo Finance or the Wall Street Journal or whatever source you have and find out what the stock is currently selling for. You then would go on your platform or call your broker and buy 100 shares of a stock.

For example, today Disney (DIS NYSE) is trading at $108.37 per share. If it is Monday and you believed that Disney stock will go up in price you could have purchased 100 shares of Disney stock for $10,837.00 or you could have purchased a Call Option in the hopes that the price of Disney Stock goes up and you can take advantage of the leverage of controlling 100 shares instead of buying shares outright. 100 shares x $108.37 = $10,837.00.

Or you could buy a Disney Call Option for the week (or for the month). A 108 ATM (At The Money) Weekly Call Option is priced at 1.54 per share so the contract (1 contract = 100 shares) would cost you $154.00. So let's say that Disney stock goes up to 112.00 at expiration next Friday afternoon. You would have revenue of $363 (112.00 – 108.37 = 3.63 x 100 = $363.00) so your total profit would be $209.00 ($363.00 - $154.00 = $209.00). If you had bought the stock shares and sold them Friday afternoon you would have $363.00 profit but would have had to have invested $10,837.00. Instead, had you bought a Call Option your profit would be $209.00 but you only had to pay $154.00 to get in on this deal.

Alternatively there is Tesla (TSLA NASDAQ). Today TESLA traded at $427.50 per share. A weekly ATM (At The Money) Tesla 427.5 Call is selling for 15.68 per share, or $1,568.00 per contract. If you wanted to buy 100 shares of Tesla it would cost you $42,750.00.

Why did the Call Option for the Disney Option cost one tenth the price of the weekly Tesla Option? TESLA has much higher Implied Volatility. That is, the market is expecting greater moves in the stock. If you are going to be buying Options, low Implied Volatility is what you are looking for. If you are selling Options you would want to sell while Implied Volatility is high.

But what if you wanted to trade TESLA and didn't have the $1,568.00 for a Call Option you could choose a higher, less expensive Strike Price. Instead of buying or selling and ATM (At The Money) 427.5 Option, you could buy or sell the further out OTM (Out of The Money) 437.5 which would cost you 9.15 per share, or $915.00. Since there is more volatility in the price movement of TESLA you still have a good probability of movement past your Strike Price of 437.5. Of course, you could go much further out and buy or sell the 457.5 Strike Price for 510 per share, or $510.00. The cost of the farther OTM (Out of The Money) Options are less expensive, but the probability that the Stock Price will have the move necessary for you to reach maximum profit is less as well.

So, why would someone pay $510.00 for a farther OTM (Out of The Money) 457.5 TESLA Option if the probability is lower of the Stock Price of 427.50 moving up and exceeding the Strike Price of 457.5? Just because your Option is OTM (Out of The

Money) doesn't mean that you aren't making some profit on it. It just means that before you can reach a 1 to 1 Delta (every move of $1 of the stock causes an equal $1 move of the price per share of the Option) which happens when the Stock Price exceeds the Strike Price, your Delta is lower, but you are still making money.

Let's say that you buy a monthly TESLA 457.5 Call Option because you really believe TESLA stock will be going up over the next month. After one week the Stock price of TESLA has gone up from 427.5 to 435.5. Your friend has heard about what you are doing and sees that TESLA stock is increasing in value, so they decide they want to also buy the same monthly TESLA Call Option that you have. Now that TESLA stock has gone up in value they aren't going to be able to buy the same Option for the same price you did. Why not? Because now that TESLA stock has gone up in value, it is also closer to your Strike Price which changes the probability of the Stock Price reaching your Strike Price. Option prices change moment by moment according to the changing probability of the Stock Price movement toward or away from the Strike Price.

The point is that even into the first week of owning that Call Option, you are already making money on the Option. You are just not making as much on your Option per dollar move in the underlying Stock Price as you would if the Stock Price moved above your Strike Price. Once the Stock Price exceeds your Strike Price, your Option is ITM (In The Money) and you will be making the most profit. But you could sell your Option after the first week for some profit if you wanted to.

I have explained that buying an Option is much like buying a lottery ticket. Let's say that you have purchased a Pick Four Lottery Ticket for $5.00 in the State Lottery. The Jackpot is several hundred million dollars and it is 4 weeks out. Now let's say that after the first week the first number is drawn and you have it. The odds have changed because now you only have to pick 3 numbers correctly. You paid $5.00 for the original ticket, but now that you have 1 correct number the odds of winning have improved. You could now sell that ticket to someone for a lot more than $5.00. You might be able to get $50.00 for it. You can grab the $50.00 or keep the ticket to see how far you can go. Let's now say that after the second week the second number is drawn and you also by chance have that also. Again, the probability has changed considerably and you can now sell that ticket for much more money or continue to hold it. Let's say that miraculously you have the third number drawn after the third week out. It's hard to say what the value of your ticket would be worth now but it's safe to say that you could sell it for many times the original $5.00 you paid for it in the first place.

When you buy an Option, either a Call Option or a Put Option, the price is going to be constantly changing based on the probability of the Stock Price moving toward your Strike Price, and other variables including the changing Implied Volatility on the Option. So, even if your Strike Price is further OTM (Out of The Money) you can still make some profit on the Option.

There are some situations when the Stock Price will move toward your Strike Price and you can actually lose money. This happens if you are buying an Option during a time of high Implied Volatility and then the price of the Option comes down as the Implied Volatility decreases.

For example maybe you want to buy an Option just before an earnings announcement or just before an important economic report comes out or before a meeting of the Federal Reserve, because you think that good news will cause the Stock Price to rise (rise for a Call Option or fall if you're are buying a Put Option) It may be that in anticipation of the news, the market has reacted with uncertainty and Implied Volatility becomes very high your Option before you buy it.

And let's say that indeed the news is good and the Stock Price increases but the level of Implied Volatility decreases bringing the price of the Option down. The lesson is to make sure that if your are buying an Option, always buy during low Implied Volatility. If you are selling an Option, then you want to sell at high Implied Volatility when Option prices are inflated. For buying Options, always buy low and sell high. For selling Options, always sell high and then buy back low.

It may not make sense for a trader to buy a far OTM (Out of The Money) Option, but if you are selling it might make a lot of sense. Remember if you are selling an Option you don't want the Stock to come near your Strike Price. If you wanted to make a quick $100.00 premium for the week and you had the money in your account to sell a Covered Call with a Strike Price of 512.50. The premium you would receive for selling the Option would be $110.00 and you would probably be safe selling so far out. But if TESLA stock did go up past $512.50 how much would make?

In the Covered Call strategy you would have first bought 100 shares of TESLA (TSLA NASDAQ) at $427.50 which is the current price. Then you would have sold the $512.50 Strike Price Weekly Option expiring on next Friday. If Tesla stock went up past $512.50 on expiration you'd receive the $110.00 premium plus a profit of $85.00 per share (512.50 – 427.50 = 85.00) or $8,500.00. Your total take for a one week investment would be $8,610.00.

If you want100 Adidas AG @ 120 GTC which would be an order for 100 shares of Adidas stock at $120.00 per share, and the order is good until cancelled (the other choice is DAY which would mean that you only want the order to be filled until the end of the trading day)

You simply have to give the number of shares, the name of the company and the price you are willing to pay and how long you want your order to stay active until it is filled or cancelled.

With a stock Option there are other components that you have to specify and concepts that you have to understand to buy or sell the right Option.

With the purchase of stocks themselves, you can make a profit only in one direction, and that's with a price increase. If the price goes up from your purchase price, you make money. If the price of the stock stays the same or goes down in price, you lose money. But since you own actual shares of stock there is no time limit. Stock shares can be held until you decide to sell them, or until you die in which case they can be transferred to an heir.

The Options Chain

Going Down the Rabbit Hole of the Stock Market

To get to an Option Chain on a trading platform, you may start with the chart and general page for the underlying stock. Here let's look at an example with Roku (ROKU NASDAQ).

This is a screenshot from the Think or Swim trading platform, but others are similar. Here you would select "Options" from the top menu bar.

Getting down to an Option Chain can be confusing the first time. You see rows of days and dates and some are marked "weekly" and others aren't. For this example we are going to select The first available weekly Option Chain. This would be for the weekly Option expiring January 31. Once you click on the 31 JAN 25 (7) 100 weekly bar.

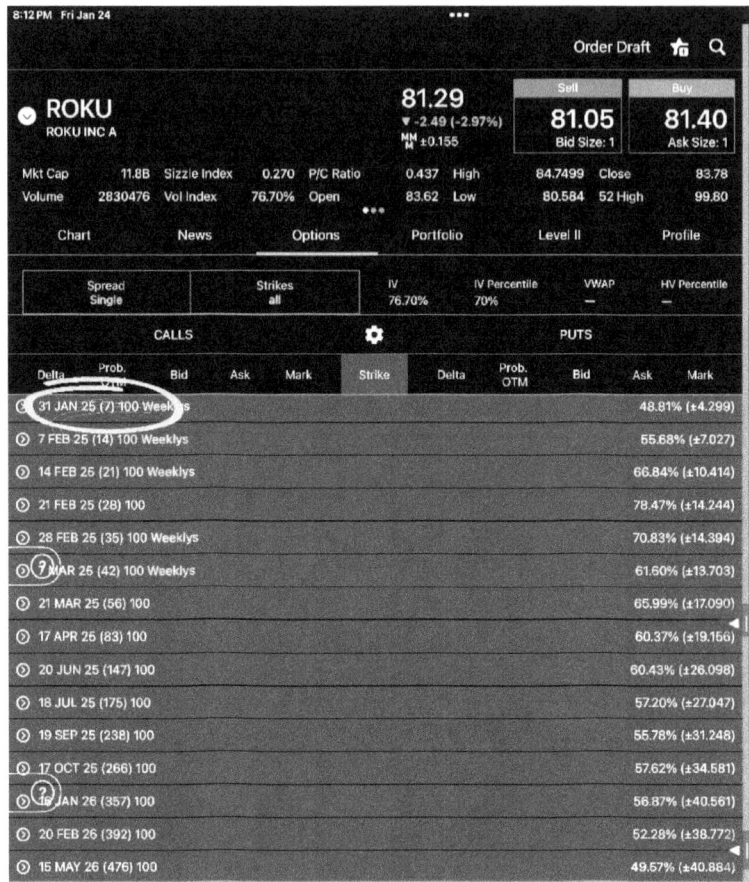

The first time you see an Options Chain it can be intimidating. Imagine this large grid in front of you with numerous columns and seemingly endless rows with numbers of varying values shaded in different colors

On trading platforms like Think or Swim you have a choice of what data you want to appear on the columns.

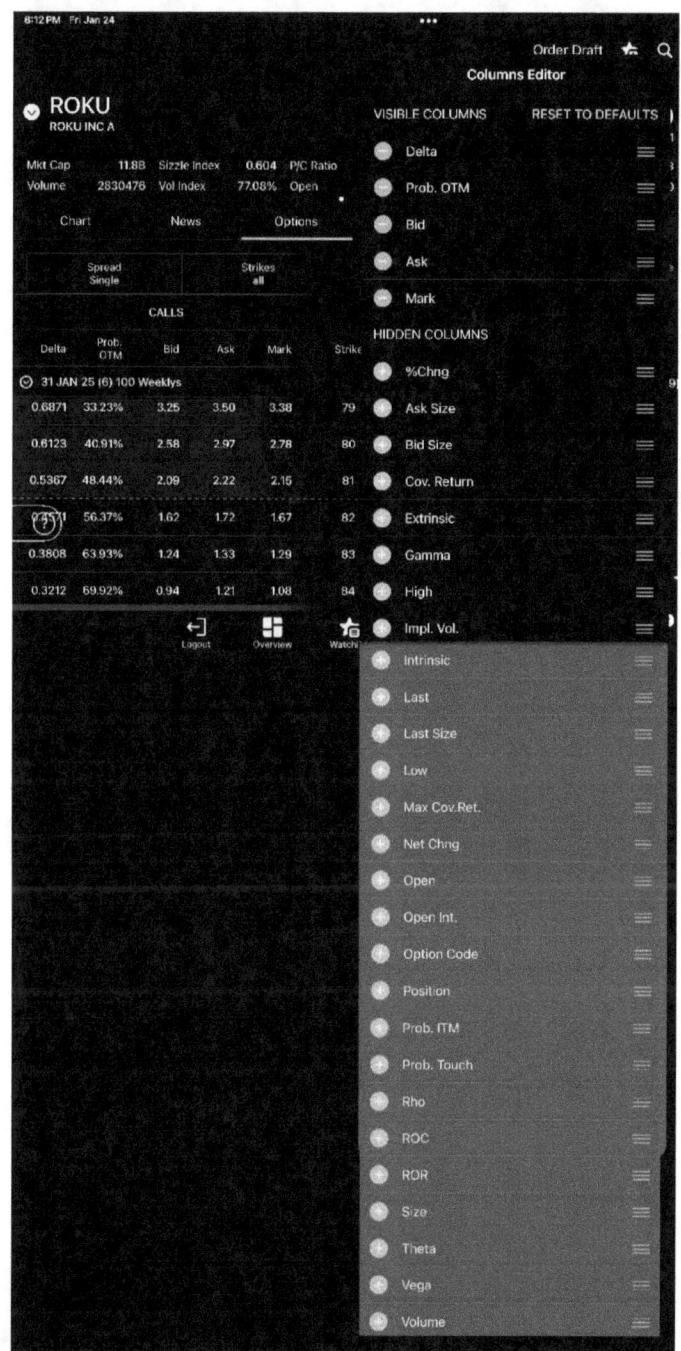

The overall chart appears to be shaded in blocks. The lighter shaded blocks are all of the Options that are right now ITM (In The Money) based on the current underlying Stock Price. The gray center column going up and down lists the different Strike Prices available for the Options. The horizontal dotted line between 81 and 82 on the "Strike" column shows the ATM (At The Money) prices for the Options.

ROKU — ROKU INC A

81.29 ▼ -2.49 (-2.97%) MM ±0.155

Sell: **81.05** Bid Size: 1
Buy: **81.40** Ask Size: 1

Mkt Cap 11.8B	Sizzle Index 0.269	P/C Ratio 0.437	High 84.7499	Close 83.78
Volume 2830476	Vol Index 76.70%	Open 83.62	Low 80.584	52 High 99.80

Chart | News | **Options** | Portfolio | Level II | Profile

Spread: Single | Strikes: all | IV 76.70% | IV Percentile 70% | VWAP — | HV Percentile —

31 JAN 25 (7) 100 Weeklys — 48.81% (±4.298)

_____ CALLS _____					_____ PUTS _____				
Delta	Prob. OTM	Bid	Ask	Mark	Strike	Delta	Prob. OTM	Bid	Ask	Mark
0.9665	3.75%	9.00	9.75	9.38	72	-0.0384	95.62%	0.06	0.12	0.09
0.9480	5.80%	8.15	8.70	8.43	73	-0.0579	93.46%	0.13	0.16	0.14
0.9164	9.28%	7.05	8.00	7.53	74	-0.0781	91.28%	0.18	0.22	0.20
1.0000	0.00%	5.50	6.75	6.13	75	-0.1066	88.23%	0.27	0.30	0.28
0.9204	8.46%	4.95	5.95	5.45	76	-0.1420	84.49%	0.37	0.42	0.40
0.8089	20.62%	4.75	5.00	4.88	77	-0.1885	79.62%	0.53	0.58	0.56
0.7547	26.21%	3.95	4.20	4.08	78	-0.2438	73.90%	0.72	0.80	0.76
0.6871	33.19%	3.25	3.50	3.38	79	-0.3102	67.09%	1.01	1.07	1.04
0.6123	40.86%	2.58	2.97	2.78	80	-0.3841	59.57%	1.35	1.44	1.40
0.5367	48.39%	2.09	2.22	2.15	81	-0.4629	51.61%	1.78	1.91	1.85
0.4571	56.32%	1.62	1.72	1.67	82	-0.5422	43.70%	2.30	2.44	2.37
0.3808	63.88%	1.24	1.33	1.29	83	-0.6265	35.52%	2.70	3.05	2.88
0.3211	69.87%	0.94	1.21	1.08	84	-0.6904	29.12%	3.50	3.80	3.65
0.2404	76.72%	0.71	0.76	0.74	85	-0.7426	23.92%	4.25	4.70	4.47
0.1964	81.81%	0.52	0.57	0.55	86	-0.7435	23.26%	5.10	6.20	5.65
0.1523	86.01%	0.37	0.43	0.40	87	-0.8371	14.71%	5.85	6.40	6.13
0.1210	89.00%	0.30	0.32	0.31	88	-0.8840	10.14%	6.55	7.35	6.95
0.0934	91.59%	0.21	0.25	0.23	89	-0.8849	9.81%	7.45	8.50	7.98
0.0712	93.39%	0.17	0.19	0.18	90	-0.9097	7.18%	8.40	9.35	8.88
0.0586	94.83%	0.12	0.16	0.14	91	-0.8979	8.13%	9.50	10.40	9.95
0.0481	95.80%	0.10	0.13	0.12	92	-0.9171	5.97%	10.25	11.45	10.85

The 5 columns you see left of the center "Strike" column are the Call Options. The 5 columns you see to the right of the center "Strike" column are the Put Options. If you are interested in buying or selling a Call Option you stick to the left side of the chart and if you are interested in buying or selling a Put Option you stay to the right side of the chart.

So for example, let's say we think that the Stock Price of Roku will not exceed $84 per share on expiration next Friday, January 31. We could go down the center "Strike" column until we find 84. The column immediately to the left of the center "Strike" column gives us a price of 1.08. This is telling us that the "Mark" (the price mid-point between the Ask price and the Bid price of the Option) is $1.08 per share, or $108.00 if we buy or sell this Call Option. If we are Bullish on Roku (we think the Stock Price of Roku will go up during the next week) we were to buy the 84 Strike Price Call Option we would pay about $108.00 and hope that Roku exceeds $84.00 per share by expiration to see some profit.

Or, if we are Bearish (we think the Stock Price of Roku will not go up in price and may even go down during the next week) then more than likely we could sell the 84 Strike Price Call Option and receive $108.00 in premium which we would keep as profit as long as Roku doesn't exceed $84 per share on expiration next Friday.

Which is more likely? There is no way of knowing for sure which way Roku stock will move, up or down during the next week. But if you look at the first Column on the left of the chart marked "Delta" you see the 84 Strike has a Delta of 0.3211. This indicates two things. Delta is a measure of how much an Option value will move with each move of $1.00 of the underlying stock. But Delta is also a fair indicator of the percentage of probability that the Option will meet the Strike

Price. So for every move of $1.00 that the Stock Price of Roku moves up in value, the Option value will increase by .32 cents.

Of course this is not a static number. If the Stock Price does move up, then the Delta will increase as well because the probability of the Stock price meeting the Strike Price increases as well. If Roku's Stock Price goes beyond $84 per share then the Delta will be between .50 and 1.00 approaching 1.0 meaning that for each dollar increase in Roku beyond $84, the Option will also increase by $1.00 per share.

But since Delta is also a fairly reliable measure of probability, it is telling us that there is statistically a 32% chance that the Stock Price of Roku will hit $84 per share at expiration next Friday. And to show us additionally, the second column on the left side of the chart is marked "Prob. OTM" This is indicating the Probability that the underlying Stock Price of Roku will stay OTM (Out of The Money), in other words that the Stock Price will remain below the Strike Price of 84. Here at the Strike of 84 the Probability of OTM is 69.74%, which means that there is about a 70% chance that if we sell the 84 Strike Call Option we will be profitable.

We might also want to be a bit more conservative and choose a further out Strike Price that would be a higher probability of profit, but a lesser Premium. We could for example choose the 86 Strike Price, and accept a premium of .55 per share, or $55.00 for selling the contract. In this case the Delta is .1964 which means that at this point our 86 Strike Call Option would increase in value about .20 cents for every dollar the Stock Price increases, and that there is about a 20% chance that the price of Roku stock will increase over the next week to $86.00 per share.

Also, the Probability of OTM (Out of The Money) is 81.81 which means that there is about an 82% chance that the price of

Roku stock will not meet the 86 Strike Price of Roku by the end of next Friday.

If you decide to sell a Roku 84 Strike Price Call Option Contract you would simply click on the actual "Mark" price of 1.08 and the following order editor box would come up.

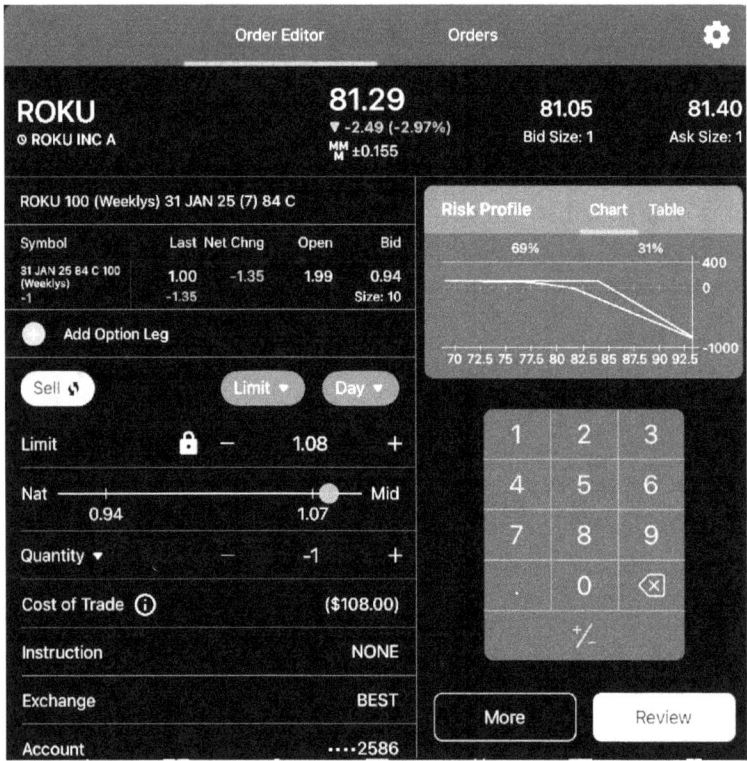

The Order Editor Box on Think or Swim allows you to select the Option Price you are willing to pay or get paid from buying or selling an Option. Here we have selected to Sell the 31 JAN 84 Call and we are asking for the mid-point price between the Ask and the Bid of 1.08. The Risk Profile is shown at the upper right as a chart or a table.

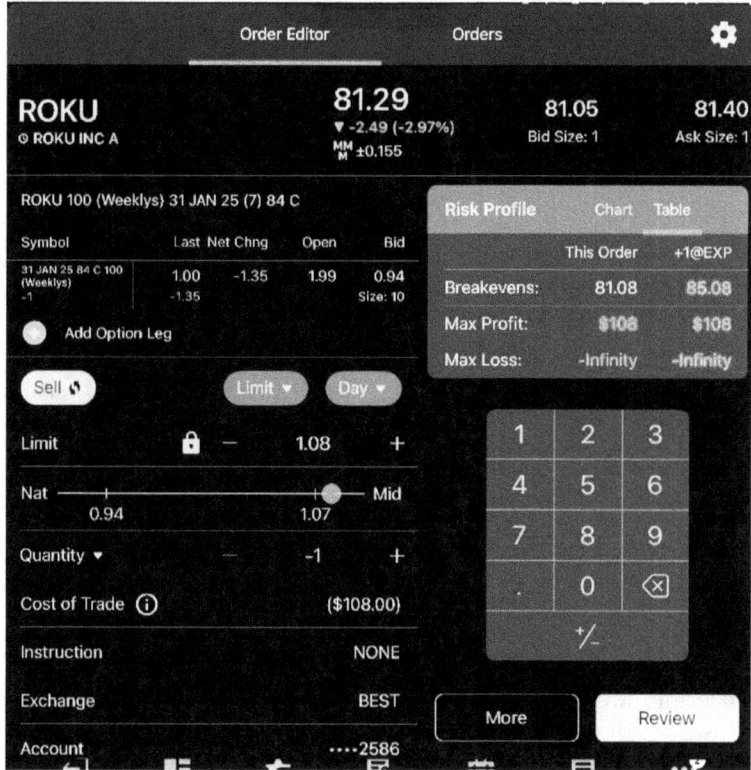

So let's say that you are interested in buying or selling Put Options on Roku for next Friday. Now we look at the right side of the chart. If we are Bullish on Roku and we think that the Stock Price of Roku will increase over the next week until Friday afternoon's expiration, we could sell a Put Option.

For this example let's look at the 79 Strike. The "Mark" for the 79 Strike Price is 1.04 which means we should be able to sell the contract for approximately $104.00. The Delta on this Strike is .3102 which means that we should have about a 31% chance that the Stock Price of Roku will go below $79.00 per share by next Friday afternoon. The Probability that the 79 Strike Put Option will be OTM (Out of The Money) is 67.09%, which means that there is about a 67% chance that the price of Roku stock will be remaining above $79.00 per share by next Friday afternoon at expiration. On the other hand if we are Bearish on Roku and believe there is a good chance that the Stock Price of Roku will go down by next Friday, we could buy the 79 Strike in spite of the Delta and Prob. OTM stats. In this case we would make profit if Roku stock drops.

Whether you are Bullish or Bearish on a stock has no bearing on whether you buy or sell Call Options or you buy or sell Put Options. You can be Bullish on a stock and either buy a Call Option or Sell a Put Option. If you are Bearish you can either Buy a Put Option or Sell a Call Option. Or in the case of the Married Put Collar Option Strategy, or the Wheel Strategy (yes, we'll get to those) You both buy Put Options and Sell Call Options at the same time, or Sell Put Options and then Sell Call Options in a cycle respectively. You have a lot of flexibility and a lot of opportunities to profit from the sales and purchases of Options, although the only time I buy Options is in conjunction with the sale of Options. Ultimately there is more profit to be made in Option sales.

Rolling an Option

Rolling Out, Rolling Up, Rolling Down

Should I stay or Should I go now?

Recently my daughter told me that she was thinking of getting a small aquarium for her dorm room in college and she was thinking of maybe getting a Beta Fish because they live such a long time. "A long time?" I thought. Beta Fish don't live more than a couple of years. Then I remembered something that to this day I haven't told my daughters.

Many years ago when they were 10 years old, they had a beautiful blue and red pet Beta Fish named "Lunar" in a small fish bowl. My daughters were quite attached to Lunar. It's normal for Beta Fish to stop swimming and rest for a while, but on one particular occasion it was clear that Lunar had passed away. At the time of Lunar's death my daughters were in school one day and my friend William Yetzer the New York hotel magnate was in town and staying with me. Bill and I went to the neighborhood Petco here in Studio City and bought a replacement Beta Fish that looked almost exactly like Lunar.

I had to repeat my trips to Petco every so often until finally when it was clear that Lunar died (probably Lunar the 3rd) we decided to bury it in the back yard. My daughter to this day still thinks that Beta Fish live a very long time because I realize that I never told her the story. So if you are one of my daughter's friends, please don't tell her.

Here it is close to expiration and the underlying Stock Price for your Option you've sold (Let's call your Option "Lunar") is moving more than you expected toward your Strike Price and threatening your profit.

If you were just trading the stock shares themselves without an Option you can always place a Stop order when you buy the stock (or anytime thereafter) so that if the Stock Price drops or rises to a certain level it is automatically sold so you can control your losses. However, there is no such Stop order that you can use that will automatically buy an Option Contract back when you are losing too much.

But there is an order that you can make so that if the price of the Option increases above a level that is comfortable for you it will be closed out. The major problem with this is that Option Prices do not necessarily correlate to the underlying Stock Prices. Your Option could be stopped out without any movement of the underlying stock just because of a rapid increase in Implied Volatility that could raise your Option Price. So, automatic Stops and Buy orders aren't practical in the world of Options Trading.

Another thing to remember, is that if you own stock shares and have an active Option sold against it, you won't be allowed to sell your stock shares while your Option is still active. So what you have to do is close out your Option by buying it back, and then you will be able to sell your stock.

The reason you can't sell your shares of stock while there is an open Option sold against them is that if the stock shares are suddenly sold by themselves, your Option position would be considered "Naked" which leaves your brokerage and you personally open to potential loss.

What are your choices? You could buy back your contract and take your acceptable losses rather than waiting it out and having greater losses. Or you could Roll Out your Option to a further contract giving the Stock Price more time to come down again. You could also Roll your Option Up either on your existing contract if there is sufficient time and Extrinsic Value left, or you could Roll your contract Out and Up to a higher Strike Price (if it is a Call Option) or Out and Down to a lower Strike Price (if it is a Put Option) and a further contract.

How does Rolling an Options contract work?

You would want to Roll an Option contract if you were losing money on it or if you could continue your trade to another contract and collect more money (additional premium). In this case you would close out your contract by buying it back. And then you would look to the next Option contract to see if there was enough premium to cover any loss so that at least you'd have some profit, or at least minimize any loss you sustained from closing it out. In other words, to Roll an Option contract you have to close out your current position and then open a new one on a farther out contract. Like Luna the Beta Fish, you're not really keeping your existing contract alive. You are just replacing it with another, hopefully healthier one.

The End Game – Exercising and Assignment

Like any contract, an Option Contract has an end date. For an Option there is an Expiration Date. For monthly Options Contracts, the expiration date is usually the 3rd Friday of the month when the market closes at 4:00PM (EST). For weekly

Options Contracts, they expire on Friday at the end of the week. But how does an Options Contract actually end? There are several ways.

If you have bought an Option, either a Call or a Put, and you are in profit or ITM (In The Money) you may want to close out your Contract during the week of expiration (or before) before Time Decay eats your profits. Time Decay is greatly accelerated during the week of expiration. To close out an Option Contract you've bought you simply sell it through your broker or platform.

It's like being at a casino for a long weekend. The end of the weekend is the "expiration" of your trip, but let's say that part way through your trip you have made a lot of money at the blackjack table and you decide you want to cash out and enjoy the rest of the weekend at shows and restaurants. Of course the casino would prefer that you continue to play, because they know that the odds are in their favor of recovering their money if you play long enough. But, you may exercise your right to cash in your chips at any time during your trip. When you cash in your chips and close out your account you are exercising your contract.

The same is true in Options Contracts. When you purchase the contract you can exercise and sell your Option as soon as the next trading day. You are not obligated to keep the Option Contract for any length of time. There is one exception, and that is, unless you have at least $25,000 in your margin trading account you are not allowed to buy and sell the same security the same day. It's called Day Trading and Day Trading is regulated.

But, let's assume that you have a monthly Options Contract and after 2 ½ weeks into the Contract you are profitable and are concerned that the underlying Stock Price might drop (if you have a Call Option), or that it might rise in price (if you have a Put Option) and so, while you are in a profit position and ITM (In The Money) you decide you want to cash out. In this case you can Exercise your Option Contract and sell it. Maybe you bought the Option Contract when there was very low Implied Volatility and therefore the Option Price was very inexpensive.

Now there was a political announcement, or a financial analyst increased the rating of your stock's company and now the Implied Volatility has increased and the price of the stock is up. Before it has a chance to go down again you might want to exercise the Option Contract by selling it and taking your profits. As long as there is ample liquidity in the market of your Option you should be able to sell your Option right away. So again, you want to make sure that when you are trading Options you choose a stock that has high liquidity.

If you've bought an Option and you have no profit through expiration, you don't have to sell it or close it out. You can just forget about it and let it expire worthless.

Whenever you buy an Options Contract, there is a seller of the Contract on the other side. Unlike the world of stock trading, in Options there is a winner and there is a loser. Most of the time, Options that are bought expire worthless. Most of the money in Options trading is made by sellers of Options. Options sellers assume greater risk than Options buyers.

In the example above the person playing blackjack at the casino made a profit and decided to exercise and cash in early. In this case the casino lost. Sellers of Options are like owners of a casino. Time is on their side for profit because of time decay and because they have a greater chance of keeping their money.

The Option buyer can only make a lot of money if the underlying Stock Price moves substantially in their direction, whereas the Option seller can make money if the stock moves down, stays the same or even moves toward the Strike Price as long as the Stock Price doesn't exceed the Strike Price. But there is limited risk for the Option Buyer. They can't lose any more than the price they paid for the Option in the first place.

For the Option seller, their risk can be a lot more. When you hear about horror stories of people losing everything in their account from bad Options trades, they were selling Options naked. This means their position had no collateral and no secondary protective position to stop their loss. Using the techniques in this book will keep any losses to a minimum, and in fact you won't be losing money with any Options you sell. At worst you may have to temporarily hold some shares of stock that almost always recover in short time. The other Option selling strategies that carry more risk are in a more advanced book. But if you only use the techniques in this book there is no limit to the profits you can make.

So, when an Option buyer sells their Option it is called exercising their Option Contract. When the buyer exercises their Contract it is Assigned on the Option seller's side. If you sell an Options Contract and it is ITM (In The Money) it has become profitable for the buyer and you might be Assigned, meaning that the buyer is cashing out. If this happens before the expiration date of the Option you have sold it is called Early Assignment. Early Assignment isn't common but it does happen on occasion. Most of the time if an Option buyer is in profit early they tend to wait for more profit movement.

But as a note this is one reason you don't want to sell an Option on a Dividend Stock during the time the company is going to pay a dividend. When a company pays Stock Dividends there is a date before they actually pay it called the Ex Dividend Date. This is the last date that a holder of the stock can qualify for the Dividend payment. If you are selling an Option on a Dividend Stock and the Ex Dividend date is before your Option's expiration date, the Option buyer could Exercise their Option so that they can own the stock before the Ex Dividend Date so they can receive the Dividend.

When you sell Options Contracts you have to pay closer attention. Since you've made your money upfront when you sold the Contract(s), Time Decay is not going to hurt your profits. In fact, if you are selling Options, Time Decay is your BFF (Best Financial Friend). This is because even though you already have your money, you only profit when you buy low and sell high.

When you sell your Options Contract in the beginning, hopefully at a high price, you are going to want to buy it back at the lowest price possible at expiration. It seems a bit counter-intuitive because in business we are all used to buying something at a low price and then trying to sell it at a much higher price for a profit. When selling Options Contracts, you are selling the Contract first, and then later buying it back at a hopefully lower price.

Although I'm explaining this to you so that you understand the mechanics of Options, the actual Options strategies that I am showing you in this book aren't going to take much management on your part. This is because the only Options strategies I am recommending at this point are all collateralized and therefore perfectly safe to trade without day to day involvement.

As I said before, the money is in selling Options but I am showing you how to do so safely. When you are selling a Call Option according to this book, you are selling a Covered Call Option. That means that if the price of the underlying stock goes crazy and shoots through the roof, you have the collateral to cover any increase in stock value, no matter how high the Stock Price goes, you can't lose money on the Option because you already own the exact number of shares to cover those in the Option.

In fact with these strategies, most of the time you want the Stock Price to exceed your strike Price and you want your Option to be Assigned and your stock to be sold in Assignment so that you have free capital to sell another Covered Call Option.

Similarly, when you are selling a Cash-Secured Put Option according to this book, no matter how far and how fast a Stock Price drops, you are protected from a loss because if the Stock Price drops below your Strike Price, you automatically are assigned and effectively own the stock at a discounted price.

Normally the price of the stock returns quickly and you can either sell Covered Call Options now that you own the discounted stock (the Wheel Strategy which I also show you in this book), or just cash out and sell the stock when it's value recovers so that you have available capital to trade and sell additional Options.

The idea is to keep selling Covered Calls and Cash-Secured Puts and Married Puts with Collars. The more Options you sell, the more Option Premium you can receive.

Sometimes Option strategies can be counter-intuitive. In the early 2000's I was working with Andrew Candelaria, one of top Advertising Art Directors in the World and he was working on a campaign for a horse wagering company. We were at the Santa Anita Park where they were preparing for one of the biggest races of the year, The Breeder's Cup.

The jockey of the favorite horse for the race, Chris McCarron was with us and he pointed out the owner of the horse that was the favorite of the race. I made the comment that I figured the owner was going to wager a lot of money on his own horse. Both McCarron and Andy explained that the owner was most likely going to wager, not on his own horse, but on the second favorite and maybe the third. I didn't understand why someone would bet against their own horse. It was to hedge against losing. You see, if his horse won the race, he'd have the winnings which were quite a lot for the Breeder's Cup winner. But if his horse lost the race he wanted to make sure that he was still able to walk away with some profit. He was not exactly betting against his own horse. He was basically buying insurance against a possible loss.

Selling Options can also be counter-intuitive. For example in the Covered Call Option strategy, you are buying Stock and then selling a Call Option against it. Much of the time in this strategy your objective is to collect Option Premium from selling the Call Option but also you want the Option to be assigned and have your stock sold automatically so that you have capital freed up to place another new trade. But this is an uncomfortable thought to some new traders. Why would you want your Option to be assigned and your stock sold out from underneath you? It's like why would you want to buy a house hoping that the bank would foreclose on it? Assignment, unlike foreclosure isn't necessarily a punitive measure. It is part of a business transaction.

In some Options selling strategies, assignment is not a good thing. However in the case of the strategies specifically discussed in this book, Assignment for the most part is simply a process of finishing a trade, hopefully with profit from either the Option Premium or the Profit from a move upward in the Stock, or both. Once the process is complete, an assignment of the stock clears the way for you to start another trade. But for some people they have trouble getting used to the idea that the stock they purchase for a Covered Call trade is there as collateral to protect the Option.

With more advanced Option selling strategies Assignment is something you definitely want to avoid because these strategies are not collateralized. They carry more risk and they can be losses if not managed on a more day to day basis.

So you might be asking, if the strategies in this book are safe and still make profit, why would anyone want to use more advanced strategies with potentially higher risk? Because higher risk Option trading strategies often require less capital and there are greater opportunities for higher profits, BUT they also require constant risk management.

If you are going to trade advanced Option strategies, even basic ones such as Debit Spreads, Credit Spreads and Iron Condors, you have to be watching the charts numerous times per day and have a really good understanding how to roll multiple leg Options past expiration, and how to close them out properly before expiration to avoid serious losses.

The strategies in this book may require more capital which could be a barrier to entry for people with smaller accounts. With one major exception, and that is my friend Ernie Varitmos's 0-DTE strategy, which is in my opinion the very best way to make potentially larger profits with very small risk and with very small capital commitment, which means it's the perfect strategy for small accounts, even very small ones. Admittedly though, there is more of a learning curve to Ernie's strategies. But they're not really that difficult and he's great at hand-holding and communication with all of his students on a one to one basis.

While I'm not big in investing in stocks with lower prices per share than say, $35.00, I understand that people reading this book may have small accounts or may want to start an account with limited finds, so if you are among them, the techniques in this book and the resources I recommend can be used well to profit from and build up an account. Aside from Ernie Varitmos's 0-DTE strategies, both the MoneyTree Visions software program and alert system can be used for smaller accounts, as well as Power Options analytics.

Options and Risk

We all know somebody who has gone to Vegas for the weekend and after a few hours on Friday night came to the room with a few hundred or a thousand or even a few thousand. Then they went back Saturday to win more and by Saturday evening they had lost all of their gains. If you play any game in a Vegas casino long enough you will most likely lose everything. Because that's the way the odds and the statistics and time work.

The next time you are in a casino, look around you. The chairs you are sitting in; the luxurious carpeting; The décor; the mere size of the place, and how about the electric bill to keep those magnificent chandeliers on 24 hours a day 7 days a week, 52 weeks a year?

The casinos didn't get built by losing money. And the casino house odds aren't large odds. Often they are only .5%, but .5% is all they need to win because statistics and time are in their favor. You may have a winning streak at the Blackjack Table on Friday night, but if you keep playing through the weekend you may find you'll eventually lose everything.

There is a great article and podcast by Kirk Du Plessis of the Options trading site, Option Alpha called, "The Casino's Edge and Options Trading" It can found at

https://Optionalpha.com/podcast/casinos-edge

There are many lessons to be learned from Casinos. Buying Options is much like going to Vegas as a visitor to gamble. Selling Options is like owning the casino. You may have small losses but if you are selling Options, both time and Implied Volatility are on your side. And you notice that casinos don't just have one game for visitors to play. They have the card games like Blackjack; Poker and even Gin Rummy. They also have Roulette Tables and Slot Machines. You as an Options

Trader will also learn to have a number of small, manageable positions rather than putting a larger amount of your capital in one trade.

So why trade Options strategies at all? If Options trading is like betting in Vegas, why give up your money? Because, unlike casinos in Las Vegas, there are ways to minimize or eliminate loss of your money in trading Options.

The success of Options trading depends on high probability trades and minimizing risk. Yes, you could buy cheap, low probability Options in the hope that there is an unexpected large move in your favor, but remember that time is against you in Options purchases. Unlike stocks, Options expire at the expiration date. Selling Options is like owning your own Casino. The odds are in your favor.

The strategies in this book are extremely low risk. In fact if you stick to the basic strategies I present here, you probably won't have any losses from the Options themselves. But there is potential loss if the stock you purchase for the trade goes down in value at expiration. But even then, you still own the stock and if it is a good stock, it should recover quickly.

It's Best Not To Trade More Than One Contract On The Same Stock At The Same Time.

There are Options Traders I know who will want larger premiums for selling Options so instead of selling 1 Covered Call Contract or Cash-Secured Put Option on a Stock, they sell several contracts of the same Stock to double or triple the amount of premium that can receive. I'm not going to tell you not to do this, but be forewarned that if the underlying stock goes down in value, for every dollar the value drops, you will be at a loss of $100 for each contract. So if you are trading 4 Covered Call Contracts on the same Stock at the same time, it means you will have purchased 400 shares of the Stock, and sold 4 Covered Call Contracts. But if the Stock goes down in value you would be at a loss of $400 for each $1 that the Stock goes down.

My advice is to stick to selling 1 Contract per Stock. If the Stock goes down in value, you are minimizing your loss and since most likely the Stock will recover in short time, you'll be able to keep more of your capital safe and be free to do other trades.

Most importantly, if you learn to cut your losses and get out of the trade when it looks like the market is going against you, you can recover minimal losses on further trades.

Only Risk a Small Percentage of Your Capital When You Trade

Financial Managers and Brokers alike will advise you not to risk more than 5% of your capital on a trade. And this is good advice. But if you have a small account and are trying to build it up, you might find that 5% is not enough to get you into a profitable enough trade.

All I can advise you to do is conserve as much of your capital as possible when trading in case the market goes against you. You will probably have to risk more than 5% of your account to build it up, but eventually as your account balance increases, you can decrease the percentage of risk that you allocate to your trading.

Try not to be impatient while building your account. Most profitable Stock and Stock Options traders take smaller profits but do so more often.

Remember, while you want to become a profitable trader. Your number one responsibility is to preserve and protect your capital.

Setting Up Your Trading Account

Before you can trade Stocks or Stock Options, ETF's, Index related trades or any securities, you're going to have to set up a trading account with a Brokerage. This is like buying chips at a casino so you can play, or buying tokens in an arcade (except that you can cash them back in later). There are Brokers who are better in dealing with Options in addition to Stocks. This is important because if you need help you want to know that your Broker is experienced enough to help you with your situation.

I was always recommending TD Ameritrade but I thought Charles Schwab was also a good fit. Recently Charles Schwab bought out TD Ameritrade but they kept the really great trading platform Think or Swim. Any Broker you sign up with will have a trading platform to allow you to make trades. My advice is to use a Trading Broker who is familiar with Options, has an intuitive, easy to access and use Trading Platform, and has live representatives who can answer questions and assist you with trades in the event you can't access your platform and need them to help you complete a trade. Having live brokers is really essential. There have been times I've been on the road and unable to access my Think or Swim and needed to absolutely buy back a short leg (a contract I sold) on a Credit Spread with minutes to spare, either because the stock was moving too quickly, or because it was a Friday afternoon on expiration day. The big Brokers will be able to take calls and assist you 24 hours a day, 7 days a week.

As of this Edition here is a list of recommended Trading Brokers for Stocks, Stock Options, ETF's, and Index related trades. The amount of money you'll need to start a brokerage account will vary depending on the Broker.

1. Charles Schwab (www.schwab.com)
2. Fidelity Investments (www.fidelity.com)

3. Tastytrade (www.tastytrade.com)
4. Webull (www.webull.com)
5. E*Trade (www.etrade.com)
6. Interactive Brokers (www.interactivebrokers.com)
7. Robinhood (www.robinhood.com)

When you open an Options Trading account with a major Broker you also need to be approved for an appropriate level of Options Trading based on your financial situation, your level of experience in Options Trading , and your investment and trading objectives. The 4 levels are –

1. Covered Calls and Cash-Secured Puts
2. Long Options, which means buying Calls and Puts
3. Options Spreads, basic Debit and Credit Spreads
4. Naked Contracts and Advanced Options

When you open your account you should request Level 2 at the minimum and if you can, you should get Level 3 approval as well. If you continue with Options Trading beyond the strategies taught in this book, and especially if you want to trade 0-DTE Butterfly Spreads or Batman Spreads you will need Level 3 approval. All you have to do is explain that you are learning how these trades work and you want the opportunity to trade them.

As for Level 4 approval, it took me some time to get approved through TD Ameritrade and honestly I've never used it. I don't trade Naked and I don't advise these trades for you. Which is why, and I've said it before and I'll say it again. Never, Never, Never leave a short leg (an Option Contract that you've sold) which is part of an Options Credit Spread or a Debit Spread open through Contract Expiration! Always buy back and close out any Options Contract you've sold before expiration.

The exceptions to this rule are the strategies I teach in this book, your Covered Calls, your Cash-Secured Puts, and your

0-DTE Butterfly Spreads. This is because these trades are collateralized and you are fully protected even through expiration of your Contract, or as with the 0-DTE trades they are based on an Index directly (SPX – or S&P 500 Index) and aren't subject to assignment. In my second book I show you how to trade Level 3 Credit and Debit Spreads and Iron Condors safely.

How Do You Buy or Sell an Option?

If you are ready to purchase a Stock or a Stock Option (including Indexes and ETF's) you can either call a Broker directly if you don't have or use a device. Or, you may use the online platform that your selected Broker offers such as the ThinkorSwim trading platform that is available if you trade with Charles Schwab. But most Brokers have trading platforms that are intuitive and user friendly. And most of the major brokers and platforms have 24 / 7 representatives to answer any questions and guide you through the trading process. You should never hesitate to ask even the smallest of questions. You are trading with them and they are making money off of you, so always remember that they are there to service you.

Either way, once you have set up and funded your trading account you are ready to go. If you are going to execute one of the Option trading strategies that I recommend and show you about in this book, you want to make sure that if you are buying shares of Stock in the strategy, such as the Covered Call Option or the Married Put Collar Option, you must first BUY your shares of stock before you are able to then SELL your Call Option.

Your ownership of the actual shares of stock is your collateral for the Option trade. Your Broker most likely won't allow you to complete an order if you are naked on your Option (naked means being exposed to possible loss by selling an Option without collateral or protection).

The exception is the Cash-Secured Put Option strategy and the Wheel Strategy, where you don't actually buy any shares of stock, but instead SELL a Put Option at a price such that that you have equal available funds in your account to cover the purchase of the stock shares if your Option is Assigned.

There are 4 ways you can place an order for Stock or an Option.

1.The Limit Order

The Limit Order places a Maximum Price that you are willing to buy or a Minimum Price you are willing to sell a Stock or an Option So, if you know the exact price you are looking for you would place a Limit Order and wait for it to be filled.

2. The Market Order

If you need to have your Stock or Option sold as quickly as possible at whatever the current Market Value is, you could place a Market Order to either buy or sell that the order would fill as quickly as possible regardless of what the Market Value is.

3. The Stop Order

The Stop Order is like a timer that you set to turn on your lights at home at a certain time when you are away. The Stop Order triggers another Market Order that you have set.

Let's say that if you are concerned that the Stock Price on shares that you own might drop quickly, you could place a Stop Order that would automatically sell the stock at a price you choose in order to limit your loss. Or it could be used to sell your stock for a profit if the stock reaches a higher price.

You would set a Stop Order to Sell the Stock when and if it reached your target price. Stop Orders allow you to be away from trading to do other things and still be protected from moves in the Market.

4. The Stop Limit Order.

The Stop Limit Order places a Stop Order that once executed places a Limit Order. But the possible disadvantage is that once the Stop Order triggers, if the Stock Price is moving too quickly, it could go through and past your Limit Order and not get filled.

With all types of the above orders, when you place them either through your Trading Platform or through your Broker directly, you can specify whether the order is good for the trading day (DAY), or whether you want the order to be good until you cancel it, or Good Til Cancelled (GTC).

For example, if you are selling an Option and you believe the best price you can get is on the Monday you are trading, you can put in your order to be good for the trading day only (DAY).

If you are looking for a specific price to close an Option Contract and you don't know when the underlying stock might reach your target price, you could keep the date open by placing your order Good Til Cancelled (GTC) which means it could take several days or even weeks but your order will execute when the price is reached.

How to use Scented and Unscented Candles

How can you profit from candles? Candles aren't for everyone, but I found that scented candles and wax melts calm me down nicely when I'm placing a trade. My favorite fragrances are the evergreens and soft spices that remind me of wintery Christmases of my youth in Michigan or the fresh cottons and ocean fragrances that remind me of the seaside California bed and breakfast inns in Santa Barbara or Pacific Grove but I also found that after watching Hugh Grant in Heretic I like to sit in front of my laptop wearing a cardigan with the aroma of a Blueberry Pie candle.

But the real profit of candles are unscented. They are the Candlestick Charts for the Stock Market. I rarely use them myself, but if you really want to get into it, the Candlestick Patterns can often help to predict stock movements. But remember, there are always outside influencing factors.

Candlestick Charting goes back to the rice markets of Japan in the late 1700's devised originally in Japan by a rice merchant named Munehisa Homma (1724 – 1803) but it was Steve Nison a top technical analyst who introduced the Japanese Candlestick Patterns and Candlestick Charting to the Western World.

The body of the candlestick has wicks coming up out of the top of the candlestick body and from the bottom. Each candlestick tells a full story about the price and activity of the Stock for the trading day. The body of the Candlestick appears as red if the Opening Price of the day is higher than the Closing Price of the day. The body of the candlestick is green if the Closing Price of the day is higher than the Opening Price of the day. The wicks, or shadows show the high price of the day and the low price of the day and the length of the body and wicks presents a precise picture of the price range for the day and where the price change is in relation to the opening and closing prices of the stock.

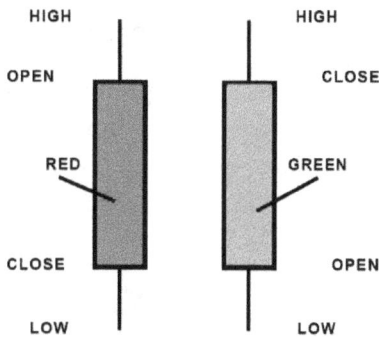

There are many complex candlestick charting patterns that can give traders an indication of where the Stock Price might be headed (or beheaded if you have a blueberry pie scented candle).

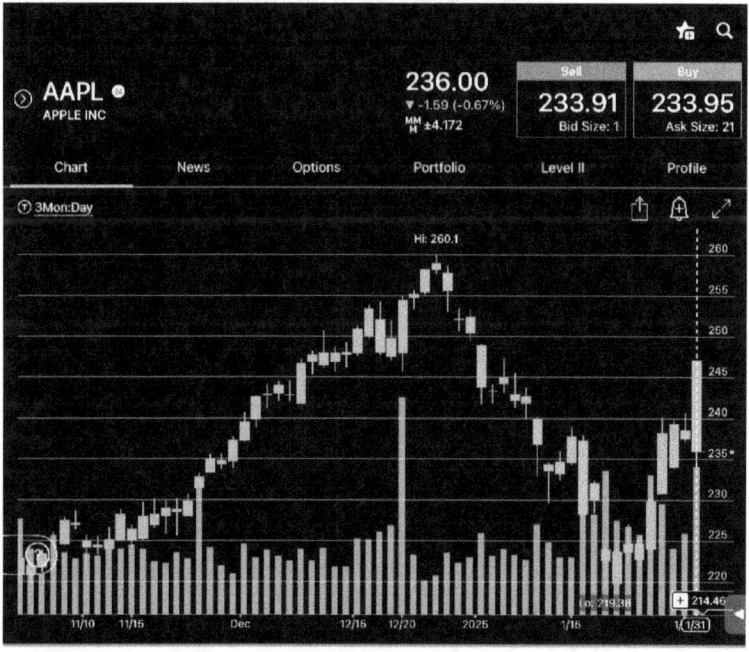

You can see in the previous chart the different variations in the length and color of the candlestick bodies as well as the wicks or shadows. Each candle is telling a story about the stock's price movement from open to close each trading day.

If you are interested in learning more about Candlestick Charting from the man who brought Japanese Candle Charting to the Western world you can visit Steve Nison's site at

https://candlecharts.com

Steve Nison, and no, his moustache is NOT a chart pattern.

Also, if you're looking for scented candles and wax melts, Winding Wick Candles has an excellent variety. . .Including Blueberry Pie!   https://windingwickcandles.com

Support and Resistance

In many ways the stock market is the perfect model of the free market system. There are sellers and buyers. If you decided one morning to buy a share of Apple (AAPL), or Google (GOOG), or perhaps even Amazon (AMZN)you would see the current selling price of the stock and you would buy 1 or 2 or as many as you would like. But every share you buy is coming from someone on the other side who is selling their shares at the same time. If suddenly one day everybody who owned shares of Apple decided not to sell them, You would have to wait until someone made a sale. But there are so many millions of stockholders around the World that the stocks for many major public corporations have high liquidity, meaning there is a lot of buying and selling activity on that particular stock.

Some people don't realize that when you buy a share of Apple, or Google, or Amazon, or Tesla, or Nvidia or any other stock you are not buying it from the company itself. Your purchase of a share of any stock doesn't come from the company or financially benefit the company directly. When the company went public some time ago their shares were put on the market in a public offering. Your purchasing a stock does indirectly help the company in the sense that the more shares a company has sold in the stock market, the better their opportunities for capitalization.

Prices for stocks are determined by supply and demand. No individuals, no corporations, no political system can set prices for stocks. When investors buy enough shares of a stock, the stock goes up in price in reaction to the greater demand and lower supply. When investors sell their stock, the prices go down due to increasing supply and lowered demand. It's really that basic.

So, when prices of stocks go up, what stops the prices from rising at some point, and when prices of stocks go down what stops them from bottoming out completely?

If you look at a stock chart going back several weeks or months or even the past several years you can mentally draw a line across the lowest prices and you might notice that although prices of the stock go up and down, there seems to be an imaginary floor that the stock doesn't want to go below.

This imaginary line is what is called Support. And during the normal trading environment, a stock might approach or even touch this Support line but it tends to bounce back from passing through, until some major event causes the stock price to puncture the Support floor level.

If the stock price continues to drop below the Support level it may have enough momentum to continue until it stops, forming a new lower level of support. But why are there levels of Support at all? What keeps a stock price from falling beyond a Support level? The market in general creates the value of a particular stock through supply and demand.

Professional institutional traders and experienced seasoned retail traders have pretty well done their research on the macro Fundamental Information including the company's earnings, valuation, capitalization, etc. and at any given moment there is wide knowledge of what a fair price for the stock is.

A price of a stock beyond this might rise or fall depending upon what you might call micro events. Maybe the market in general is reacting to a political announcement, or the earnings of the company or earnings for a competitive company in the same sector has been announced, Maybe one of the hundreds of financial analysts has upgraded or downgraded the stock. Events like these and countless others happen unexpectedly on a daily basis and cause the price of the stock to move up and down throughout any trading day, and the market reacts.

Remember that the stock market is actually an auction. There are those who sell stocks and the prices they ask for are called the Ask Price. The buyers of the stock are offering or bidding on the stock at a different usually lower price called the Bid Price. Most often the price that the stock actually is purchased for is around the middle between the Ask Price and the Bid Price.

So knowing that the market is an auction, if an event occurs that holders of the stock don't like, they very well might sell off some or all of their shares. As the shares are sold two things happen. First, there is an increase in supply of the stock in the market which would naturally bring down the price, but also other traders in the market see the sell-off and probably the reason for the concern and they also, anticipating a lowering of the stock price start to sell off their stock before the prices fall too far.

And now there is downward momentum as the price of the stock continues to drop, but when the price hits the Support Level (previously established lowest recent price) traders realize that the stock has now entered an area where it is perhaps at a low price and a good buy. So, traders who are interested in the stock and wanting to buy it at a discounted, low price have good reason to anticipate the price will either bounce up form Support or at some point reverse direction and head up again. Once traders start buying the stock again the supply of the stock decreases as demand increases and the price of the stock begins to rise again.

The same is true for rising stock prices. What stops a stock's price from rising beyond a certain point? That point is called the Resistance Level. And again, if you look at a stock chart going back in time, you will see the recent highest price the stock has attained. You might see the stock going up and down after that day but often you will see the stock price approach the top Resistance level, but bounce back down. This is again caused by a general knowledge of the fair price of the stock within the marketplace and supply and demand.

Once the stock has reached a certain high price, the market feels that any further increase in price is not worth the price asked and so buyers of the stock are reluctant to pay any more for the shares. Demand for the stock has slowed down and so the prices stop rising and there is increased supply of the stock in the market.

Stocks in the short term will tend to stay within the range of Support and Resistance Levels until some event causes the stock price to break though one way or the other. In the long run, depending on whether the market is in a growth economy (known as a Bull Market) or in a shrinking economy (known as a Bear Market) stock prices may move outside of the previously established Support or Resistance Levels.

Image by Sabrina Jiang. Copyright Investopia

The Winning Strategies

Sell A Call

The Covered Call

The Covered Call strategy is in many ways the most popular of Option strategies and one of the least risky of Options selling strategies.

Do you remember when I told you that buying an Option is like a Lottery Ticket, and selling an Option is basically writing an insurance policy, for which you as the seller get paid an insurance premium? Here is a good example. In this strategy you are going to have the opportunity to make a profit two ways. First you buy stock. Depending on how you structure the trade, the stock may provide some additional profit because the stock price is fluid. It moves up and down.

Stock in and of itself is something of value that can be used as collateral in a trade. Once you have the stock, You can sell an Option against your stock at a specific, safe Strike Price far away from the stock movement. Think of the stock as you would a moving car. When you sell the Option you are basically writing an insurance policy. You don't want the actual stock to increase and collide with your Strike Price.

You buy 100 shares of stock and then sell 1 Call Option against the shares. The goal is to collect the premium from the sale of the Option contract while using the stock as collateral against the stock price rising above the Option Strike Price.

In this strategy, you start by BUYING 100 shares of an underlying stock that you believe will increase in value over the period of the Options contract you will be selling. Once you purchase the stock you are going to SELL an Options contract in order to collect the premium.

The stock itself is purchased as a form of collateral. In other words, owning the stock is not your primary goal. The expectation is to have the stock Option you are selling assigned at expiration causing a sale of your 100 shares of stock, freeing up capital for a new trade. Your main profit comes from the premium collected by the sale of the stock Option, or in some cases a combination of the premium and a profit on the stock.

When you initiate a Covered Call you buy 100 shares of stock at the current market price. You can buy more shares of stock, but the shares need to be purchased in lots of 100 since each contract you sell against the shares represents exactly 100 shares. Then you can Sell 1 Call Option contract against each hundred shares of the stock that you have bought.

There are different techniques for selling the Call Option(s). I'll go through each and show you through actual examples with NIKE (NKE) stock.

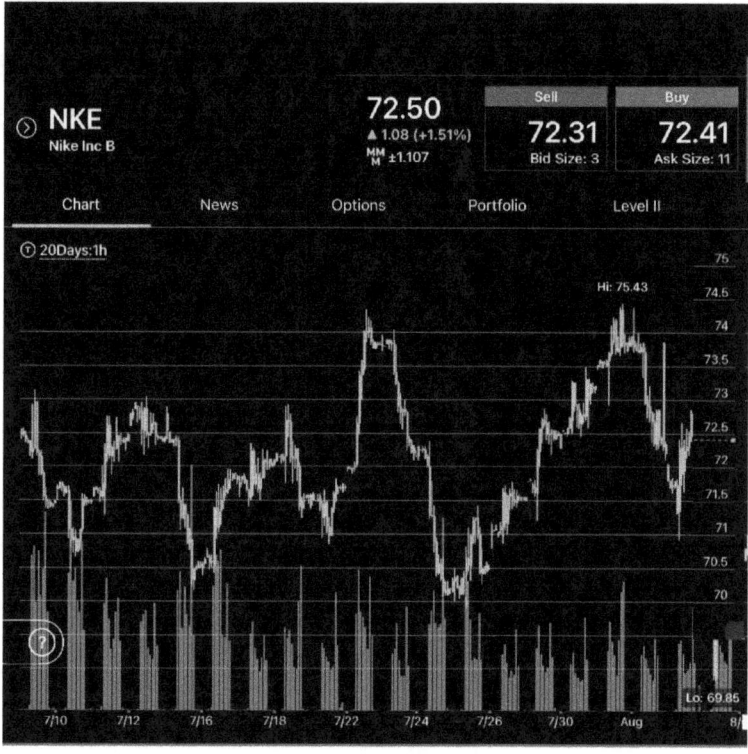

OTM (Out-Of-The-Money) Strategy

1. Some people like to sell out-of-the money Options. With this technique the Options contract Strike Price is above the market price of the stock so that you receive the premium from selling the contract, but also have the opportunity to profit from an increase in the stock's price if the stock increases higher than your Strike Price at expiration. In this case, upon expiration the Call Option would most likely be assigned and your stock would automatically be sold at the Strike Price of your contract. The upside of this strategy is that you profit from the premium from selling the Call Option and

you also could profit from the stock sale when assigned if your stock price has increased at expiration.

The downside of this strategy is that if the stock price decreases by expiration, you still receive the premium from selling the Call Option but you will still own the stock after expiration and you may have a loss on the decrease of the stock's price if it goes below what you paid for it.

The premium you would receive from selling an out of the money Call Option would be less then other strategies as your Strike Price is farther from the stock's market price, so the probability of the stock reaching your Strike Price is less.

In our NIKE example, you can see from the chart above Nike stock is selling for about $72.50 per share. So let's say that you buy 100 shares.

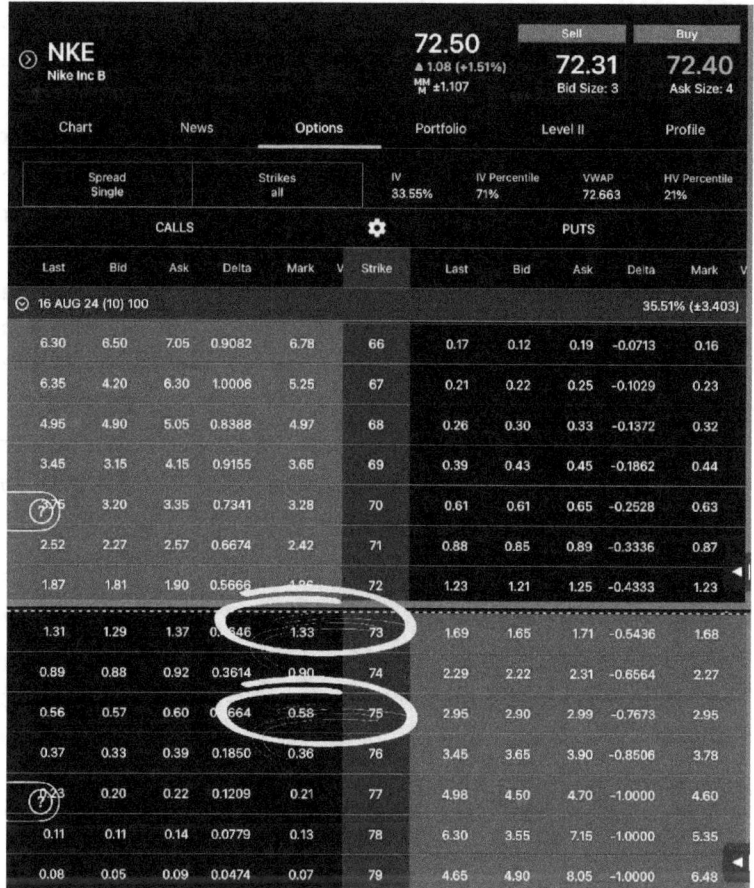

In the Option Chain chart above, the middle gray vertical column shows the strike prices. There is a horizontal dotted line at the current market price of the stock, $72.50.

The columns and rows to the left of the gray center Strike Price column are for the Call Options available to buy or sell. The columns and rows to the right of the gray center column are for the Put Options available to buy or sell. The rows with the blue background represent in-the-money Options and the rows with the black background are the out-of-the money Options.

Now you'll notice the columns titled "Bid". "Ask" and "Mark". The Bid represents what the buyers are offering to pay for the Option. The Ask is the price the sellers of the Option are asking for the contract. The Mark is the midpoint and the fair market price for the Option. The first out-of-the-money Call Option available is the 73 Strike. The Mark (mid-point price) to buy or sell this Option contract is $1.33 (listed as the price per share). If you were to sell 1 Call Option at the 73 Strike Price you would receive $133.00 as a premium. Remember though that you purchased the stock at $72.50. So, if at expiration of the contract, Nike stock increases beyond $73.00, your Call Option would exercise automatically selling your stock at $73.00 per share, giving you an additional profit of $50.00 (73 – 72.50 = .50 per share). Your total profit would be $183.00 (133 + 50).

Let's look at the 75 Strike. By selling1 Call Option at the 75 Strike you would receive a premium of $58. But additionally if Nike stock rose to beyond $75.00 per share by expiration, your Call Option would be exercised and your Nike stock would be sold for $75.00 per share giving you a profit on the sale of the stock of $2.50 per share, or $250.00. Your total profit on the contract would be $308.00 (58 + 250).

Now remember, in order to receive the full profit, the actual price of Nike stock would have to increase by the contract's expiration beyond the Strike Price. In the event in the above examples, Nike stock does not increase beyond the Strike prices, you would still receive the premiums paid for selling the Call Option contracts and after contract expiration you would still own the stock. With this strategy there is a lower probability that the actual market price of the stock will meet and surpass the Strike Price of your Option contract because it is farther from the actual Stock Price. But, there is the opportunity to profit from an increase in the stock price. Lower probability, lower premium.

ATM (At-The-Money) Strategy

2. You could sell a Call Option at the money. In this case you would sell a Call Option with a Strike Price as close to the market price of the stock you purchased. In this case your profit would come from the premium from selling the Call Option. You would not receive any profit if your stock increases in value at expiration. The upside is the higher premium you would receive for having your Call Option's Strike Price so close to the stock's market price. The downside of this strategy is that if the price of the stock decreases by expiration you will have a loss on the stock but you will still own the stock beyond expiration.

An ATM (At The Money) Option has a Delta at about .50 which means that the probability of the Stock Price moving in EITHER direction is about 50%.

For a short term Covered Call such as a weekly expiration, you don't worry too much about Delta because there is very little extrinsic value. Even though there tends to be more volatility in your trade because you're dealing with such a short period of time, the premium you receive when you sell the Option at the beginning of the week is the Premium you will keep.

The advantage of selling an ATM (At The Money) covered Call Option over an OTM (Out of The Money) Call is the higher premium. Yes you are taking more of a chance of the Stock Price increasing above your Strike Price, and you are sacrificing any gain of the Stock Price itself, but you already know what the Premium you are receiving is, and there is a chance that the Stock Price may go down slightly which would net you the Premium at expiration and you would still be able to keep the Stock, if that's what you wanted.

		CALLS				Strike			PUTS		
Last	Bid	Ask	Delta	Mark	V	Strike	Last	Bid	Ask	Delta	Mark
16 AUG 24 (10) 100											35.51% (±3.403)
6.30	6.50	7.05	0.9082	6.78		66	0.17	0.12	0.19	-0.0713	0.16
6.35	4.20	6.30	1.0006	5.25		67	0.21	0.22	0.25	-0.1029	0.23
4.95	4.90	5.05	0.8388	4.97		68	0.26	0.30	0.33	-0.1372	0.32
3.45	3.15	4.15	0.9155	3.65		69	0.39	0.43	0.45	-0.1862	0.44
3.25	3.20	3.35	0.7341	3.28		70	0.61	0.61	0.65	-0.2528	0.63
2.52	2.27	2.57	0.6674	2.42		71	0.88	0.85	0.89	-0.3336	0.87
1.87	1.81	1.90	0.5456	1.86		72	1.23	1.21	1.25	-0.4333	1.23
1.31	1.29	1.37	0.4646	1.33		73	1.69	1.65	1.71	-0.5436	1.68
0.89	0.88	0.92	0.3614	0.90		74	2.29	2.22	2.31	-0.6564	2.27
0.56	0.57	0.60	0.2664	0.58		75	2.95	2.90	2.99	-0.7673	2.95
0.37	0.33	0.39	0.1850	0.36		76	3.45	3.65	3.90	-0.8506	3.78
0.23	0.20	0.22	0.1209	0.21		77	4.98	4.50	4.70	-1.0000	4.60
0.11	0.11	0.14	0.0779	0.13		78	6.30	3.55	7.15	-1.0000	5.35
0.08	0.05	0.09	0.0474	0.07		79	4.65	4.90	8.05	-1.0000	6.48

To continue our Nike stock example, let's assume that you actually purchase Nike stock at $72 per share. If you look at the Option Chain chart above you'll see that an at-the-money Call Option should be selling for approximately $1.86 (price per share). So, if you sell 1 at-the-money 72 Strike Call Option you would receive a premium of $186.00. If the price of Nike stock at expiration is higher than 72, your Option will be exercised and the stock automatically sold.

No matter how high the Nike stock price has risen at expiration, you would only receive the initial premium of

$186.00. The upside of this strategy is that the premium is higher because the Strike Price is as close as possible to the actual market price of the stock, making the probability of a stock increase higher. Higher probability, higher premium.

In-The-Money Strategy

3. You could sell a Call Option in the money so that the Strike Price of your Call Option is below the market price of the stock you purchased, Since the price of the stock is already in the money and profitable, the premium you would collect for selling the Call Option is higher.

Another great advantage of selling an ITM (in the money) Call Option is the downside protection you have if your stock goes down in value. Since the Option's Strike Price is below the market value of the stock you are already agreeing to sell the stock for less than you paid. If the stock price stays above your Option's Strike Price through expiration your stock will be assigned and sold for the lower Strike Price but the much higher premium you receive for selling the Option ITM (in the money) will give you a profit even with the loss of the stock.

An additional advantage of selling a Call Option ITM (in the money) is that you have additional downside protection in case the price of the stock decreases by expiration. You've already figured in a loss on the stock.

The ITM (In-The-Money) strategy requires a little more calculation at the beginning, but offers the highest premiums and lowers the downside risk involved in case of a decrease in the value of the underlying stock. Sometimes it's hard to understand the logic of a strategy where you accept a loss on your stock at the beginning, but you are taking a loss on the stock to receive a much higher premium. The stock will be sold at the Strike Price upon expiration at a loss, but once the loss of the stock is subtracted, you should still be able to profit.

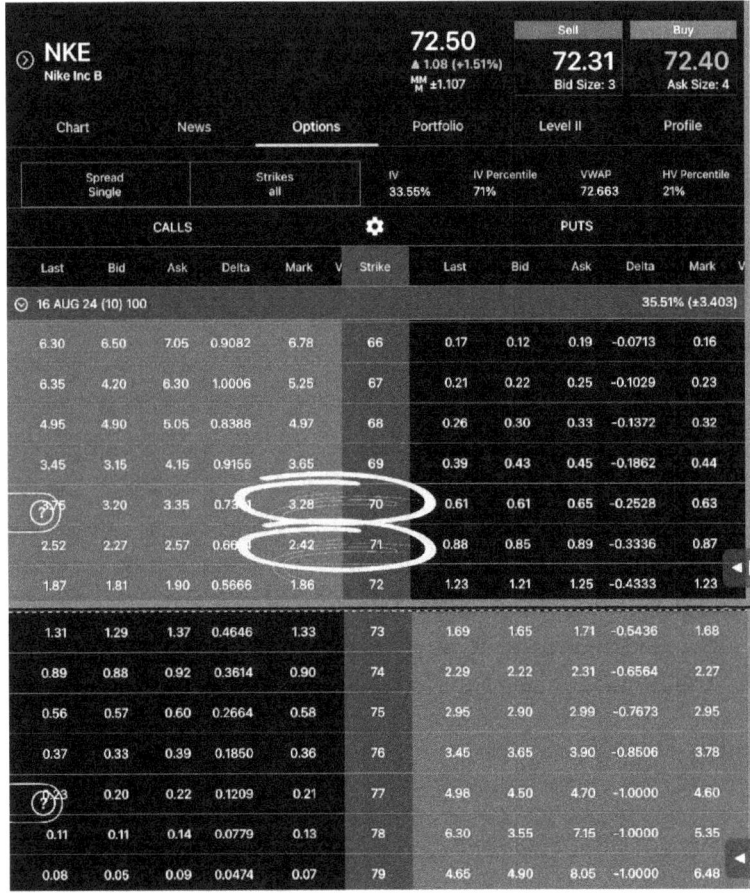

In our Nike example, let's again assume that you purchase 100 shares of Nike stock at $72.50 per share. Now look at the upper left area of the Option Chain chart above to see your Options that are already ITM (in-the-money). The 70 Strike Call Option is selling for approximately $3.28 (price per share). If you sell the 70 Call Option the premium you would receive is

$328.00, but the built-in loss of the stock is $2.50 per share, or $250.00 (your purchase price of $72.50 - the Strike Price of $70.00 = $2.50) If the Nike stock price is above $70.00 at expiration your Option will be exercised and your stock will be sold automatically for the Strike Price of $70.00. Your total profit on the trade would be $78.00 ($328.00 - $250.00 = $78.00). Highest probability, highest premiums with added downside protection against a loss in the stock price.

Some people prefer this strategy because while their net profit might be lower after the subtraction of the initial stock loss, the additional downside protection is worth it. For the Covered Call strategies, there is no risk in terms of selling Options because the stock purchase is the collateral to protect against any stock movement. You can't get hurt selling Options this way. BUT because you own stock you are subject to the gains or losses on the stock while you own it. If at expiration your Option is not exercised you will continue to own the stock and if the price of the stock decreases you can suffer the loss though you're stock will probably recover.

Let's say for example that you purchased 100 shares of Nike at $72.50 and you sold an out-of-the-money 73 Call Option for a premium of $133.00. During the Option term the price declines to $70.00 per share at expiration. You received $133.00 but you suffered a loss on the stock of $250.00. So, after expiration you will have a net loss of $117.00 but you also still have the stock and you now have the choice of either waiting for the stock to recover, selling another Call Option on the stock, or selling the stock to reduce any further loss of value and preserving capital for another stock and trade.

But now let's say that you had bought the Nike stock for $72.50 and sold an in-the-money 70 Call Option for a premium of $328.00 and the stock had declined in value to $70.00. upon expiration your Option would be exercised at $70.00 per share and you would have a stock value loss of $250 ($2.50 per share x 100) but you would still have a net profit from the trade of $78.

In both examples the loss due to the devaluation of the stock price was the same as the purchases of stock were at the same market price of $72.50 and both had the same value decline to $70.00. But the downside protection offered by selling the in-the-money Call Option kept the trade profitable.

Most Options traders use the Covered Call strategies to profit from the Option premium and the hope is that at expiration the Option will be exercised and the underlying stock will be sold so that capital can be recovered and used for further trades.

But what about people who already own over 100 shares of a given stock in their portfolio. Can stockholders take advantage of extra income if they already own stock?

The short answer is of course selling Call Options are a great way to make additional income from stock that is already in your portfolio. However depending on how long you've owned your stock, the original cost basis and how much your stock value has appreciated you may be subject to Long Term Capital Gains Taxes. One way investors and stockholders can take advantage of the selling of Call Options is by making sure the stock is traded within an IRA account. This way profits can increase in the account but are not taxed until a distribution is taken.

Sell A Put

The Cash Secured Put

One of the most asked questions from investors is, "How does Billionaire Investor Warren Buffet make his money, and what is his strategy for buying value stocks at discounted prices?" Mr. Buffet uses this strategy, The Cash Secured Put so that he can make money on his Options on a stock he likes, until he is Assigned and then owns the stock at a discounted price. Just as he has made a lot of money from this strategy, you can too.

Not to be confused with a Naked Put, the Cash Secured Put is an Option selling strategy where you would sell an out-of-the-money Put Option with a Strike Price below the current market value of the stock. The hope is that the Strike Price of your Option stays below the stock price so that upon expiration of the Options Contract you keep the premium. If the stock price decreases and goes lower than the Strike Price of your contract at expiration, then your Option will be exercised and you will own 100 shares of stock purchased at the Strike Price.

As opposed to the Covered Call where you purchase the stock first as security against the Call Option that you will then sell, The Cash Secured Put Option does not require you to purchase stock first before you execute the sale of the Option, BUT you must have enough liquid cash in your account to cover the purchase of the stock if your Put Option is exercised at expiration.

		CALLS				Strike			PUTS		
Last	Bid	Ask	Delta	Mark	V	Strike	Last	Bid	Ask	Delta	Mark	V

NKE Nike Inc B — 72.50 ▲ 1.08 (+1.51%) — Bid 72.31 (Size: 3) — Ask 72.40 (Size: 4)

Chart | News | Options | Portfolio | Level II | Profile

Spread: Single | Strikes: all | IV: 33.55% | IV Percentile: 71% | VWAP: 72.663 | HV Percentile: 21%

16 AUG 24 (10) 100 — 35.51% (±3.403)

Last	Bid	Ask	Delta	Mark	Strike	Last	Bid	Ask	Delta	Mark
6.30	6.50	7.05	0.9082	6.78	66	0.17	0.12	0.19	-0.0713	0.16
6.35	4.20	6.30	1.0006	5.25	67	0.21	0.22	0.25	-0.1029	0.23
4.95	4.90	5.05	0.8388	4.97	68	0.26	0.30	0.33		0.32
3.45	3.15	4.15	0.9155	3.65	69	0.39	0.43	0.45	-0.1862	0.44
	3.20	3.35	0.7341	3.28	70	0.61	0.61	0.65	-0.2528	0.63
2.52	2.27	2.57	0.6674	2.42	71	0.88	0.85	0.89	-0.3336	0.87
1.87	1.81	1.90	0.5666	1.86	72	1.23	1.21	1.25	-0.4333	1.23
1.31	1.29	1.37	0.4646	1.33	73	1.69	1.65	1.71	-0.5436	1.68
0.89	0.88	0.92	0.3614	0.90	74	2.29	2.22	2.31	-0.6564	2.27
0.56	0.57	0.60	0.2664	0.58	75	2.95	2.90	2.99	-0.7673	2.95
0.37	0.33	0.39	0.1850	0.36	76	3.45	3.65	3.90	-0.8506	3.78
	0.20	0.22	0.1209	0.21	77	4.98	4.50	4.70	-1.0000	4.60
0.11	0.11	0.14	0.0779	0.13	78	6.30	3.55	7.15	-1.0000	5.35
0.08	0.05	0.09	0.0474	0.07	79	4.65	4.90	8.05	-1.0000	6.48

Let's look again at our Nike stock example. On the above Options Chain chart since you are now selling a Put Option you want to look on the right side of the chart. The out-of-the-money Options available are in the black section on top. Let's again say that the current market value of Nike stock is $72.50. You want to collect premium but stay below the stock value in case of a price decline. In this example you choose the $69.00 Strike Price and collect a premium of $44.00 (.44 x 100 shares). As long as the value of Nike stock stays above $69.00 at expiration your Put Option won't be assigned. In the worst case scenario, the stock price would fall below $69.00 let's say for example to $67.50 or even lower. At expiration your Put Option would then be assigned and exercised and you would own 100 shares of Nike stock at your Strike Price of $69.00. Once you own the stock, if the current stock price of Nike moves at or above $69.00 you can sell the stock for a profit or hold the stock to sell a Call Option at a higher Strike Price.

If you try to Sell a Put Option on a stock without having enough cash to cover the cost of the stock you get into dangerous territory known as a Naked Put Option and unless your broker has cleared and authorized you to be able to sell naked Options (unsecured) your broker may not allow you to complete the transaction. As long as your sale of the Put Option is covered by your account you're safe to trade Put Options.

Again the goal of selling Put Options is not to own stock, but to make income selling premium. In this case you are selling an insurance policy, just as you would to a driver if you were selling automobile insurance. And the driver is paying the premium for that insurance. You are in effect insuring against a drop in price of the stock.

No matter what the stock does during the term of your Options contract, you have the premium you sold the Option for. If the stock price stays above your Strike Price, you have additional income from the sale of the Put Option. If however the stock moves down farther than you anticipated you also now own 100 shares of the stock at a discounted price. Again, most people in this position either sell the stock as it goes higher for additional profit, or now that they own the stock, they can sell a Covered Call Option at a higher Strike Price. Selling a Put Option until you own the stock at expiration and then selling Covered Call Options on the stock until the stock sells at expiration is called the Wheel Strategy.

Sell A Put, Acquire the Stock, Sell A Call

The Wheel Strategy

The Wheel Strategy starts with the sale of a Cash Secured Put. If the Option remains unassigned at expiration, another Cash Secured Put is sold and this process continues until the Option is assigned and you own 100 shares of the stock.

Then you start to sell Covered Call Options on the stock and if the stock is not assigned you continue to do so until the Option is Assigned and the stock is sold.

You've come full circle from selling Put Options and owning the stock, to selling Call Options and selling the stock. Now you can start again with the same stock or a different stock.

		CALLS						PUTS		
Last	Bid	Ask	Delta	Mark	V	Strike	Last	Bid	Ask	Delta	Mark
16 AUG 24 (10) 100										35.51% (±3.403)
6.30	6.50	7.05	0.9082	6.78		66	0.17	0.12	0.19	-0.0713	0.16
6.35	4.20	6.30	1.0006	5.25		67	0.21	0.22	0.25	-0.1029	0.23
4.95	4.90	5.05	0.8388	4.97		68	0.26	0.30	0.33		0.32
3.45	3.15	4.15	0.9155	3.65		69	0.39	0.43	0.45	-0.1862	0.44
	3.20	3.35	0.7341	3.28		70	0.61	0.61	0.65	-0.2528	0.63
2.52	2.27	2.57	0.6674	2.42		71	0.88	0.85	0.89	-0.3336	0.87
1.87	1.81	1.90	0.5666	1.86		72	1.23	1.21	1.25	-0.4333	1.23
1.31	1.29	1.37	0.4646	1.33		73	1.69	1.65	1.71	-0.5436	1.68
0.89	0.88	0.92	0.3614	0.90		74	2.29	2.22	2.31	-0.6564	2.27
0.56	0.57	0.60	0.2664	0.58		75	2.95	2.90	2.99	-0.7673	2.95
0.37	0.33	0.39	0.1850	0.36		76	3.45	3.65	3.90	-0.8506	3.78
	0.20	0.22	0.1209	0.21		77	4.98	4.50	4.70	-1.0000	4.60
0.11	0.11	0.14	0.0779	0.13		78	6.30	3.55	7.15	-1.0000	5.35
0.08	0.05	0.09	0.0474	0.07		79	4.65	4.90	8.05	-1.0000	6.48

Let's go back to the example of Nike stock above. On the date of this Option Chain Chart, NIKE stock was going for $72.50. In this example you would sell a Cash Secured Put Option at a Strike Price of $69 and receive a premium of $44.00 (44 x 100) Let's assume that the price of Nike stock decreases to $68 per share at expiration. Because the stock price decreases below your strike price, your Put Option is assigned and exercised. You now own 100 shares of Nike at $69 per share which was your Strike Price.

Come Monday morning, Nike stock is selling for $73.74. Since you effectively purchased the stock for $69.00 per share you could sell your stock for a profit of $474.00 ($4.74 per share) or you could use the Wheel Strategy and since you already own the stock, sell a Covered Call Option.

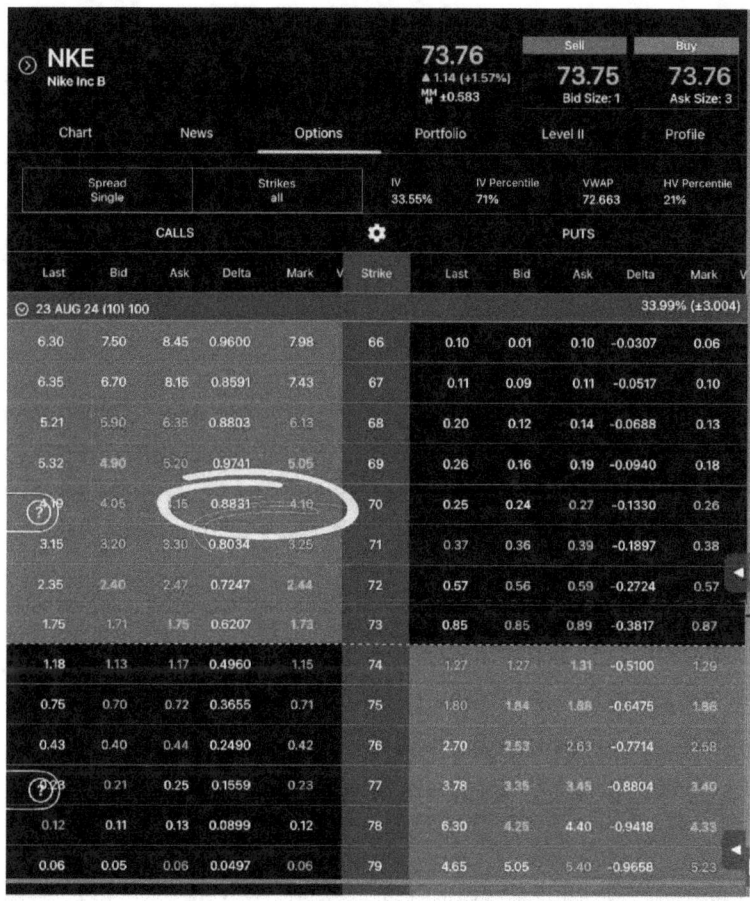

You have the opportunity to receive a large premium, as you didn't purchase the Nike stock for the current market price of $73.74. You received the stock at the lower price of $69,00.

The Covered Call Option available with the highest premiums are the in-the-money Options (blue area on the left side of the chart). The Call Options with the highest premiums available are those with a Strike Price below $70.

The $70 Call Option would give you a premium of $410.00 and the $69 Call Option would give you a premium of $505.00.

To figure out your net premium below $69 you have to subtract the difference between the cost of the stock at $69.00 per share and the lower Strike Prices. In this case the $68 Strike Price has a listed gross premium of $613.00 ($6.13 x 100). Since there is $1.00 difference between the $68 Strike Price and the $69 cost of the stock, you would subtract the $1.00 difference and your net premium received would be $513.00 ($6.13 - $1.00 = $4.13).

There is a $2.00 difference between the $67 Strike Call Option and the $69.00 cost of the stock, so you would take the listed gross premium of for the $67 Strike Price of $743.00 ($7.43 x 100)and subtract $2.00 to receive a net premium of $543.00.

The difference between the $66 Strike and the $69.00 cost of the stock is $3.00, so you take the gross premium of $7.98 and subtract $3.00 to get a net premium of $4.98

In this example you would have a number of choices of high premiums to sell a Covered Call Option.

You could Sell the $67 Strike Price Call Option which offers the highest premium, or you could Sell the $66 Strike Call Option which has a slightly lower premium but offers more downside protection in case the price of Nike stock drops.

If you want to take advantage of premium as well as possible profit of the stock, you could sell an out-of-the-money Call

Option (the black area on the left side of the Options Chain Chart). In the out-of-the-money scenario, you could sell a Call Option at the "Mark" price.

The farther up you go from the actual current market price of the stock, the lower the probability that the stock will move up to meet your Strike Price by expiration, so the premium is lower as you see higher Strike Prices. For example on the Options Chain Chart above Nike is currently selling for $73.74 per share. If you were to sell an in-the-money 74 Strike Price Call Option, you could receive a premium of 1.15 ($1.15 x 100 = $115). $115.00 might not seem like a large premium for being so close to the current market price of the stock, but remember that you also have the profit from the stock because you bought 100 shares at $69.00 and the stock has risen in price to $73.76. So you are in profit $591.00 ($73.76 - $69.00 = $4.76 + $1.15 x 100 = $591.00).

If you decided to select a higher Strike Price you would receive less premium but also reduce your probability of being assigned in case you want to keep the stock past expiration.

While the Nike 74 Strike Price Call Option has a premium of 1.15, the Nike 75 Strike Price Call Option has a premium of .71 and the Nike 76 Strike Price Call Option has a premium of .42

Selecting a Strike Price closer to the actual market price of the stock increases the probability that your Covered Call Option will be assigned and your stock sold at expiration. Most Option traders want this so that their initial capital is returned from the stock sale and they can try another trade. But, if you decide that you might like to keep the stock and just make extra money continuing to sell Option premiums from week to week or month to month, you can always select a higher Strike Price for a slightly lower premium since you're already profitable on the stock itself. Selecting a higher Strike Price decreases the probability that the stock price will meet your Strike Price and you may be able to keep the stock beyond expiration of the stock Option.

But most Options traders who are using the Wheel Strategy want to sell a Cash Secured Put and keep selling them until they are assigned and own the stock. Then they sell a Covered Call Option and keep selling them until they are assigned and the stock is sold. Once this Wheel Strategy cycle is complete, they start all over again.

Buy Stock, Buy a Long Put, Sell Numerous Calls

The Married Put with Collar

I do trade a number of strategies, including some of the more complicated Debit and Credit Spreads and the Long Butterfly that you will learn about later. But by far my favorite strategy is called the Married Put Collar.

Here is an analogy for this strategy that Ernie Zerenner of PowerOptions uses. Let's say that you own a video rental store (remember those?) You buy a DVD of The Godfather. When you buy the DVD you purchase an extended warranty against damage or wear and tear. Now that you own the DVD, you rent it out on a weekly basis for income. The income that you receive from your weekly rentals is more than enough to pay for the extended warranty and have profit.

This Option strategy is much the same. You buy 100 shares of a Stock and then you buy a long term Put Option (your warranty) which will protect your stock from a loss in value. Then you can sell Covered Call Options against the Stock, but this time you are also protected from a loss in Stock Value. In other words, depending on the Strike Price you select for your long term Put Option, you aren't going to lose money.

Remember that in order to trade a Covered Call, you first buy 100 shares of the stock you are interested in trading. Then you sell a Call Option against that stock. Any problem doesn't come from the Call Option, but rather the possible issue from the price of the stock declining.

Enter the Married Put. In this trade you would first buy 100 shares of stock but then you would buy an ITM (In The Money) long term Put Option, going out preferably about 6 months. An

ITM (In The Money Put Option is preferable to an ATM (At The Money) Put Option or an OTM (Out of The Money) Put Option, because if it is already In The Money, it has a high Delta, meaning that for every one dollar drop in the price of your stock, the In The Money Put will increase in value at or near the same amount. So, from the moment you buy your Put Option your stock value is protected from a drop in price.

If you were to choose an OTM (Out of The Money) Put Option it would be less expensive for you to purchase, but the Put would protect your stock value only after the stock drops in value past your Out of The Money Strike Price.

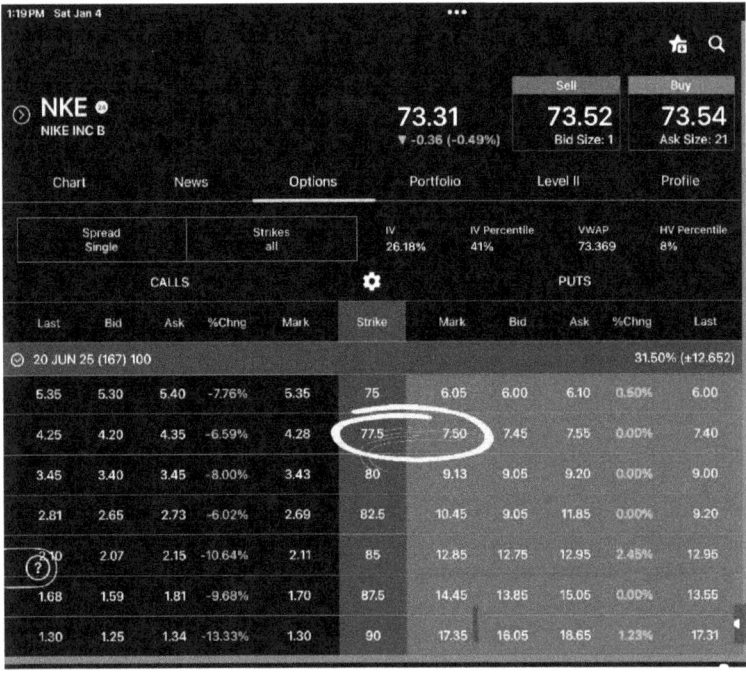

In the above example, on January 06 You would have bought 100 shares of Nike Stock (NKE NYSE) at $73.31 per share. Then you would have bought a long term ITM (In The Money) protective Put Option going out six months with a June

expiration date. You'd want to go several strikes In The Money so you could choose the 77.5 Put Option which is going for $7.50 per share, or $750 for the Option Contract.

Once you have bought your Put Option, then you can sell weekly or monthly Covered Call Options.

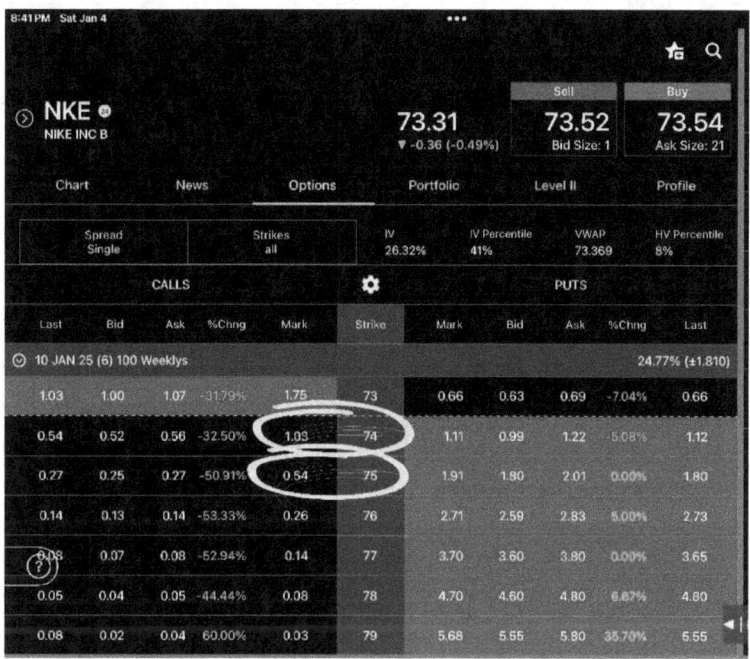

In the example above, you have your shares of Nike Stock and have purchased a long term In The Money Protective Put Option with a 77.5 Strike Price. Now you can sell Weekly or Monthly Covered Call Options against the Nike Stock. If you were to choose the next weekly Options Contract you could sell a Covered Call Option for $1.03 at the 74 Strike Price, or $.54 at the 75 Strike Price.

If you were to sell the 74 Strike and If at expiration next Friday Nike Stock Price has risen above $74.00 per share, you would receive your premium of $103.00 plus the profit on the stock of $69.00 ($74.00 - $73.31 = $.69 per share) for a total of $172.00.

If you were to sell the 75 Strike and if at expiration next Friday Nike Stock Price has risen above $75.00 per share you would receive your premium of $.54 per share, or $54.00 for the Options Contract and the profit on the stock of $1.69 per share or $169.00 ($75.00 per share - $73.31 per share = $1.69 per share or $169 for 100 shares). Your total profit would be $223.00.

Assuming the stock price of NIKE increased and your stock was assigned, you could simply buy the stock again on the next Monday morning and sell another Covered Call Option.

If the NIKE Stock doesn't increase in value over the coming week by expiration, then you would still receive a premium of $103.00 for the 74 Strike, or $54.00 for the 75 Strike, but you would still own the stock.

You can see how you could pay for the Long Term Protective In The Money Put Option in just a few weeks out of the total 24 weeks that you have available to sell weekly Covered Call Options for profit.

This strategy is great for a number of reasons.

1. You own the underlying stock but are protected from a decline in the stock price because of your protective Put Option that you bought.
2. You don't have to sell any ITM (In The Money) or ATM (At The Money) Covered Call Options because there is no downside that you have to protect the stock price from. OTM (Out of The Money) Covered Calls not only give you

the premium from selling the Option, but you can also profit from the stock price increase if you choose a higher Strike Price when you sell your Call Option.

3. If you buy a long term ITM (In The Money) Put Option going out six months, you have the opportunity to sell 24 weekly Covered Call Options, or six Monthly Covered Call Options, or a combination of both. And you'll be able to offset the price of the long term Put Option and still make plenty of profit. This strategy is called a Bullet-Proof Trade because you have the potential to make unlimited profit while being protected against any loss in the stock.

Protecting The Risks of
Covered Call and Cash Secured Put Options

Every investment opportunity has some degree of risk. The Options strategies selected for this book are those that have the smallest risk in terms of downside from Options trading. It is possible however to lose money on these Options trading strategies, not from the Options themselves, but from a sudden devaluation of the underlying stock.

The risks are no different than the downside of buying the stocks themselves since all of these strategies involve buying stock or having stock assigned to you through Option exercise. Option premiums are easy to calculate and once purchased or sold, Option premiums when sold are immediately deposited into your account where they remain yours. There are occasions when the price of the underlying stock will move against your position and not only threaten your profits, but may create a loss.

A value loss of stock during the term of an Option is often not a major problem because you continue to own the stock after the Option has expired, and stock almost always has an opportunity in time to recover and even show profit.

Following the strategies in this book will prevent loss from Options trading because we use stock as collateral against large moves. BUT we can't predict or control the stock market itself and a drop in stock prices can create a loss while you own the underlying stock.

1 In case of a fall in stock prices at Option expiration, you still own the stock and wait for the stock prices to recover.

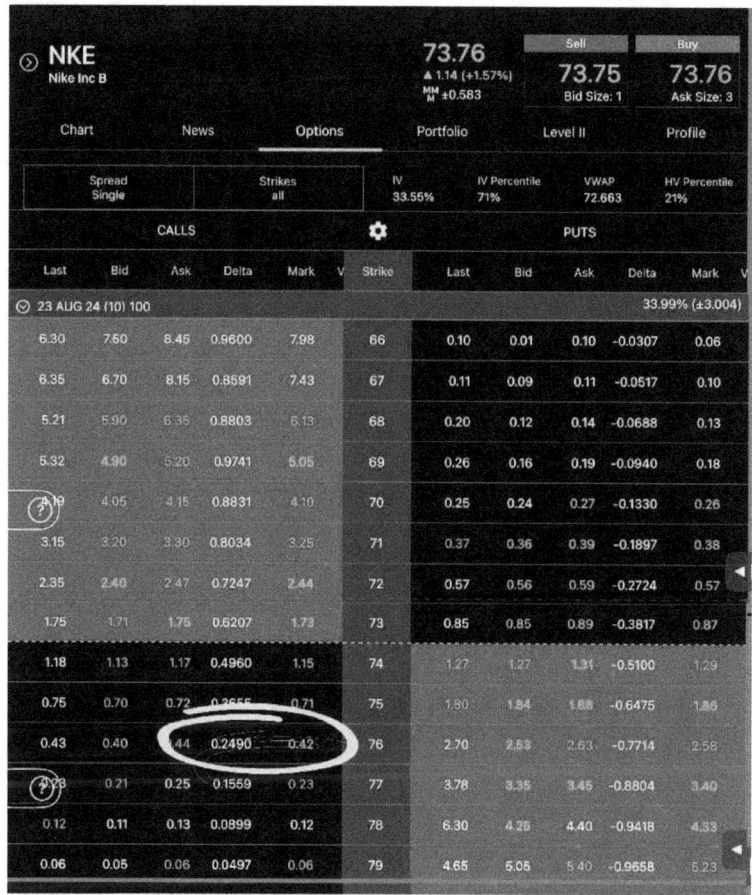

In the example above let's say that after purchasing 100 shares of Nike at $73.76 per share you also then sell a Covered Call Option with a $76 Strike Price. You receive a premium of .42 which means that immediately you receive a premium of $42.00. The hope in the best case scenario is that by expiration of the Covered Call Option the price of the Nike stock will increase beyond $76.00 per share, at which time the Option will be assigned and the stock will be sold for a profit of $2.24 per share x 100 + the premium of $42.00 = $266.00. Another acceptable scenario would be receiving the premium of .42 per share but having the price of Nike stock reach some price between what you paid at $73.76 and $76.00. In this case the Option would not be assigned and your stock would not be sold by being exercised. On Monday morning after expiration of the Option you could sell the stock for the profit and of course you would still have the premium you received of $42.00 on top of whatever profit your stock realized by selling it.

But what if after you purchase the Nike stock for $73.76 per share and the 76 Call Option, the stock price drops during the Option period to $70.00 per share. You now have a loss of $3.76 per share or $376.00. Your instinct might be to sell the stock before it decreases in price further, however you can't sell the stock and still have an open Option contract. This would leave you naked in the market, without the stock collateral to protect you and most likely your broker will not let you complete the stock sale until you first buy back your Option. This can be done but it will cost you some or more than your collected premium on top of the loss of the stock.

There are several ways you can minimize a loss of stock value during the term of an Option.

2 If the stock price decreases too far and too quickly, buy back your Call Option and sell the stock.

Normally when you decide to exit an Option strategy you close the contract by buying back an Option if you originally sold it. In some cases the price of the Option might be expensive to close unless you roll it out to another future Contract. If you have sold a Call Option and the stock price has gone way above your original Strike Price you are now deep in the money

Standard Deviation

What is a Standard Deviation and why should you care? Simply, if you are going to invest in a stock or an Option wouldn't it be great if you could know that you could be successful within a 70% probability? If you knew how far the stock price is likely to go up or down you could make more successful trades. And without having to know anything about statistics or even much about math there is a really easy and quick way to calculate what the expected move is of a stock within a period of time.

In statistics, the Standard Deviation is a measurement of how far something is going to drift away from its mean or average. Specifically, it is really useful in trying to estimate how far a stock will rise in price or fall in price in a certain time. Let's say for example that you know the current price of a stock that you want to invest in. If you could have a measurement of likely that stock will move up or down your chances of being profitable increase and more importantly your chances of losing money on the stock are greatly decreased. Let's take an example of Nvidia Stock (NVDA NASDAQ)

This chart shows Nvidia stock for the last 180 days of trading. If you wanted to invest in NVDA and buy stock, or buy or sell stock Options it would be helpful to know how far the stock might rise or fall from its current position.

About 70% of the time (68.4%) a stock will move within a range called a Standard Deviation. In the stock market we refer to this possible move up or down as the Expected Move. Take a good look at the above chart. Do you think NVDA will be moving up or down? How far do you think it might move? These are rhetorical questions because nobody has a clue which way NVDA will go or whether up or down.

But history and a little math can give us an idea a range and how likely that NVDA might move. According to a 2 minute calculation of the Expected Move of NVDA over the next month I found that there is a 70% chance that NVDA could move up to $130.63 or it could move down to $99.76, in other words, the calculated Expected Move is + or – 15.43.

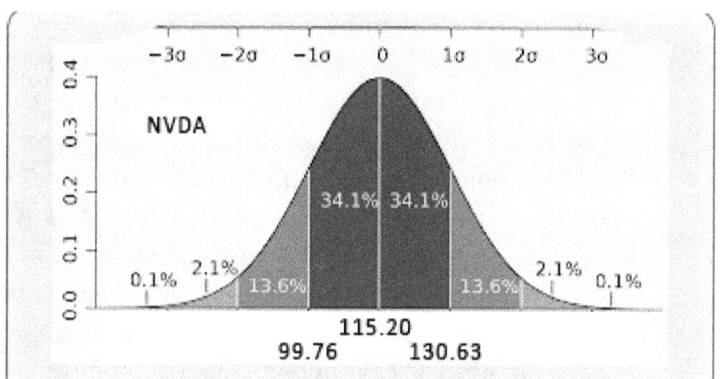

The Expected Move

The Expected Move is a simple calculation which indicates how far a stock is likely to move in either direction over the period of the Option. This calculation shows the movement of the stock within 1 Standard Deviation.

To calculate the Expected Move, you first go to the Stock Option Chain and select an Option period that is of interest to you. It doesn't matter whether the Option date you are choosing is a weekly Option or a monthly Option and you want to be sure to use the actual Option chain of the actual Option you are interested in buying or selling, not necessarily the closest one in time (unless that is the Option you are interested in).

1. Take the actual current market price of the underlying stock.
2. Now open the Option chain that you are interested in and find the closest Call Option strike price to the actual current stock price.
3. Take the Bid price of that Option strike price, add it to the Ask price of that same Option and then divide by 2 to get the mid point or average of the call Option. Note that depending on your broker and the trading platform you are using, on many Option chains the midpoint or average is already in a column of its own called the "Mark". For the purposes of illustration I am showing you the complete calculations anyway since the Mark may not always appear on your Option chain.
4. On the same strike price, go to the far right in the Options chain and find the Bid price for the Put Option and add it to the Ask price of the put Option and then divide by 2 to get the mid point or average of the put Option.
5. Add the "Mark" or mid point price of the Call Option to the "Mark" or mid point price of the Put Option.
6. This number is the Expected Move of the stock over the term of the Option contract. Notice that there is no way of knowing whether the stock will move up or move down, but within an approximately 70% probability (68.2%) the stock will move within the upper and lower range of the Expected Move.
7. Remember to always use the closest strike price to the actual current value of the stock.

Here is an example.

Example 1

Dick's Sporting Goods (DKS NYSE) is currently trading at 208

And let's say that you want to trade a weekly Option expiring Friday afternoon, September 13

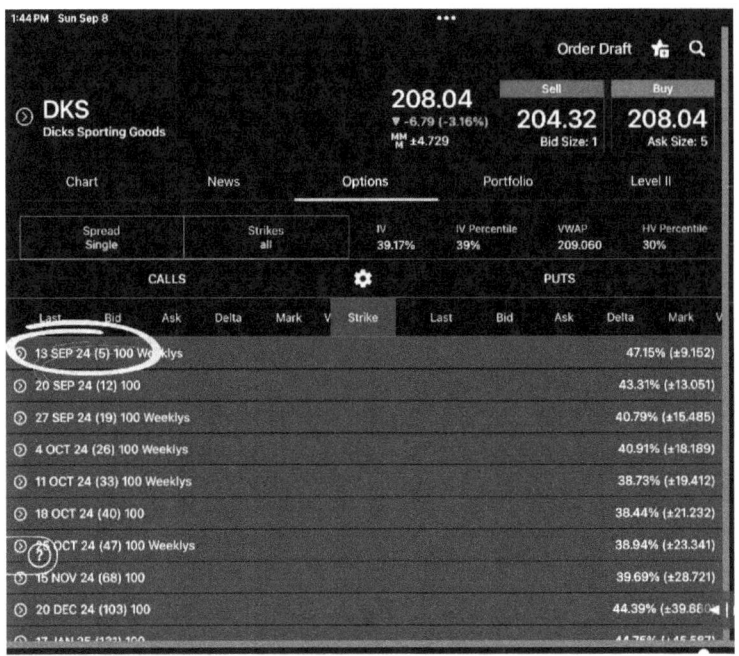

Open the 13 Sept 2024 weekly Option chain. Notice in the above illustration right underneath the 13 Sept 24 Weekly Option there is the closest monthly Option in case you want to work with a monthly Option. But in this case we are going to be interested in the weekly September 13, 2024 Option chain.

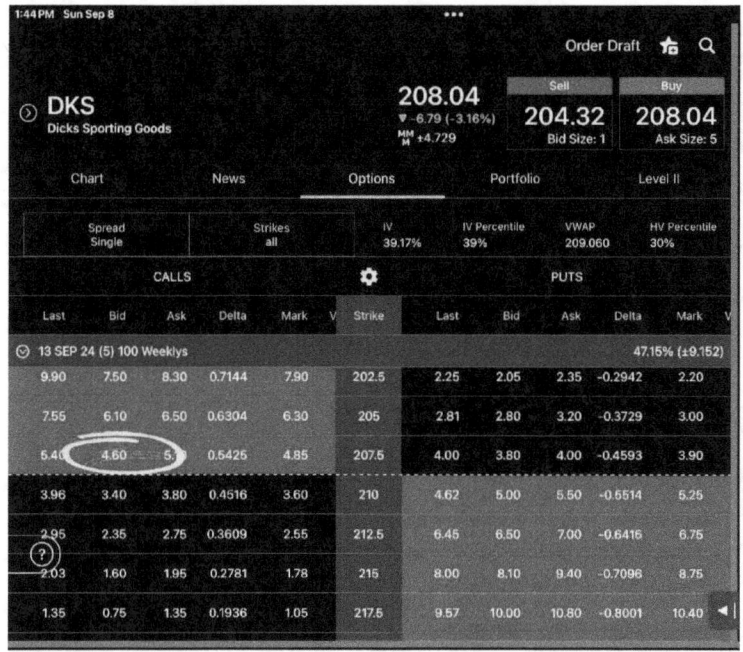

You can see above that the closest Option strike price to the actual current stock price of $208 is the 207.5. So first on the Call Option side you would take the price of the Bid on this Option which is 4.60 and then you would add the Call Option Ask price.

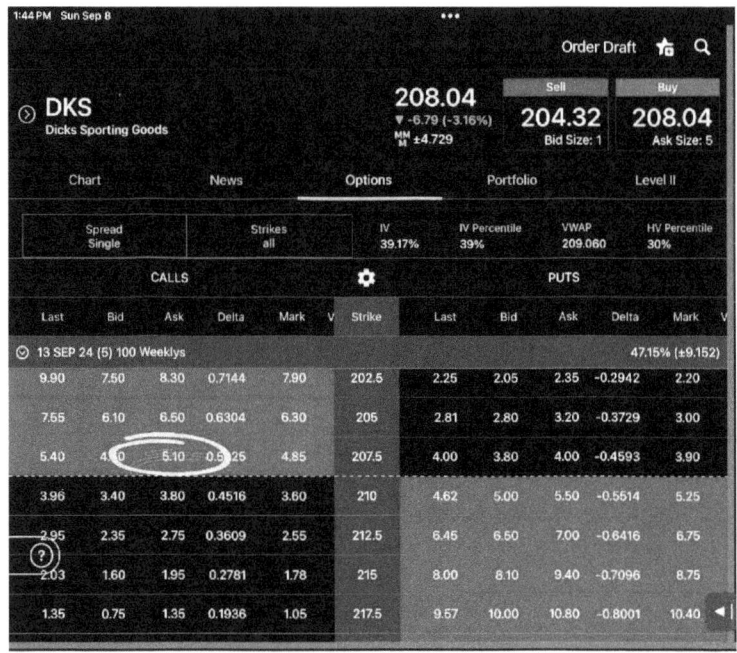

The Bid price of 4.60 is added to the Ask price of 5.10 and then you would divide by 2 to get the mid point price or average. In this case the mid point average of the Call is 4.85.

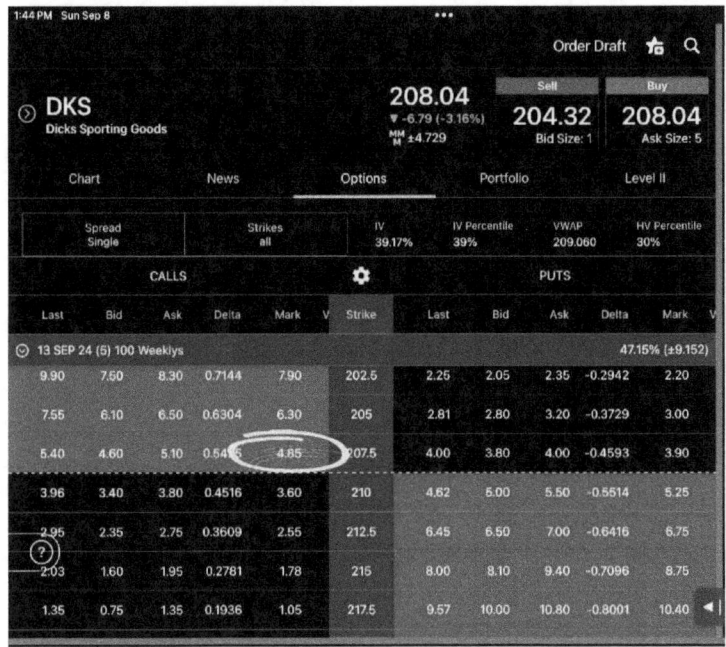

Notice that on this platform which is Think or Swim there is already a column labelled "Mark" which has the midpoint of 4.85. Not all platforms will have this so you might have to do the calculations.

Now you have to do the same to the Put Option side of the chain.

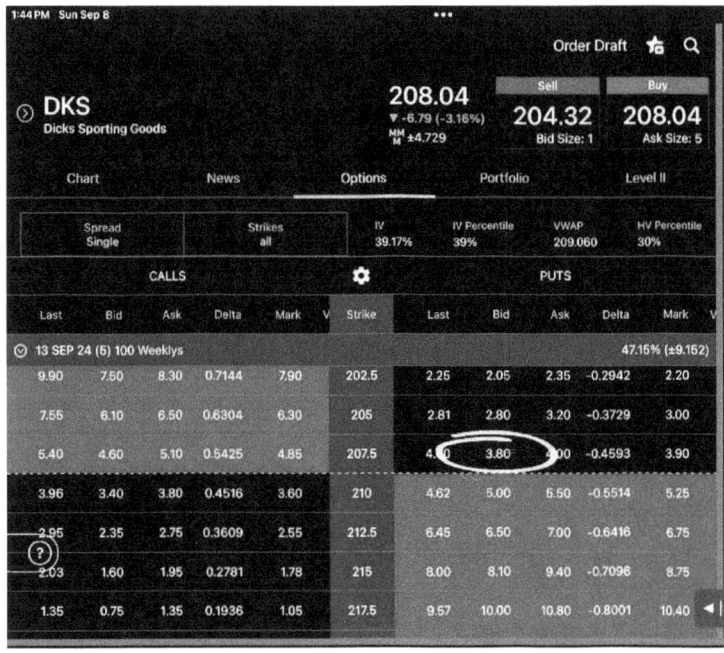

As you can see the Bid price on the Put Option is 3.80.

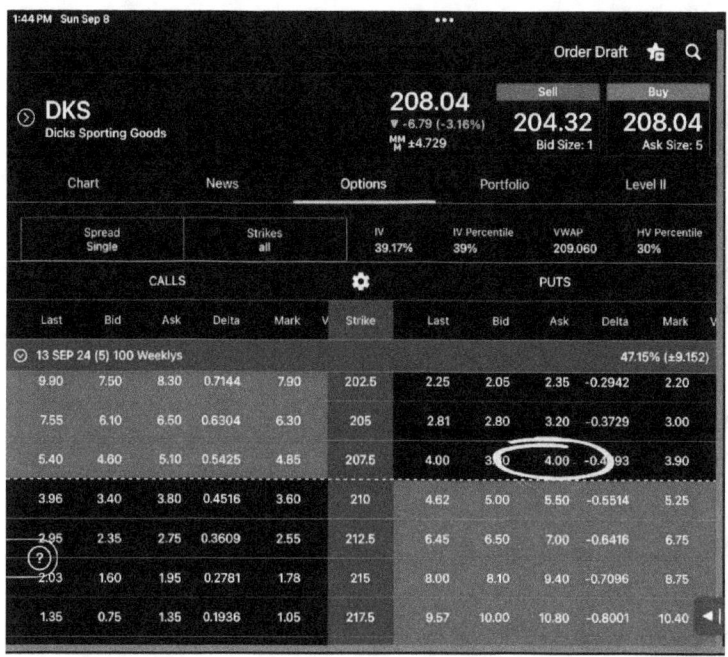

You add the Bid price of 3.80 to the Ask price of 4.00 and divide by 2 to get the mid point price of the put which would be 3.90

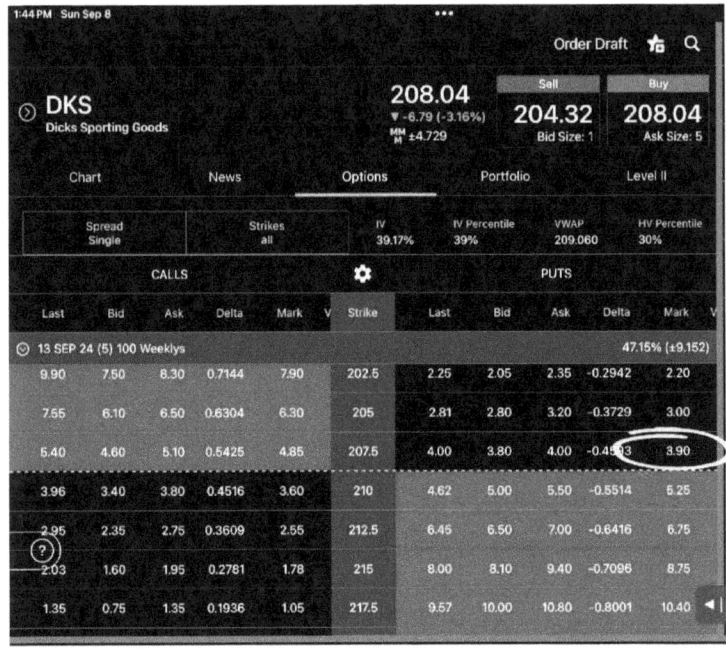

Again, in this illustration there is a column for the Mark at 3.90.

So now you would take the mid point Call Option average from above of 4.85 and add it to the mid point Put Option average of 3.90 and your Expected Move for the price of Dick's stock over the term of this contract would be + or – 8.70. This means that within a range of about 70% probability, the price of Dick's Stock might move up or down 8.70 from where it is now at $208.

Within the range of the Expected Move or 1 Standard Deviation, Dick's stock could rise as high as 216.70 or could drop as low as 199.30.

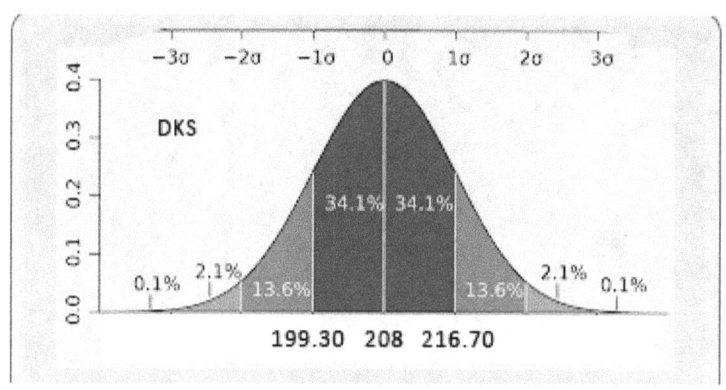

Example 2

Acushnet Holdings Corporation (GOLF NYSE)

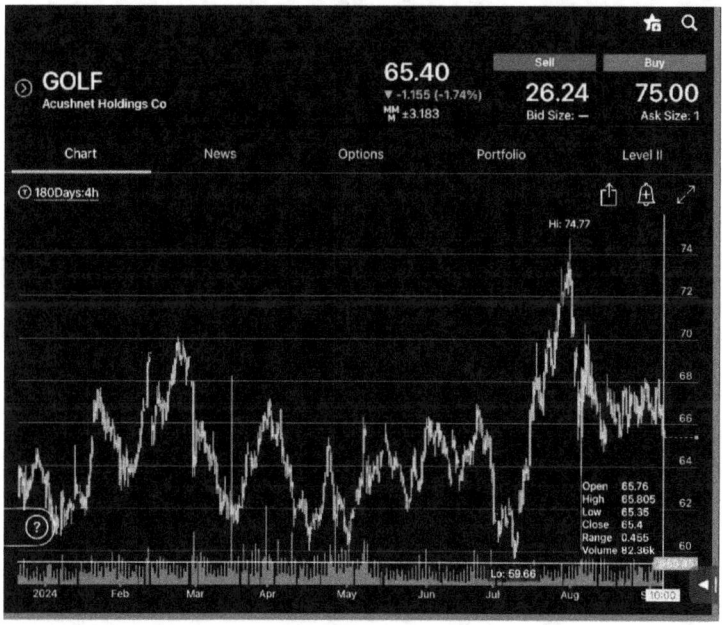

Current price per share of 65.40

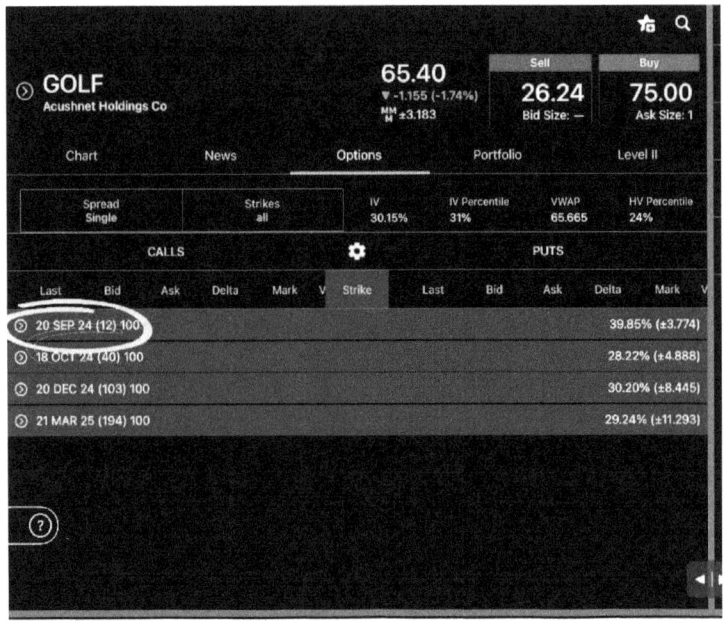

In this example you see that GOLF (Acushnet Holdings Corp) does not offer weekly Options to trade. They only have the monthly Options available. You could choose any of the monthly Options to trade. You don't have to choose the closest one, but let's say for example that you want to trade the Option expiring September 20, 2024. You would first open the Option chain for the 20 SEP 2024 Options.

Here the closest Option strike price to the actual current trading price of $65.40 would be the 65 strike price Option. If the stock had been trading at $65.50 you'd probably choose the 70 strike price. But here the Bid price of the Call Option is 3.10.

You would take the 3.10 Bid price and add it to the 3.60 Ask price as seen above. Then divide the number by 2 to get the midpoint Call Option price of 2.35.

The Mark or mid point of the Call Option is 2.35.

Now you go to the other side of the Option chain to the Put Option grid.

The Bid price of the 65 strike price Put is .05.

You now add the Bid price of .05 to the Ask price of the 65 Strike Put which is 2.80 to get the mid point or average of the Put Option of 1.43.

In this case the Mark or mid point of the 65 strike Put Option is 1.43. So you would add the mid point value of the 65 strike Call which was 2.35 to the above mid point Put Option value of 1.43 to get an Expected Move of + or – 3.78. This means that during the term of this monthly contract, there is within a 70% probability that GOLF stock might move up or down by 3.78.

Within the range of the Expected Move or 1 Standard Deviation, Acushnet's stock could rise as high as 69.18 or could drop as low as 61.62.

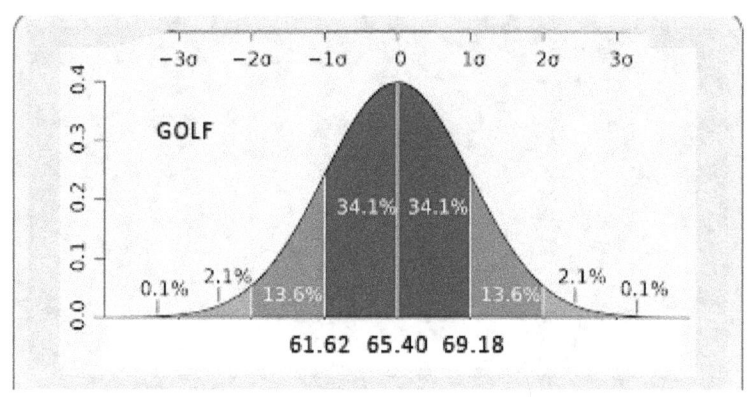

Example 3

Topgolf Callaway Brands Corp (MODG NYSE)

Topgolf Callaway is trading currently at $10.20 per share.

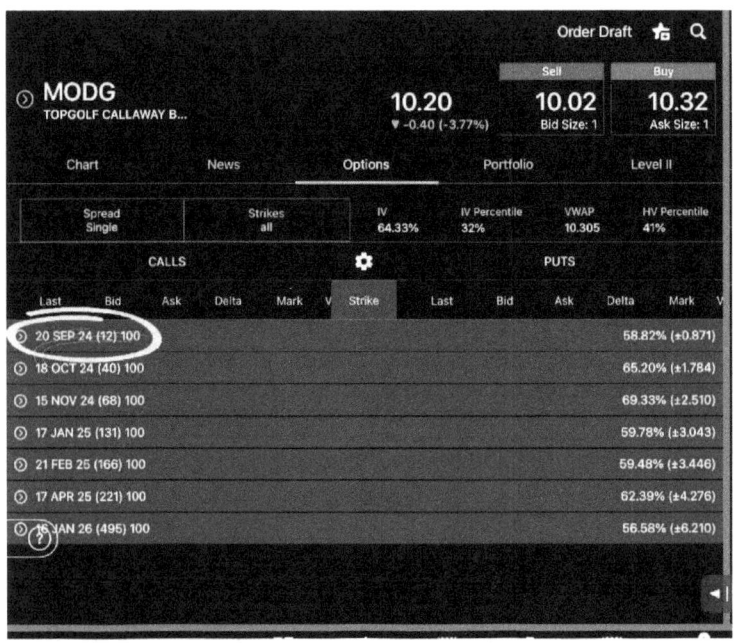

Here again we have only monthly Options offered in the chain. And again we'll pick the September 20, 2024 monthly Option.

The closest strike price is the 10.00 Option. On the Call side, the Bid is going for .50.

The Call Ask price is .60. So, when you add the Bid price of .05 to the Ask price of .60 you would have .65 and if you divide that by 2 you would have .325. This is one of those cases where if you offered .33 to buy or sell the 10.00 Call it probably wouldn't fill at that price, meaning your order would not be accepted. Why not? Because as you can see there is such a wide difference between the Bid price and the Ask price, and more weight here is given to the Ask price.

The Mark here for the Topgolf Calloway stock is going at about .55. While it is not the mid point of the Bid price and the Ask price, it is the more acceptable price for this Option. But for the purposes of calculating the Expected Move we are going to go with the actual mid point average price of .325.

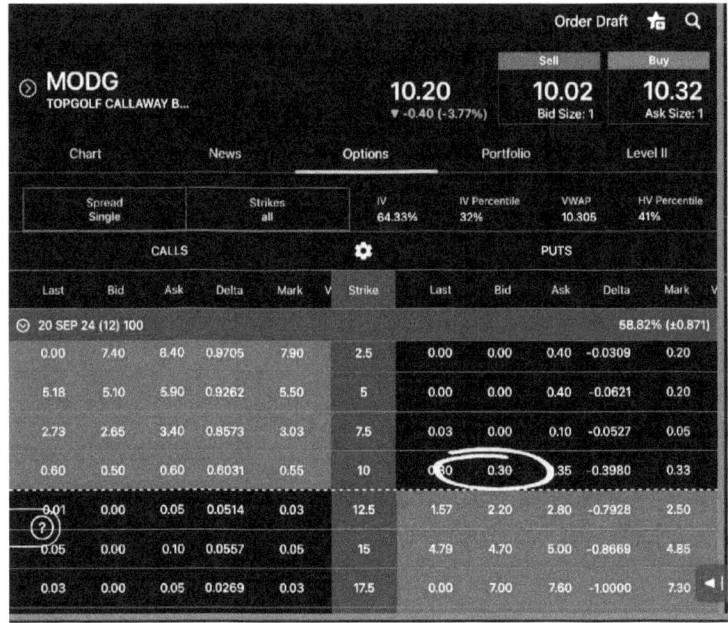

On the Put side the Bid price for the 10.00 strike Option is .30.

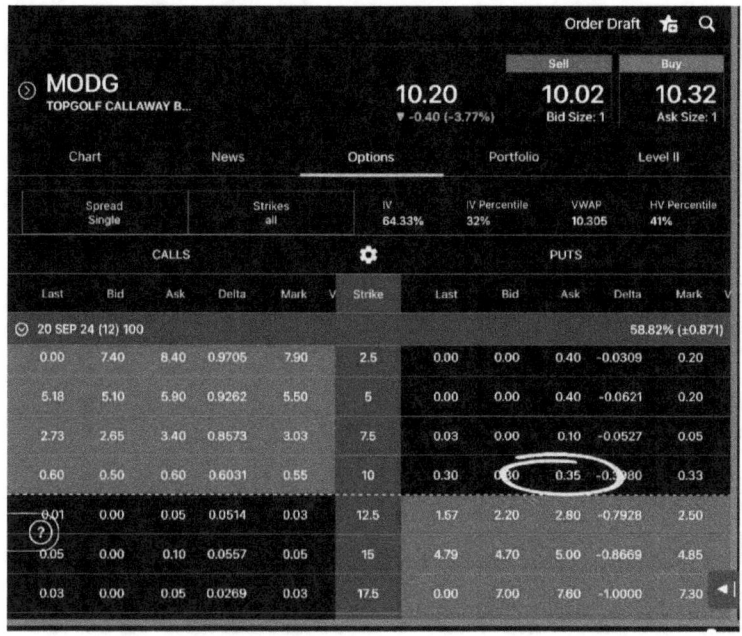

The Ask price for the Put is .35. When you add the Bid price of .30 to the Ask price of .35 and divide by 2 you will get .325 or realistically, .33.

In the case of the Put, the Bid price and the Ask price were closer together, so the actual Mark on this Option is .33. So to get the Expected Move for the underlying stock during the term of this Option, you would add the Mark of the 10.00 Call Option which is .55 to the Mark of the 10.00 Put Option which is .33 and you will have an expected Move for the stock of + or - .88. Within the range of the Expected Move or 1 Standard Deviation, Topgolf Callaway's stock could rise as high as 11.08 or could drop as low as 9.32

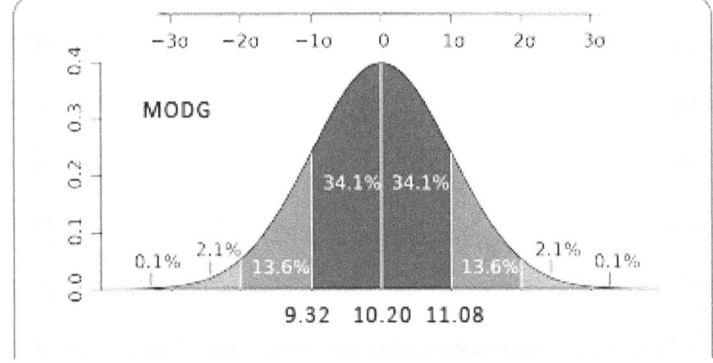

Technical Analysis

I've stated many times that you need to be careful not to rely too heavily on technical analysis indicators to make decisions on your investing. No matter how sophisticated they appear to be, indicators can only help clarify past information for a stock, there is no way to predict a future movement for the stock market. And as time goes on it becomes even harder to predict. Decades ago, before social media and easier instant access to so many news outlets, stock market trends though never completely predictable were more stable.

Now, every analyst making a grade or recommendation, every news outlet and business news magazine, or podcast has a direct impact on stock investors. Every comment made by a corporate CEO, or financial Analyst, every governmental bulletin or announcement or economic outlet report gets filtered down to business reporters and within seconds becomes part of the social media and newsfeed that millions of investors around the world digest in an instant. And to make it worse a simple post from forum sites such as Reddit; Instagram; X (formerly Twitter); TikTok, and bulletins that come through LinkedIn can have a major impact on stock prices even though temporary.

It is ironic that the more technologically advanced and connected we become as a society the more that predictability evades us. But that's exactly what has happened in many aspects of life, not just the stock market.

The lesson in this for you is that no matter what kind of advertisement you see about an advanced stock indicator, the less that product is likely to be able to be effective in heling to predict a stock trend. I see ads on the net and on YouTube from would be stock gurus who have a new AI driven product that "will predict tomorrow's stock moves for you".

The question I have always had about technical analysis in the stock market is, If Stock market indicators actually work, then why isn't everybody in the stock market rich? If these indicators were even partly reliable for predicting stock market trends and prices, then everybody would be rich. And that is not the case.

So, when you hear ads for software or subscriptions services or even books on Fibonacci Retracements; Elliott Waves, Bollinger bands; Stochastic Relative Strength Index (RSI; Exponential Moving Averages; Volume Profile and the Moving Average Convergence Divergence (MACD), don't be intimidated. None of these tools are going to predict the stock market movements tomorrow.

In fact there have been several experiments carried out on the randomness of the Stock Market. Starting in 2019, the Writers of the Wall Street Journal threw darts at a list of stocks, and based on the random hits, they created portfolios around those selected stocks. When compared to top financial institutional investors, they beat them by an average of 27 percentage points.

In 1973 Princeton University Professor Burton Malkiel stated in a book, "A blindfolded monkey throwing darts at a newspaper's financial pages could select a portfolio that would do just as well as one carefully selected by experts.". As it happened, a company called Research Affiliates chose 100 portfolios containing 30 stocks from a 1,000 stock universe completely at random. They replicated and repeated the exact process every year from 1973 through 2010 of 100 monkeys throwing darts at the stock pages every year. An average, 98 of the 100 monkey portfolios beat the 1,000 stock universe each year.

The lesson in this that I am trying to share isn't to completely disregard technical analysis. History is important and very much so in the financial markets. But learn that famous phrase you hear and read in ads from financial investment institutions, "Past performance isn't indicative of future results" and then yes, learn how to use some of the financial technical indicators **NOT** to choose your stocks but rather to help you make decisions based on what the market has done. Take the information that the indicators tell you, and then use your own common sense and intelligence to make your decisions. Once your decisions are made and you've executed your trades know best when to close out the trade for your best profit and know when to get out of a trade that isn't going well. These are the only true secrets of successful trading.

The technical indicator tools I will be showing you are the most popular and the ones used most by retail stock traders. Everybody who is really into stock market investing uses the top several I will show you. And yet most retail stock investors aren't rich or highly successful because of them.

One of the more useful tools for examining stock market trends are the moving average lines. In fact the moving averages have become part of other tools we'll talk about.

Moving Averages

How Moving Averages are Used

The Moving Average (MA) or Simple Moving Average (SMA) or Exponential Moving Average (EMA) are tools designed to even out price data over a period of time. Since they are changing along with current pricing it is easier for an investor to see history of the stock's price and trends. A Moving Average can be measured over different time scales. The most popular are the 200 day Moving Average, the 100 day Moving Average and the 50 day Moving Average and even the 20 day Moving Average. The longer the time scale, the smoother the line representing the Moving Average will appear as the longer Moving Average is less responsive to sudden and temporary changes in prices along the way.

Moving Averages on their own can often help investors determine trends in a stock's price and also help establish clear support and resistance levels for stocks.

At those moments when a stocks actual price crosses over a Moving Average line, it may be a buy or a sell signal. When the price of a stock crosses above the Moving Average line it may be an indication the price will be trending upward and provide a signal for investors to buy the stock. Alternatively, when a stock's price crosses below the Moving Average line this might be a sign of a downtrend and it might be a signal to sell the stock.

Some investors use Moving Averages on their own to look at basic stock trends and lines of support and resistance. But Moving Averages also form the basis of other stock indicators used in technical analysis including Bollinger Bands and the moving average convergence divergence (MACD).

Why Use a Moving Average?

The Moving Average clarifies the stock's price information over a period of time and defines a single line. Many times the Moving Average line itself is all that's need to determine directional trend for a stock. If the Moving Average line is moving toward an upward direction then much of the time the stock might be also moving in an upward direction.

If on the other hand the Moving Average line is moving in a downward direction that might be a signal that the stock itself is trending downward. If the Moving Average line is steady it might indicate that the stock will be in a range and trading sideways for a time.

Another feature of a Moving Average line is that it can provide a good idea of where support and resistance is for a stock. In an upward trending direction, the Moving Average line can usually be found below the stock actual movements and you might see the stock prices coming down but then bouncing back up as they hit the support of the Moving Average line.

Likewise if the stock is moving in a downward direction you would probably see the Moving Average line staying above the stock's actual movement and the stock prices might come up to the Moving Average line's resistance level and bounce back down. Whenever a stock's price breaks through a support line or a resistance line it could be a sign of a breakout to further push the stock past support or resistance to gain further momentum.

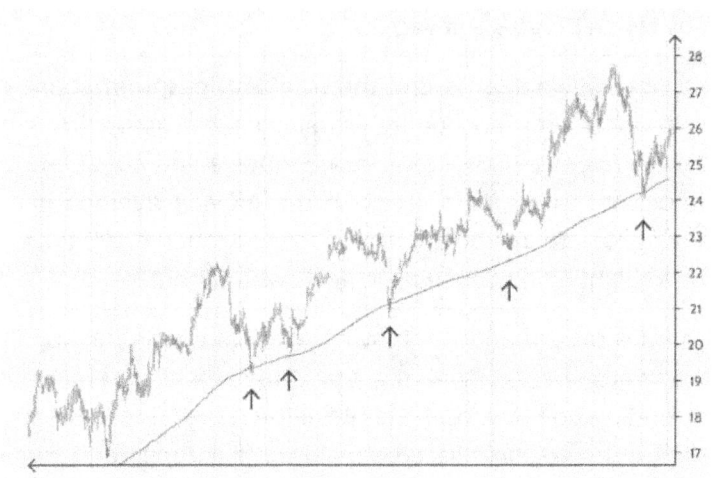

In the illustration above a Moving Average line creates support
Image by Sabrina Jiang © Investopedia 2020

In general, if the stock's price is above a Moving Average then one would assume that the stock price is upwardly trending, and if the stock price is below the Moving Average line then stock's price would be downwardly trending, but since different Moving Average timelines are representing different pricing, it is possible that a stock that is above or below a Moving Average timeline might be different for a different Moving Average timeline. A 200 day Moving Average line might show a stock in a different position than a 50 day Moving Average line, so it might be wise to check the stock's price level at several different Moving Average timelines.

SMA or EMA? What are they and Which is Better?

In the World of moving Averages, there are basically two types. There is the basic straightforward Simple Moving Average (SMA) and there is the Exponential Moving Average (EMA).

First let's see what ach one is. The Simple Moving Average (SMA) is exactly that. The closing price of each previous day is added together times the number of days in the timeline and then divided by the number of days.

For example if you have a 20 Simple Moving Average you would take yesterday's closing price of the stock and add it together with the previous 19 days' closing prices and divide by 20 and plot it on a chart. Each day that passes, you would do the same. Take the closing price of the stock at the end of the market trading day and add it to the closing prices of the previous 19 days and then divide by 20 to plot the next point.

If it sounds a bit messy and time intensive, you don't have to worry because you don't have to do any of the calculations or plot any points. Any trading platform will automatically plot the 20 day Simple Moving Average (SMA) and place it on your stock chart. I went through the explanation of what it is to help you understand how they arrive at numbers that are plotted.

With a 50 day, 100 day, or even a 200 day Simple Moving Average (SMA) it is the same process except for a 50 day Simple Moving Average (SMA) you would have the previous 50 closing prices added together and divided by 50; for the 200 day Simple Moving Average (SMA) the previous 200 closing prices added together and divided by 200 and so on.

Remember that the longer the timeline, the more smooth the Moving Average line will be because it is less responsive to sudden temporary jumps or drops in the price.] of the stock.

There is another type of moving average measurement called the Exponential Moving Average (EMA). The calculation of this Moving Average measurement is more complex because it weighs more recent price data of your stock more heavily. Again you don't have to worry about calculating the Exponential Moving Average yourself. Your trading platform will place an Exponential Moving Average (EMA) on your chart for you.

Either the Simple Moving Average (SMA) or the Exponential Moving Average (EMA can work for your trading. Deciding on which one you want to use is more a matter of experience and style. Because the Exponential Moving Average is more responsive to recent stock activity, it might be better used for shorter term trades, although a lot of traders will use short term Simple Moving Averages like a 10 day Simple Moving Average or a 20 day Simple Moving Average (SMA) just as well.

One major use of the Moving Average in trading is the Crossover Strategy. In this strategy you would watch for a stock price to cross over a Moving Average line. If the stock price crosses above the Moving Average it may be a good signal that the stock price will stay above the Moving Average line and might continue on an upward trend. If the stock price crosses the Moving Average line heading downward it might be a signal that the stock price will remain below the Moving Average and continue in a downward trend.

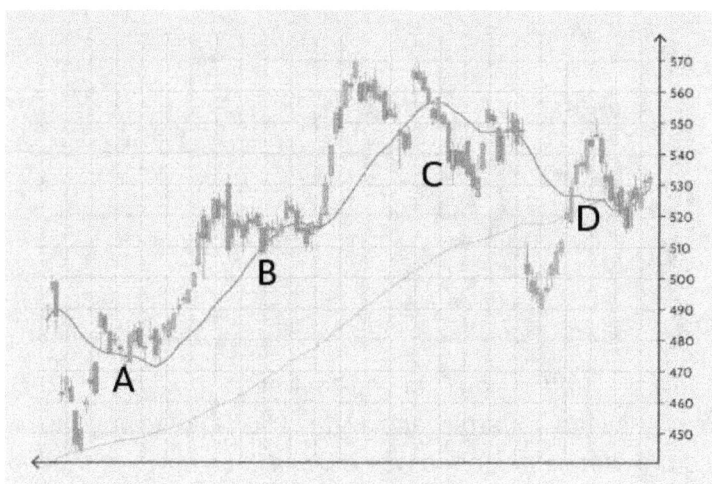

In the above illustration, you can see the stock prices cross over the Moving Average line (The blue line) and continue a trend. When the stock prices cross at A, they continue in an upward trend and use the Moving Average as support at B. At C the prices break support and continue downward until D when they cross the Moving Average again.

Image by Sabrina Jiang © Investopedia 2020

Which takes us to the solution of which timeline is better to use, a 20 day Simple Moving Average (SMA) or a 200 day Simple Moving Average (SMA) timeline. Why not use two different timeline Moving Average measurements?

You can use two different Moving Average lines for a different strategy. You would use a longer timeline Moving Average such as a 200 Day Moving Average and then add a shorter term timeline such as a 50 Day Moving Average. What this does is show how shorter term price of your stock reacts to a longer term average. If the shorter term Moving Average line crosses above the longer term Moving Average then this might signal an upward movement of the stock price. When this happens it is called a Golden Cross.

In this illustration you can see that even though the 50 Day Moving Average started above the 200 Day Moving Average and therefore stock price was moving in an upward direction, as the 50 Day Moving Average moved to come down toward the 200 Day Moving Average the stock's price started to drop. Once the 50 Day Moving Average once again crossed above the 200 Day Moving Average (the Golden Cross) the stock price started an upward movement.

Of course the opposite is true as well. If the Shorter term Moving Average crosses down over the longer Moving Average that can be a strong signal that the stock could be on a downward trend. In this case the cross of the shorter Moving average down across the longer Moving Average is known as the Death Cross.

In this chart, the 50 Day Moving Average is above the 200 Day Moving Avraage

In this illustration, the 50 Day Moving Average is initially above the 200 Day Moving Average but then crosses under the longer 200 Day Moving Average and signals a downward movement of the stock price. The point at which the shorter 50 Day Moving Average crosses under the longer 200 Day Moving Average is known as the Death Cross.

One problem with indicators such as Moving Averages is that there is lag time between the move of the price and the Moving Average reflecting it. So all too often a stock will make a move before the Moving Average shows it on the line. And of course, as always, there are so many other factors that affect stock pricing on a daily basis.

One mistake that new traders make when they learn about indicators such as the Moving Averages is that they put too much confidence in them. If stock and Option trading could reliably use these indicators then every stock trader would be profitable and simply place the Moving Average lines on their charts and wait for Moving Average lines to cross over each other to buy or sell stocks or stock Options.

Real life movements of stocks are much mor complicated unfortunately. Still, the use of Moving Averages with other indicators can give traders an edge on their trading and every little bit helps.

The MACD

Moving Average Convergence Divergence is a Moving Average momentum tool invented in the 1970's by Technical Analyst Gerald Appel.

The MACD is a next generation take on the 2 line Moving Average tool. You remember above we talked about the Golden Cross and the Death Cross that occurs when one shorter term Moving Average line crosses over another longer term Moving Average line.

The MACD is a more sophisticated tool that uses Exponential Moving Average lines and an additional calculation to create a signal line.

With the MACD a 26 Day Exponential Moving Average is subtracted from a 12 Day Exponential Moving Average to form a MACD Moving Average or MACD line. What?!! You say? Why would you subtract a larger number (the slower 26 Day Exponential Moving Average line) from the smaller (the faster 12 Day Exponential Moving Average line)? That's crazy! Well not really so crazy. You see, the shorter 12 Day Exponential Moving Average is a faster line and more active because it is more sensitive and responsive to more recent price action of the stock. And so it carries more weight in the equation.

So, once the 26 Day Exponential Moving Average is subtracted from the 12 Day Exponential Moving Average that is called the MACD Exponential Moving Average.

But Wait!, There's More! The MACD Exponential Moving Average is now plotted on a chart with a 9 Day Exponential Moving Average (which is a faster Moving Average and even more responsive to recent price changes of the stock). The 9 Day Exponential Moving Average will cross over or under the MACD Exponential Moving Average and where the 9 Day line crosses over the MACD line This should be a signal of the stock momentum increasing upward. Conversely when the 9 Day Line crosses underneath the MACD line, it should be a signal that there is downward movement of the stock prices.

On the MACD Chart there is a histogram so you can actually see the 9 Day line (also called the Signal Line) converge with the MACD Line and then diverge again. As the lines converge, the histogram bars are shorter indicating decreasing momentum of the Stok prices and when the two line diverge the bars on the histogram are longer and indicate increasing momentum for the stock.

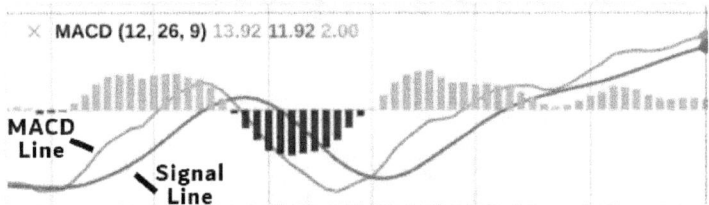

Figure 1: ZOOMING IN ON MACD. The **MACD** (gray line) is the difference between two exponential moving averages (EMAs)—the 12-period and the 26-period. The purple **signal** line is a 9-period moving average of the MACD. The faster-moving gray line gives more weight to recent prices, while the purple line smooths them out by taking the average over nine periods. Note that when the two lines diverge, the histogram bars become larger. That's not a coincidence. *For illustrative purposes only.*

Image source: Barchart.com

Again, You don't have to worry about calculating any of the differences between any of the Exponential Moving Averages. All you have to do is go to the dashboard of your trading platform and indicate that you want the MACD histogram to be a part of your chart.

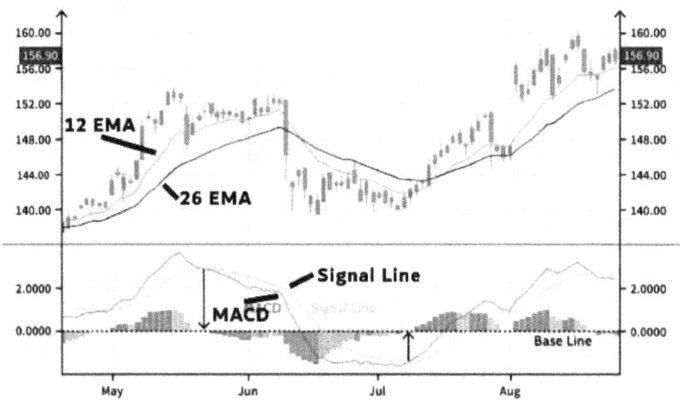

Image by Sabrina Jiang © Investopedia 2020

Although Gerald Appel retired from finance in 2012 he has become an award winning photographer.

Gerald Appel
Photo courtesy of traders.co

Stochastics and RSI

Sorry to throw a word like "Stochastic" out at you. I've pledged to keep this guide rally down to Earth and simple. But at least the word stochastic has a very simple meaning. Stochasticity is randomness. And since I've said many times the stock market is a series of random events that affect pricing, it is no surprise that there is an indicator tool that takes the seemingly random things like stock prices and using an oscillator shows a pattern that has useful information.

Oh, there he goes throwing out expensive words. What's an oscillator? And Oscillator is an indicator tool that creates lines between two extreme values and then has a trend indicator that moves up and down between the two extreme value lines. Wait! Before you throw down this book because of the lines and extreme values and trend indicators, let me show you something that you know that is an oscillator that you see and use every Sunday and probably enjoy it.

A football field is an oscillator! And it doesn't matter whether we're talking about American football or European football. You have two extreme values, or in this case the goal lines on each side. In between the goal lines you have football players moving the ball back and forth toward each goal during the game. As Team A moves the ball closer toward the goal line of team B, the probability of team A scoring increases. And conversely (having nothing to do with Converse shoes, although players might be wearing them) the closer Team B gets the ball toward the Team A goal line, the greater the probability that they will make a goal.

What I've describes is a perfect example of an Oscillator used in the stock market. Over the time of the game the ball being moved back and forth from one goal line toward another is a trend indicator. The trend being the area the ball stays in most of the time. So if you have Kansas City and the Detroit Lions, The ball would be moving back and forth, but might stay in one end zone more often.

So now imagine a stock chart with a line that moves up and down every day. At the top of the chart is a strong horizontal line which represents the top extreme of price and at the bottom is a horizontal line that represents the extreme low price of the stock. In between the extreme lines there are more lines from top to bottom at 10 degree intervals, just like the 10 yard line or the 30 or 40 yard line on the football field.

As the price of the stock goes up toward the upper extreme line it means that the stock is becoming more expensive, and if it approaches the upper extreme line it is considered to become overbought, meaning that the price is too high for the value of the stock and at some point it should be coming down. Likewise if the price of the stock is very low toward the lowest extreme then the stock is thought to be oversold, meaning the stock is considered too cheap and will probably initiate a buy signal.

Normally the lines from the lowest extreme to the top extreme are in units of ten starting from 0 to 100. At the bottom, if the stock is anywhere below 20 it is considered in the oversold territory, and if the stock price is above 80 it is conserved to be in the overbought territory. The farther the price goes into the extreme territories and the longer the price stays in there, the greater the possibility of a reversal of price.

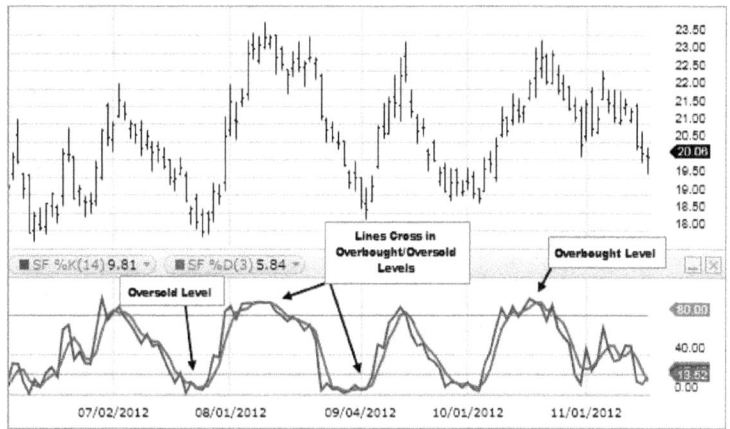

The above illustration shows the actual stock prices on the top part of the chart and the Stochastic Oscillator on the bottom part of the chart.. The overbought levels are signaled at above 80 and the oversold levels are at about 20 on the chart. Illustration courtesy of Fidelity.

RSI – Th Relative Strength Index

The Relative Strength Index was invented by John Welles Wilder, a mechanical engineer / real estate developer, / technical analyst. His brother Bert was a defensive tackle and defensive end with the New York Jets football team. (you see, there we go with football again!)

The Relative Strength Index (RSI) is also an oscillator that is trying to show similar overbought oversold trends. The difference between the Stochastic Oscillator and the Relative Strength Index (RSI) is that the Stochastic Oscillator measure price closes over a number of days to establish a trend in price movement. The RSI measures the velocity of price movement by measuring recent gains of the stock prices against recent losses of the stock prices

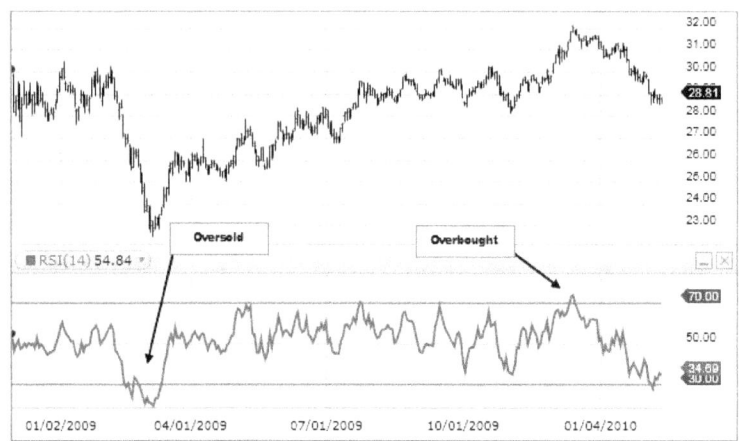

Not unlike the Stochastic Oscillator, The Relative Strength Index aims to show overbought and oversold areas of stock pricing.
Illustration courtesy of Fidelity.

So, for those who want to know if a stock is overbought or oversold but they can't decide on whether recent closing prices confirming the stock's trend is more efficient and accurate than examining the stock price gains against the stock price losses, the solution is a combination of both. Introducing the new and improved Stochastic RSI.

Tushar Chande, a Registered Commodity Trading Advisor in Des Moines Iowa decided he was tired of counting rows of sweet corn along highway 70 and decided to invent a stock momentum oscillator in 1994 that was more responsive and faster that either the Stochastic Oscillator or the Relative Strength Index (RSI) and he created the Stochastic Relative Strength Index, or for short they call it StochRSI (almost sounds like a crime investigation TV show like CSI or NCIS).
Instead of having an oscillator measure stock price data, the StochRSI measures an oscillator against an oscillator which is able to show more responsive data in a faster period of time. The drawback is that the data from the StochRSI can give false

readings in a volatile market. But because it is more responsive and faster to changes in price, a trader might be able to react faster to price reversals and changes in the stock direction.

In this illustration you can see that the Stochastic RSI are much smoother and more frequent data interpretations of stock prices.
Illustration courtesy of barchart.com

Tushar S. Chande PhD
Inventor of the StochRSI

Bollinger Bands

Bollinger Bands were invented by Financial Management Specialist John Bollinger in the 1980's Bollinger had a background in both mathematics and engineering and devised a tool that could show stock price volatility and movement.

The Bollinger Bands consist of 3 lines that move along with the price movement of a stock. The center line is usually a 20 Day Simple Moving Average (SMA) and there is an upper line that is set 2 standard deviations above the center line. The lower line is usually set 2 standard deviations below the center line. Depending upon a traders specific needs, the Bollinger Bands can be adjusted to a different Simple Moving Average, or a different set of Standard Deviations. The standard use though is the 20 Day Simple Moving Average for the center line and the outer line of 2 standard deviations each. The reason 2 Standard Deviations are used is that the bands need to expand to show statistically high and low areas of price movement. The bands expand and contract automatically with both stock movement and volatility.

If the Bands expand it means there is a period of high volatility and conversely if the bands contract it usually means there is a period of low volatility. This is important to see because generally following a period of high volatility it will be followed by a period of low volatility. So when the bands have expanded it signals that the bands are likely to contract, and vice versa if you see the bands tight and squeezing the price on either side this contraction period is usually followed by a period of higher volatility.

There are several ways Bollinger Bands can be of great use to traders. One is to watch the actual prices of stock within the bands. If the stock goes up and hits the upper band it might be a sign of a coming reversal in prices and that either the stock will reverse and come back down to the center line, or could even go further toward the lower band. The converse is also true. If a stock price is hitting the edge of the lower band, it might be a sign that the stock is ready for a reversal back up toward the center line or even further toward the upper band.

Another great use of the Bollinger Bands is to watch the price of the stock to see if it goes up beyond the upper band. This means that the stock might be overbought and the price being too high might be ready to come down. It is probably not a good time to buy the stock. On the other side, if the price of the stock is reaching beyond the lower band it means the stock is probably oversold and is ready for a move up again.

Sometimes patterns can be seen more clearly in the Bollinger Bands. For example there may be a Double Bottom formation and without the use of the Bollinger Bands it may appear that the stock is ready for a downward move, however if the first price move down goes past the edge of the lower band, but the second price move is within the lower band, even though it may be a lower price then the first low, it may indicate a possible price reversal is coming..

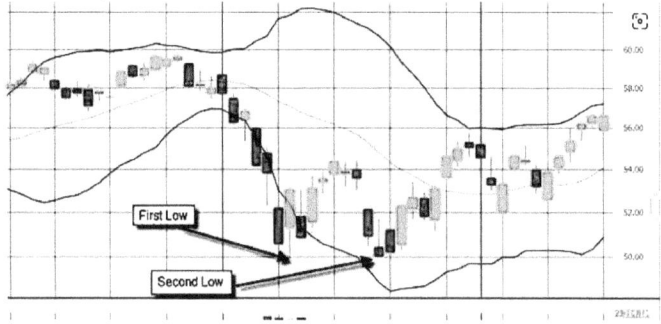

In this illustration, you can see a familiar Double Bottom formation. Without the bands it would appear that the price is trending downward after the second low, but as you can see,

the first low went beyond the lower band, but the second low, even though lower than the first, was within the lower band. This signaled a price reversal and the stock went up.
Illustration courtesy of Charles Schwab.

In similar fashion here is an example of how a price that makes several highs can signal decreasing stock momentum and a reversal of stock prices. A stock may hit a price high beyond the upper edge of the upper band, come down a bit and then make another higher high, and then come down a bit before the price makes and even higher high. Without the bands it might appear as if the price is trying to break a resistance level to continue upward. However the first price that made a high was beyond the upper band and then the next high although it just barely broke the upper edge, and the third high was within the upper band. In this case this is a sign that the stock may be losing momentum and a reversal might be signaled.

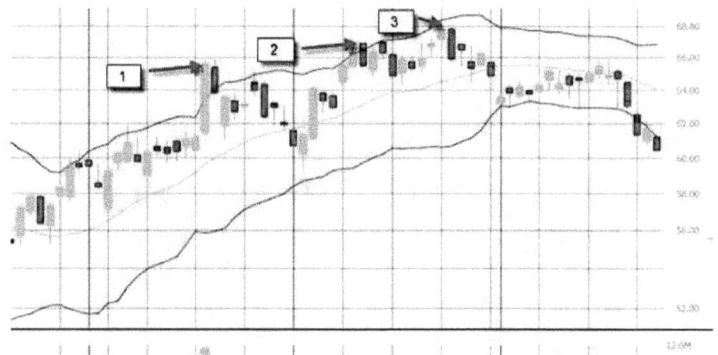

Here in the above illustration you can see the price making a new high and breaking beyond the upper band (1). Then there is a pullback and the price once again reaches a new higher high just breaking the upper band, but not going as far beyond the upper band as the previous high (2). There is an even small pullback on price but then there is another higher high, but this time the new high is within the upper band. This indicates a reversion back to the center line and then even further down

toward the lower band. Also note that as the price is coming down, the bands are narrowing indicating lower volatility.
Illustration courtesy of Charles Schwab.

Here is another example of a contraction of the Bollinger Bands signaling that a squeeze of pricing might be a sign of higher volatility ahead.

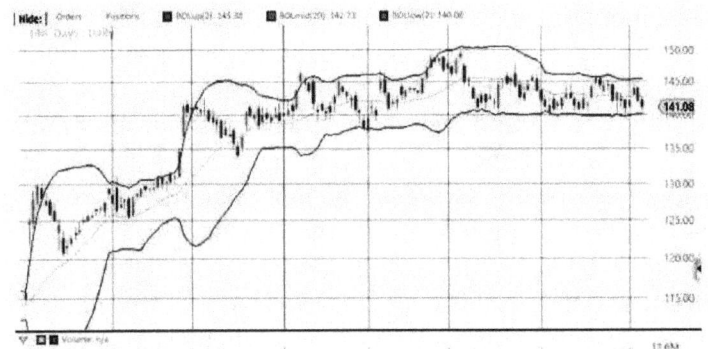

You can see in the above illustration that the bands are significantly wider on the left side of the chart and as the bands constrict, the price is being squeezed. Most likely there will be increased volatility in the near future.
Illustration courtesy of Charles Schwab.

John Bollinger
Photo courtesy of bollingerbands.com

Fibonacci Retracements, The Fibonacci Sequence and The Golden Ratio

As I said before, I am a believer in sciences and I especially love physics. Studying the patterns and laws of physics helps us understand life and the universe on many levels, but not the stock market. The laws of gravity can explain the way bodies fell from office buildings when stock traders in despair jumped from windows after the great stock market crash of 1929. But neither gravity or any other physical law or mathematical system can describe why, how far and when stock prices fall or rise and certainly there is no way to use mathematics or hard science to predict when and where they will retrace their movements.

There are a lot of scenes in films where the hero is running from someone or something or a lot of someones and ends up on the edge of a cliff very high above a river, ocean whatever. They wait until they have no choice and then jump, free-falling way way down until they plunge into the surface of the water. They continue falling down into the body of water, then come up, break the surface and gasp for air. In the stock market on a fairly regular basis a stock can have a sudden surge upward or a correction downward. These sharp moves tend to often be temporary and can last a matter of hours or maybe a few days, and then there is what's called a retracement. A stock that has suddenly surged will come down again to some level between the starting point and the top of the surge. A stock that drops suddenly may come back up to some level between the starting point and the low point of the drop.

Some opportunist who wanted to take advantage of the volatile nature of the occasional sharp stock price movements and especially the vulnerability and the superstitious nature of stock investors exploited the brilliant and serious work of a 13th century mathematician named

Leonardo Pisano Bigollo of the Bonacci family is Pisa, Italy. Long after his death in 1240ish, Leonardo's name became more commonly known as Leonardo Fibonacci, shortened from "Filius Bonacci" which meant "Son of Bonacci".

Leonardo Pisano "Fibonacci"

Leonardo's father Guilielmo of the Bonacci family was a secretary of the Republic of Pisa in the Province of Tuscany but also spent a of time as a merchant Customs Officer stationed in Algeria and other places in the Mediterranean and Middle East. During his time traveling assisting merchants, He brought Leonardo who learned about Indian and Arabic numbers and the entirely different mathematical systems used in other parts of the world.

You have to remember that at the time in the Roman Empire, Roman numerals were used and it was Leonardo Pisano who brought Indian and Arabic numbers to Europe.

I'll show you the difference.

Before Leonardo Pisano brought math to the Roman Empire and Europe –

Add these numbers together

   CXLIV
+ CCLXXVI
_____

= CDXX

Here is the same math problem using the Indian and Arabic number system that Leonardo Pisano showed us all

   144
+ 276
_____

= 420

Which system is really 420 friendly?!

You can't use Roman numerals to add and subtract and multiply and divide. It was the Merchants of the Mediterranean and Middle Eastern countries who taught Leonardo Pisano how they were able to calculate their transaction in the marketplace.

Leonardo Pisano also had many such great mathematical accomplishments during his lifetime, but he is probably best remembered for another discovery of his that he brought back to Europe known as the Fibonacci Sequence and the Golden Ratio. Although Fibonacci did not come up with the numerical sequence which dates back to 200 BC and credited to The Indian Mathematician Pingala, Fibonacci brought the sequence to Western Europe.

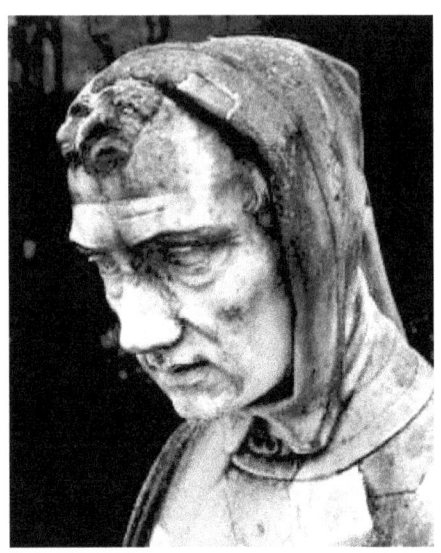

Statue of Leonardo Pisano in Pisa, Italy

The Fibonacci Sequence describes a sequence of numbers in which each number is the sum of the two preceding ones.

0, 1, 1, 2, 3, 5, 8, 13, 21, 34, 55, 89, 144, etc.

The reason the Fibonacci Sequence is important in science is that the Golden Ratio of the sequence is found in many parts of nature and physics.

The pattern of branches and leaves on branches of trees follow the Fibonacci ratio. As do the pattern of seeds in many fruits and vegetables including bananas, cucumbers, pineapples, broccoli, The arrangements of leaves on artichokes and pinecones follow the Fibonacci sequence. The pattern found in the spirals of seashells also follow the Fibonacci Sequence.

Knowing how important and how relevant the Fibonacci Sequence and code and the Golden Ratio is to the physical properties of nature on so many levels, how does the Fibonacci Sequence relate to the Stock Market?

IT DOESN'T

Using the Fibonacci Numbers or any mathematical formula to predict price movement of stocks is complete nonsense and total fantasy created by market investors who desperately and superstitiously want to believe that a sophisticated mathematical formula can be applied to something as irrational, random and non-scientific as the stock market.

There. I've said it. But now that I've said my piece, what are the Fibonacci Retracements in the stock market?

So, as per the example I showed you above of the film hero jumping into a river from a high cliff, he plunged to the bottom of the body of water and came back up again to the surface. He didn't come all the way back up to the cliff, he came up to the surface of the water, which is probably part way up to the cliff. Stocks are similar. An event can and often does cause a reaction from the stock market and a stock or even a sector or even the market as a whole can see a sudden dip in the stock price. Maybe there is an announcement that the Justice Department is going to investigate a company for anti-trust. Maybe the Federal Reserve is about to announce an interest rate hike. Maybe the President has announced a policy that affects some part of the market. It could be an individual stock drop or increase when one of the many hundreds of Stock Analysts announce a change in their assessment of the company. There are so many factors that can and do affect stock price movement on a daily basis, and this is just a part of the market's unpredictability.

So let's say a stock drops suddenly in price. Most of the events that affect the stock market are temporary and it is normal and expected that the stock will recover in short time whether in hours or in a few days. The problem that investors deal with is where and when will the stock recover? If you go back over charts of different stocks you can see sudden stock movements and the "retracements" after.

Some investors who use the Fibonacci Retracement theory in technical analysis actually believe that the Fibonacci numbers sequence can predict where a stock will return.

To their partial credit (not much) it is true that often when stock move suddenly up or down, they try to return to find levels of resistance and support. You can look at past charts and see this retracement attempt over and over. The issue is determining exactly where these levels of support and resistance will end up. And there is no way to predict this.

But I don't want to be a total downer, so I am presenting you with a nice recipe of a dish that would have been served during Leonardo Pisano's time in the Tuscan region. And the recipe uses Fibonacci ingredients, that is, all have Fibonacci patterns in them, Romanesco Broccoli, Pine Nuts, Garlic, Olive Oil and the peperoncini.

This recipe is from our family friend and my daughters' informal Godfather, William "Bill" Gotti

And as you increase your wealth using the methods I present in this book, you will have plenty of opportunity to celebrate your gains and enjoy more of Bill Gotti's recipe and wine recommendations.

Spaghetti Aglio e Olio

Ingredients: First, a brief chat about the ingredients needed to make spaghetti aglio e olio (pronounced "ah-lee-oh eh ohlee-oh")...

• Spaghetti: Or linguine, fettuccine, or any other shape of pasta noodle you prefer.

• Olive oil: Since olive oil is the main ingredient in this sauce, I really recommend using the best-quality extra virgin olive oil you can find. It will make a difference!

• Garlic: I admittedly like tons of garlic in this pasta (like, closer to 10-12 cloves). But it is traditionally made with between 4-8 cloves. So you do what sounds best to you!
• Broccoli. Lightly steamed.

• Toasted pine nuts

• Crushed red pepper flakes: Traditional spaghetti aglio e olio is made with fresh peperoncini (red hot chili peppers) that are commonly found throughout Italy. But since they are harder to find in other countries, I have written this recipe using dried crushed red pepper flakes, which we will simmer in the olive oil to bring out their best flavor.

• Optional garnishes: The two most popular toppings for this classic Italian dish are finely-minced fresh parsley and/or freshly-grated Parmesan. I love adding both, but they are totally Optional.

How To Make Spaghetti Aglio e Olio:

To make classic spaghetti aglio e olio, simply...

1. Cook the spaghetti. Cook the spaghetti in a generously-salted pot of boiling water until it is just one minute shy of being al dente.

2. Sauté the garlic. Meanwhile, about 3 minutes after you add the pasta to the boiling water, heat the olive oil in a large sauté pan over medium heat. Add the sliced garlic and crushed red pepper flakes and sauté for 3 to 5 minutes, or until the garlic is lightly golden.

3. Toast the pine nuts in a 350 degree (F) oven and check every 4 minutes or so until toasted to your liking.

4. Toss the pasta in the sauce. Once the pasta is ready to go, use tongs to transfer the pasta immediately to the sauté pan, along with 1/2 cup of the hot starchy pasta water. Toss the pasta continuously until it is evenly coated in the garlic sauce. If the sauce looks a bit too dry, add in another 1/4 cup of the starchy pasta water.

5. Add lightly steamed broccoli. Chop broccoli florets to small pieces.

6. Taste and season. Give the pasta a quick taste add an extra pinch of salt and/or crushed red pepper flakes if needed.

7. Serve. Serve immediately while it's nice and hot, garnished with any toppings that sound good.

8. Serve with a good wine. I suggest a Fiano di Avalino (Naples) or an Etna Bianco (Sicily)

A little wine is good. More is better – Bill Gotti

Probability of Expiring Cones

One indicator tool that has come from the Expected Move is the Probability of Expiring Cone. The Probability Cone uses statistical historical data to predict and graphically map future forecasts of prices in terms of probability.

To make it simpler, the Probability cone is a bell curve placed sideways to expand into the future showing projected stock prices within a selected number of Standard Deviations.
Like the Expected Move, he cone can't predict whether stock prices will move up or down, or even sideways. But what they show is the likelihood given current data on stock prices and implied volatility of the range of where the stock price should be over time in the future.

Since the data used to form the Probability Cone is based on Implied Volatility, it's possible that the cone will expand or contract from day to day as Implied Volatility changes.
You may set the parameters of the Probability Cone to show how far out in time you want the forecast, It could be 30 days or 100 days or even 1 week if you are doing weekly Options. You can also set the number of Standard Deviations you want the data to be presented in. You may select prices within 1 Standard Deviation to see where the stock price is likely to be within 68% probability or 2 Standard Deviations which would show the stocks anticipated future prices within 80% probability.

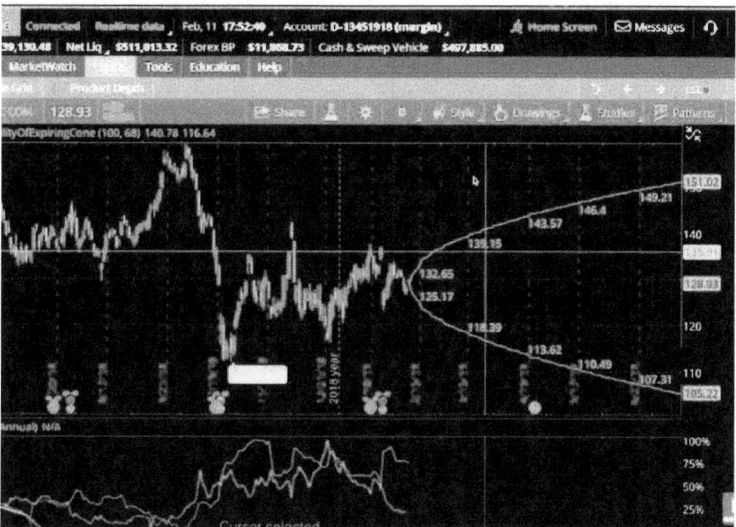

In this illustration you can see the Probability of Expiring Cone expanding from the current stock price. The parameters of this Probability Cone were set to forecast 100 days out into the future and within 1 Standard Deviation or 68% probability.
Illustration courtesy of Tackle Trading.

So anything within the inside of the cone up to the edge of the cone on any given day will have a probability of 68% being inside the cone. For those traders who are selling Options rather than buying stock or buying stock Options want to be outside of the curves of the cone.

In this illustration a second Probability Cone has been added on top of the first Probability Cone. The forecast term is still 100 days out but the outer cone is wider because the probability parameter has been set to between 1 and 2 Standard Deviations at 80%.

Illustration courtesy of Tackle Trading.

Another nice feature of the Probability of Expiring Cone is that along the edges of the cone as it expands, the estimated price range for each upcoming Friday are listed with the high price in the range on the upper curve and then below on the lower curve with the low price

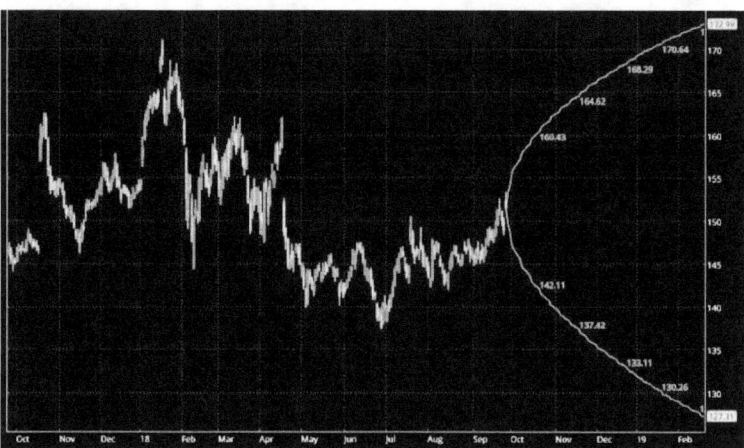

In this illustration you can see the expected prices on both the top and the bottom curves for each Friday within the future time range.

Illustration courtesy of Think or Swim.

TTM Squeeze Indicator

One of the most famous and successful traders in the world of stocks, Options and commodities is John Carter of Simpler Trading. He has been trading since 1996 and not only does he have a genius level understanding of the markets, but he has a sincere passion for helping others. He is the author of the bestselling "Mastering the Trade" now in its Third Edition. He also founded Simpler Trading (simplertrading.com)

John developed an amazing tool called the TTM Squeeze Indicator which is available as a standard add-on on some trading platforms including Thinkorswim and Tradestation and available for sale on his site.

The TTM Squeeze Indicator measures volatility and momentum for a stock in an extremely easy to see oscillator pattern. The Indicator takes volatility data from a combination of the Bollinger Bands and the Keltner Channels of a stock. The idea is that when price of a stock is compressed and volatility is low for example when a stock is in consolidation, the indicator is looking for a "firing" of the stock either up or down. The breakout if shown on a visual histogram with either green or blue lines of the stock is breaking out upward, or red lines of the stock is moving downwards.

It sounds like a dream come true to be able to see exactly hen a stock will begin to move in an upward or downward direction. The problem though, is that often a stock might begin to push upward, or downward and then reverse its direction. So, it might be hard to know exactly when the price is a true breakout in either direction. It's easy to look at the below TTM Squeeze Indicator and say that a breakout is obvious to see. But remember as with all indicators and charts, you are looking into the past. Watching an indicator or chart unfold in the present in real time is not as predictable.

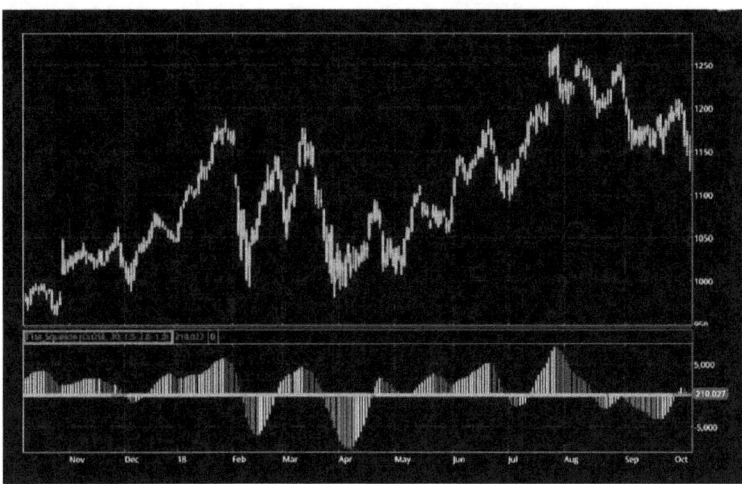

John Carter / Simpler Trading

Advanced Option Spreads

I wrote this manual to only show traders how to trade Options that are safe and affordable. But I found that many of the people who read earlier versions of this book had encountered information about more advanced Options trading strategies with the lure of high profits (people seem to ignore the higher risk) and they were tempted to try some of them.

In the beginning of this book I mentioned how Options Trading was in many ways like the Casino business. Generally when you sell Options you are more like the casino than a customer. But even selling Options can result in losses if not managed carefully and then you could become like a casino customer who loses by statistics.

When you get into more advanced Options trading strategies risk management that the casinos use become vital both to your survival and your success. The Options markets are the same. With trading strategies like Credit Spreads and Iron Condors, you may have a high probability of winning, but at some point the market will move unexpectedly against you and the way risk / reward and pricing works on Options and Options spreads, you can win 9 out of 10 deals and then lose everything you've gained (and perhaps more) on the 10th trade.

I have a second book on more advanced trading strategies. They are not included in detail in this book, not because I don't think you would understand the strategies. They aren't that complicated to learn quickly. But while they might not be complicated to learn, you have to remember that higher profits mean higher risk and after spending the better part of more than 35 years in both commodity and stock Options trading I've seen my share of losses as well as profits with these advanced trading strategies. Because invariably the risk to reward ratio on higher profit trades is usually so high, traders frequently make money on a number of trades until the inevitable losing trade wipes out all of their previous gains.

There are ways to manage risk and losses in these more advanced strategies but you'll have to find them in detail in my other book on the subject or in some of the listed resources I am providing at the end of this book.

The world of advanced stock Option trading includes some commonly used strategies including

- Bear Call Spread
- Bull Put Spread
- Iron Condor
- Bear Put Spread
- Bull Call Spread
- Calendar Spread
- Diagonal Spread
- Ratio Spread
- Strangle
- Straddle
- Long Butterfly Spread

But then there are the exotic, and sometimes more complicated Spreads

- Albatross Spread
- Double Diagonal Spread
- Ladder Spread
- Gut Spread
- Jade Lizard
- Twisted Sister
- Skip Strike Butterfly

Some of these exotic stock Options trading strategies sound more like a chocolate bar from Wonka's like the Scrumpdiddlyumptious Bar or the Whipple Scrumptious Fudgemallow Delight. So I'm just going to select the most commonly used advanced Option strategies that you might actually use one day.

I am at least introducing you to some of them and basically how they work in this chapter for two reasons. First, when you read this manual and start to explore the resources I have in this book (and I hope you will) especially on Youtube, you are definitely going to be bombarded repeatedly by unscrupulous salespeople who have expensive software that they claim can predict where the stock market will go; over-priced courses; AI Systems which will supposedly select your winning stock picks, and subscriptions to trade services to keep you on the hook and cost you thousands of dollars.

I promise you, if they are out there I know about them. I am constantly on top of the latest in Options education and I am in touch with dozens of other professional traders many times throughout the week. We all share information.

Now onto some of the trading strategies that you may need to know about if you continue Options Trading.

Again the reason this is only an introduction and I am not recommending them at this level is that you have to be more careful with these strategies. On the face they seem like they are clearly defined risk strategies, but they require constant management of your account and in reality they can be very dangerous.

I'm talking here about the Credit Spreads, Debit Spreads and the Iron Condor.

Yes I do trade them, but with a lot of risk management techniques that I have learned and share in the more advanced book.

The other important reason I am sharing the basics of these more advanced Options strategies, is that after this chapter I am going to introduce you to a completely different strategy that is a little more advanced, but very low risk and very high profit potential. It's great for small accounts and it's great for people who have limited time and want to earn profits with Options in as little as a few hours. But to help understand the strategy, it will help to understand the following more advanced Options strategies.

Debit Spreads

Formally they are known as the Debit Spreads including the Bear Put Spread and the Bull Call Spread.

The Bear Put Spread means that you are Bearish, or that you think or hope that the price of the stock will go down. It's a Put Spread because you are going to buy a Put Option and then sell a Put Option farther out to stop you out. Because the Put Option that you buy is closer in distance to the Stock Price. It is more expensive than the farther out Put Option that you will sell and therefore it will cost you money to get into this trade, hence a Debit.

The Bull Call Spread means that you are Bullish, or that you think or hope that the price of the stock will go up. It's a Call Spread because you are going to buy a Call Option and then sell a Call Option farther out to stop you out. Because the Call Option that you are buying is closer in distance to the Stock

Price it is more expensive than farther out Call Option that you are selling it will cost you money to get into this trade, hence a Debit.

Don't be confused by the titles. You can just refer to them as Debit Spreads.

When money comes into your account, in accounting terms it is called a Credit. When you sell an Option, the money you receive as a premium is credited to your account. When money comes out of your account, it is called a Debit. So, when you buy an Option, the cost of the Option premium is debited from your account.

The idea of spreads are to allow you to trade with protection, if managed well. In the case of a Debit Spread, you can buy an Option and sell another Option at a slightly farther distance which will sell the Option you bought, which caps your profit.

Going back to the football analogy that I used earlier to explain different strike prices I'm going to use it again to show you how a Spread works.

Let's say that your offense is on the 30 yard line and of course your goal is to get the ball toward the 20 yard line, the 10 yard line and hopefully score a touchdown. The other team has a line of defense which is going to try to stop you at some distance so you can't make it further. The distance your team gains between the yard line where the ball starts and where the ball touches the ground at the end of the play is the number of yards your team gained, or the spread distance.

In a stock Option Debit Spread, it is much the same. You are buying an Option because you want the stock to move up if it is a Call Spread, or down if it is a Put spread. But either direction, you buy the Option, and then a bit further out you will sell an Option that is meant to stop you out. The obvious question is, if you have bought an Option, and it is going in the direction you want it to, why on Earth would you want to stop it at a certain point and cap your profits? Why not just let it continue to move and make more money?

Because usually with a Debit Spread, traders buy more than one contract for added leverage and more opportunity. Buying more than one contract can be really expensive and there is a chance they won't profit at all, and the contract(s) will be worthless at expiration. A Debit Spread caps the profit a trader can make, but it also dramatically reduces the cost of the deal.

Here's an example with TESLA (TSLA NASDAQ the chart below is a 20 day look at the stock price.

It's hard to say whether TSLA will be going up in the coming days or down, since this is a chart from the final week of the year 2024. It's not unusual for the stock market to go down in the final days of the year. The tax season ends for a lot of businesses, and they might want to take profits or even losses. It's hard to predict where TSLA's stock price will be at the end of next week if we were to buy or sell weekly Options with next week's expiration.

Now let's look at the Option Chain for the next week's weekly expiration contracts

This chain is giving Option information for single Option contracts. So, if you were to buy or sell a single price contract or even several of those single price contracts, this is the chain that you would use if you were going to buy a Call or a Put Option or sell a Covered Call or a Cash Secured Put Option.

There's a very good chance that TSLA will be moving up by the end of next week you could buy a Call Option. The current price of TESLA stock is $403.88 per share and the first ITM (In The Money) Strike is the 402.5 Option. As long as TESLA remains over $402.50 per share and continues to climb you could make a lot of profit on the single contract. But the price of a 402.50 Call Option is $17.88 per share which is $1,788.00 for the contract. If that's too expensive you could buy the 412.50 Strike which is $13.48 per share or $1,348.00 for the contract.

So a more affordable alternative might be a Debit Spread.

Here is the Option Chain for TESLA for the same expiration but now you are looking at the prices of the Vertical Spreads instead of the Single Options.

Now instead of a 402.50 Strike Call Option for $1,788.00 you can buy a 402.50 / 405.00 Debit Spread, which means you are buying the 402.50 Call Option and then Selling the 405 Call Option. It gives you a window of profit. Certainly it isn't the great profit that you would gain if you bought a straight single contract and the price of TESLA stock continues to climb, but it only costs $1.20 per share, or $120.00 for the contract. If the price of TESLA climbs into your spread by expiration you could make several hundred dollars and if the Implied Volatility goes up during that time you could make a lot more.

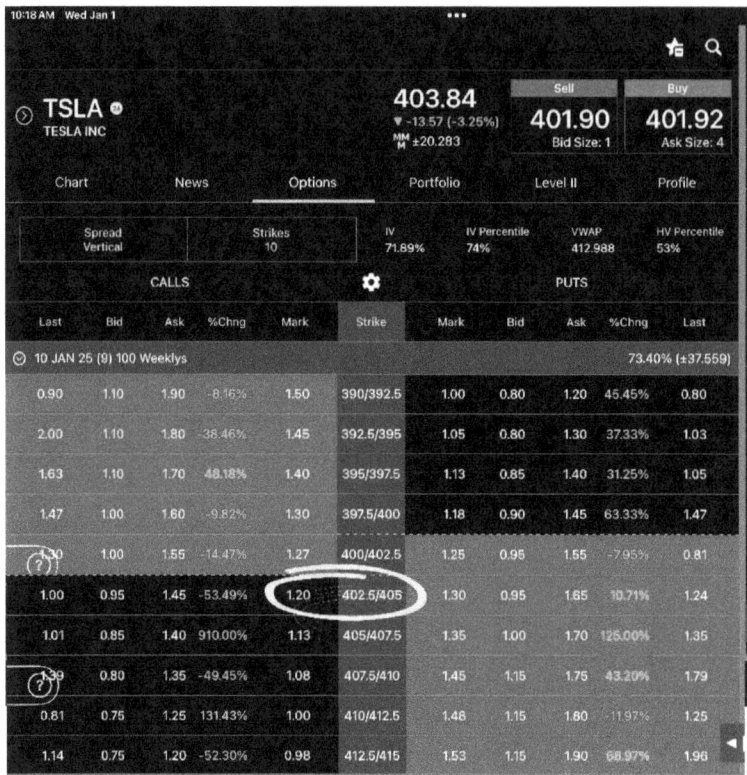

Since most traders trade more than one contract with Spreads, usually 5 or 10 at a time, you can easily control 500 shares or even 1000 at a time for less than the cost of a single contract. It's still a gamble though, because we don't know what TESLA will do during the next week. TESLA could continue to decrease in price over the next week and you'd be out the entire premium you paid on the contract(s).

Credit Spreads

Since Option sellers tend to make more money than Option buyers the other alternative is to sell a Credit Spread which is the opposite of the Debit Spread.

The most common Credit Spreads are the Bear Call Credit Spread and the Bull Put Credit Spread.

It is called a Bear Call Credit Spread because you are Bearish, meaning you are expecting or hoping that the Stock Price will go down and so you are selling a Call because you think the Stock Price won't go up. So, you are selling a Call Option and then buying a further out Call Option to use as a stop in case the Stock Price does come up through your Strike.

But because the Call Option you are selling is closer in distance to the Stock Price it is more expensive and when you sell the farther out Call Option which is less expensive, you are actually paid a premium. You make money the moment you make the trade.

The other common Credit Spread is called a Bull Put Credit Spread. This means that you are Bullish and believe or hope that the Stock Price will be going up and so you are willing to sell a Put Option and then buy a farther out Put Option as a stop in case the Stock Price actually goes down to meet your Strike Price.

With Debit Spreads you are buying so you pay to have the opportunity to profit. With Credit Spreads you are selling so you get paid to make sure the Stock Price stays far away from your Strike Price.

In stock Option terms, with a credit spread you are going to choose a strike price as far away from the actual stock price as you can and still collect decent premium money for it.

Remember that as an Option seller, you are selling an Option to someone else who believes that the stock will go up past your strike price. You are selling the insurance policy against the stock going up in price as far as your strike price.

Looking again at the TESLA chart, you can see that the price for TESLA stock can easily move up from 50 to 80 points in a 5 day trading cycle. The price can also drop.

The 2 vertical lines to the left of the chart above the price line of TESLA show the amount of increase in TESLA stock over the next 5 trading days. The horizontal line at the right shows the drop in TESLA stock and this is why I want to emphasize that no technical analysis tool could have predicted this drop, and it wasn't just a drop in TESLA stock. The market in general slumped over this period. Several World events occurred that had a direct effect on the stock market prices going down.

First there was the Federal Reserve Bank deciding that in light of future economic plans from the President and a sluggish inflation report, they would be cutting interest rates at a slower pace into 2025. The market did not react well to this news. It was followed by the possibility of a government shutdown as legislators were in disagreement over a spending bill. The market sell-off (investors selling large amounts of stock suddenly often affects overall market prices) continued to the end of the week.

So, the drop in TESLA and the drop in the market in general couldn't have been anticipated days before. But, in situations like this the market frequently comes back quickly from the losses at least part way. And then either continues to drive upward or might just consolidate and stay within a range before either breaking out up or down again.

You could choose any price you want to if you are going to sell a Credit Spread. And the normal desired risk to reward for a Spread is 1 to 4 or 1 to 5, meaning that you might make a dollar but you could risk 4 or five dollars.

In the case of TESLA I would want to get up as far away from the current price as possible as TESLA can move up pretty quickly. Even though the risk to reward isn't optimal I wouldn't want to sell any Call Option below 440 or even 450. The 440 / 442.5 Credit Spread is selling for .43 per share, or $43.00 for the contract. This means I am selling the 440 and then buying the 442.5. Most Spread traders trade in either 5 contracts or 10 contracts.

The risk, which is the length of the Spread is $2.50 per share, or $250. This risk to reward is about 1 to 6 and while this is not optimal, going up farther away from the current stock price reduces the probability that TESLA will invade my Spread.

I could also try to go up farther and sell the 450 Credit Option with a 450 / 452.5 Credit Spread. If I sold this Spread I would receive a premium of .33 per share, or $33.00 for the contract. If I sold 10 contracts I would receive a premium of $330.00 with a risk of $2,500.00. This is about a 1 to 8 risk to reward. While it doesn't seem great, but when you are calculating risk to reward on Option Spreads, there are other important things to take into consideration than just the cost versus the potential profit or loss.

It's just as important to weigh your potential profit or loss against the probability of touch. The probability of touch is the probability that the stock price will move enough to meet your closest leg in a multi-leg spread. When you are buying Options you are hoping that the stock price meets and exceeds the Strike price of your closest leg. If you are selling Options then you want the stock price to be as far away from your strike price as you can to avoid the stock price meeting or exceeding your closest leg.

The Iron Condor

There is another strategy that will give you additional premium and allow you to put a Credit Spread out farther from the Stock Price. It's called the Iron Condor.

Iron Condor Spreads are best used when you think that the Stock Price is not going to make a major move up or down. In other words, it's what's known as a Neutral Strategy play. And it can be very profitable if it's managed properly.

An Iron Condor is a Double Spread. You would sell a Call Credit Spread above the Stock Price and at the same time you would sell a Put Credit Spread underneath the Stock Price. If the Stock Price remains below the Call Option and above the Put Option by expiration you get the profit from both of the Spreads.

This is good for a couple of reasons. First, because after selling your first Credit Spread (either Call or Put), your broker has put aside the margin. But your second Credit Spread in the opposite direction doesn't require any additional margin or security. And the reason is simple. The Stock Price can't move in both directions at the same time. If you aren't lucky on one of the Spreads it means that the Stock Price has to be farther away from your other Spread. If you lose one of the Spreads, you can't lose the other.

The other reason Iron Condors make sense is that since you are collecting two premiums in the same expiration period, you can afford to move your short legs (the ones you are selling) a little further away from the Stock Price and still hopefully get some decent premium money from the safer Strike Prices.

Here is an example on TESLA.

In this example I wanted to make sure I am safely away from the current Stock Price of 403.84 on both the up and down sides. I am selling the 450 and then buying the 452.5 on the Call side and then simultaneously I am selling the 350 and then buying the 347.5 on the Put side.

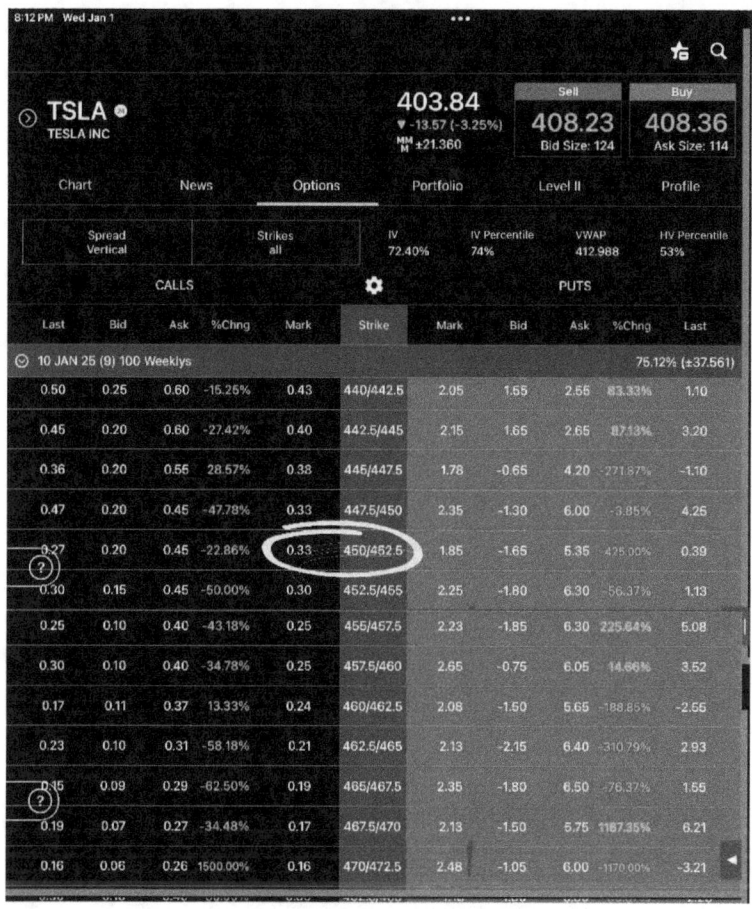

Selling the 450 and then buying the 452.5 will give me a premium of .33 per share or $33.00 per contract.

On the Put side I am selling the 350 and buying the 347.5 which will give me a premium of .38 per share, or $38.00 per contract.

Both Call and Put Spreads are about $50.00 equal distance up and down from the current Stock Price in terms of Strike Price. Both Call and Put Spreads are $2.50 between the Short (Sell) Strike and the Long (Buy) Strike, so there is a maximum at risk amount of $250.00 on either side, but not both sides since the Stock Price can't be in two places at the same time, only one side can lose in the worst scenario. Because of this your

Broker will only margin or put aside the maximum loss from one side. In essence the second Spread is free in terms of collateral held from your account.

Assuming TESLA stock price doesn't go above $450 or drop below $350 by expiration, your total premium received would be .71 per share, or $71.00 per contract. And your total risk would be $179.00, (maximum loss of the Spread $250.00 − your received premium $71.00 = $179.00) a little over 1 to 4 risk to reward ratio.

But an Iron Condor, as any Option Spread trade is not a set-it, forget it type of trade, but this is why I emphasize that Spread trades have to be managed a lot.

Over the years I've sold many Spreads, both Bear Calls and Bull Puts and have never lost the full amount of the Spread when the trade went against me (and they have, plenty of times).

The trick with Spreads is to know when to get out and either just buy back the contracts that you've sold, or roll them up, or down, or out to another expiration date. You have to do this type of management when you trade Spreads and it means you need to be checking on them several times per day. You can't just set them and forget them or you're likely to have great losses. In fact, this is exactly why I say that Option Spreads are not risk defined and can be dangerous.

You might get to expiration with your Credit or Debit Spread safely where you want it in relation to the actual closing stock price, and you might be expecting to end the week's market close with a profit from your premiums. What you don't know, and what some unlucky traders have found out the hard way is that when the market closes Friday at 4:00pm (EST) your Long Options (the Options you bought) can't be traded anymore, but your Short Options (the Options you sold) are still in play. And as frequently happens, if there is a move in the stock in afterhours trading you are involuntarily trading naked (unprotected). So if you had a Bear Call Credit Spread, hoping that the stock would not go up, and if after hours the stock goes up beyond your Strike you could find on Monday morning that your account had to cover a huge, unexpected loss. In some cases traders have lost everything.

The Rule with any Options you are selling, is to make sure you close them before expiration. Never let a sold position go past expiration without closing it out!

The exceptions are the strategies earlier in this book including Covered Calls; Cash-Secured Puts; Married Puts and Collars because they all have collateral attached to them that are independent of the Option's expiration, and in terms of the Options, in most cases you can't get hurt.

The Three Greatest Resources

Choosing the best stocks for a trade is usually done in a two step process. First is to thoroughly research the company's or index's fundamentals and then once you narrow down your top candidates, then to use technical analysis to try to catch the best timing for your trade.

Seasoned traders develop a knack for selecting the best stocks to trade with from week to week or from month to month. But even still there are tools which can reliably do most of the important selection work for you. In later chapters I will show you how to do your own fundamental research and introduce you to the techniques of technical analysis. Even veteran stock Options traders use the tested and proven resources I'm going to review in the next three chapters.

To be considered a reliable and favored resource,

- it has to be a time-tested product, system or service that has been established and successful in the stock market community for a number of years.
- It has to be a simple and easily usable system or service
- It has to be accessible on all devices from desktops and laptops, to tablets and cellphones.
- It has to be affordable (for a service no more than $100.00 per month) and can be a month-to-month subscription paid monthly if desired and be able to be cancelled at any time.
- It has to produce a substantial win rate in terms of the numbers of successful trades and in overall profit.
- The owners / designers of the service must be easily accessible and available personally for questions,

guidance and issue solving at least during regular business hours by phone as well as by E – Mail; text or other communication platform. (I'm old fashioned and prefer to speak in person by phone, so that is a requirement of mine.)

- It should provide a regularly scheduled forum for members and subscribers to meet other subscribers and members to communicate with the service owner and each other and ask questions about trading.

Each of the three resource services I've selected I actually use and have used for years. I know the owners / developers personally and have had great success with their tools.

MoneyTreeVISIONS

Ron Groenke showed an early passion for life, learning, and hard work. In ninth grade, his algebra teacher gave him some advice that would shape his future: "Learn all you can about computers; it's the wave of the future." Inspired by these words, Ron pursued a degree in mathematics from the University of Minnesota, graduating with distinction. His studies focused on data communications and software engineering, fields that would become the foundation of his career.

Ron's work became legendary during the Apollo missions. He developed the communication software for Apollo 7 and Apollo 8, two groundbreaking spaceflights. Apollo 7 was the first crewed mission to launch into space and included the first live TV broadcast from orbit, captivating the world. Apollo 8 made history as the first mission to orbit the moon, completing eight lunar loops and paving the way for future lunar landings.

Later, Ron shifted his focus to the financial world. He wrote five books on stock Options trading, including The Money Tree: Risk-Free Options Trading, Show Me the Money and Show Me the Trade. These books detailed his innovative strategies for earning income through covered calls and cash-secured puts, making complex financial concepts accessible to everyday investors.

To further support investors, Ron created a unique software program called VISIONS. This tool simplifies the process of analyzing stocks and Options, allowing users to find trading opportunities that match their goals. VISIONS became a cornerstone of Ron's work, evolving over time with feedback from its growing user base. The software is available through a monthly subscription from MoneyTreeVISIONS, LLC.

Tommy Brown followed in his father's footsteps by going to college and leaning civil engineering. After service in the military, he became an engineering consultant, and was licensed in Virginia, California, Georgia and Florida. He discovered Ron's first book, The Money Tree, while attending a professional conference. Years later, when Tommy was considering early retirement, he realized the need to generate reliable monthly income. He purchased Ron's fourth book, Show Me the Money, and began using Ron's strategies seriously. Over time, the two met, became friends, and formed a business partnership. Ron gave Tommy an exclusive license to host seminars and training sessions for the VISIONS software. Together, they have now expanded MoneyTreeVISIONS, LLC to include not only educational events but also a weekly Trade Alert service. They are currently working on a daily AI-driven trading signal program called MTVAID (MoneyTreeVisions Artificial Intelligence Decisions). This is a system focusing on market trends, volatility, and making adaptive investment decisions based on current data. It is a sophisticated, automated approach to investment education under the MoneyTreeVISIONS umbrella, emphasizing artificial intelligence algorithms.

VISIONS Software

VISIONS is a powerful software program designed to help investors analyze stocks and Options efficiently. It eliminates the tedious process of gathering financial data and evaluating multiple Options manually. Instead, VISIONS provides tools to identify the best opportunities for covered calls and cash-secured puts.

The full-featured version of VISIONS includes the following components:

- Stock Screener: A search engine that helps investors find stocks meeting specific fundamental criteria.
- VISIONS Scout: A comprehensive stock search engine.
- Stock Chart Search Engine: For analyzing price trends and patterns.
- VTAM Black Box: An advanced tool for optimizing trade entry and exit points.
- Call Option Search Engine: Helps identify the best call Options.
- Put Option Search Engine: Focuses on cash-secured puts.
- Trade Planner: Assists in creating detailed trading plans.

Although VISIONS was originally designed for covered calls and cash-secured puts, it has since been upgraded to support more complex trading strategies, such as call and put spreads and iron condors.

Key Features of VISIONS

The VISIONS software includes several unique tools and concepts that set it apart from other trading systems:

1. Fundamentals

Ron believes that successful trading starts with choosing stocks that have solid financial health. He uses strict criteria to define "good fundamentals":

- Annual revenue of at least $250 million (preferably $500 million or more).
- A market capitalization of $500 million or higher (preferably $750 million).
- Positive revenue growth of at least 10–15% per year.
- Positive earnings in at least three of the last four quarters.
- An average daily trading volume of at least 250,000 shares (500,000 shares is preferred).
- At least $100 million in Bare Cash (cash and marketable securities minus long-term debt).

Here are the screening results for the DOW 30 that meet the

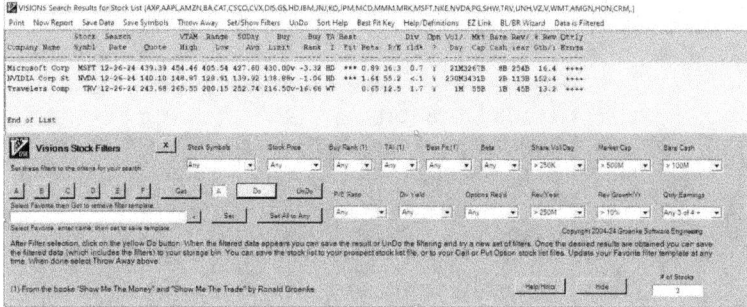

criteria in Ron's books.

2. Magic Chart

Selecting the best premium for covered calls can be tricky. This area is mostly science and a little art. It involves balancing the strike price and expiration date to maximize returns. If you want a large premium, choose a strike price close to the current price. If you keep the strike price constant, then the further out in time, the greater the premium. How do we strike a balance between time in the

Trade Duration (weeks/months) to Expiration	if sold	if expir
week 1	0.49	0.
week 2	2.19	1.
week 3	3.89	3.
week 4	5.59	4.
month 1	6.80	5.
month 2	8.40	6.
month 3	10.00	8.
month 4	11.60	9.
month 5	13.40	10.
month 6	15.00	12.

overall game? Ron developed the Magic Chart to help traders make these decisions. The Magic Chart shows potential returns for both possible outcomes of selling a call: assignment or expiration.

By visualizing these returns, the chart helps users find the ideal strike price and duration for their trades. VISIONS further simplifies this process with its Call Option Search Engine, which generates detailed analyses for each call Option, including expected returns and a graphic summary. What you are looking to find are the strike price/expiry that provides a *** or <-> Best Fit. Shown below is the output from the Call

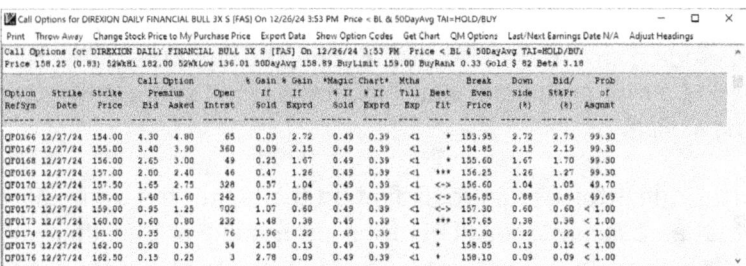

Search Engine. The *** or <-> are 'good' Options to be selling.

3. Probability of Assignment

Many experienced Options traders use a measurement called Delta to predict if an Option will end up "in-the-money" (when the Option's strike price is reached before it expires). Delta is based on a mathematical analysis of probabilities. While this is a helpful way to trade, Ron created a different approach called the Probability of Assignment (PofA), which focuses on how the stock's price has moved in the past.

Here's how it works: the program looks at the stock's price behavior over a number of days equal to the Option's time until expiration. For example, if an Option expires in 31 days, the program examines how the stock's price behaved during the last 31 trading days. It checks how often the stock's price went above the chosen strike price and adjusts this count based on how many days are left until the Option expires. This gives a more practical view of whether the Option is likely to be assigned.

The longer the period to expiration the higher the probability that an assignment will occur. A probability of less then .01 (1%) is possible when a stock has not traded above the strike price for the period under consideration.

Remember, assignments are always possible on good news and analyst upgrades.

4. VTAM Black Box

The VTAM Black Box (short for Visions Technical Analysis Model) is an advanced algorithm that optimizes entry and exit points for trades. This is an optimization tool to find the best entry and exit points for a Buy-Hold-Sell strategy. It can also be used to determine the opportune time to enter a covered-call position, since buying the stock is the first step to establishing a covered-call. Initially, Ron's trading strategies relied on 52-week price ranges, but he later refined his approach to identify and capture the opportunities to 'buy the dips'. The Black Box uses optimization techniques and simulations to provide the best settings for maximizing annual returns.

5. Groenke V

Ron's years of analysis led him to believe that stocks follow predictable cycles, especially within the most recent 50 trading days. The Groenke V is a visual tool that tracks stock price movements within this window.

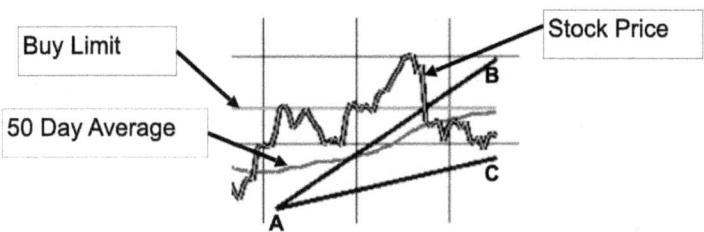

Using optimized data from the VTAM Black Box, VISIONS constructs a V-shaped pattern to analyze price action. Point A is drawn using the optimum trading range low, and is placed fifty trading days from today. Using the Buy Limit and the V Fraction, Point B is drawn at the Buy Limit plus 1/2 the fraction time the High minus the Low. Point C is drawn at the Low plus 1/2 the fraction times the High.

VISIONS will analyze the price action using the V. The items it utilizes are the number of days the stock has traded in the V, if the stock is currently inside the V, and what the price action has been for the past three days. The ideal case is when:

    1) A stock has traded in the V for 20 days or more;

    2) Is moving up for the past three days;

    3) Is in the V or within +/- 5% of the 50-day moving average.

A stock meeting these criteria is often an excellent candidate for investment right now.

6. Portfolio Income Explorer (PIE)

Can you really generate income from a stock portfolio? Absolutely, and PIE will help you learn how much income can be generated per month (and likewise, per year). Enter your portfolio and let VISIONS do all the work. It will get the Options information and select the expiration date. The resulting graphic will show you the income from call selling and the capital gains from assignment.

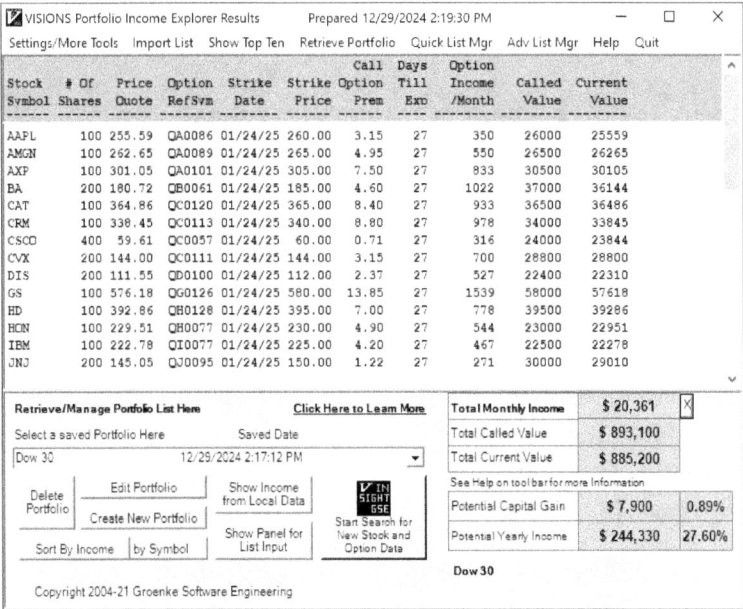

Here is the output from looking at the DOW 30.

MoneyTreeVISIONS Services

Learning the VISIONS program can take some time, and not all traders have the hours to fully master it right away. Some people want to start using the software and earning money as soon as possible. Contained on the MoneyTreeVisions website are educational videos and archived webinars with specific topics to help users get 'up to speed' quickly. Additionally, a one hour one-on-one session is included with each trial of the software and Trade Alerts.

1. Trade Alerts

Tommy and Ron recognize that using the VISIONS software is a great tool for finding potential covered calls and naked puts. Not everyone has the time or dedication to use it day in and day out. They are using VISIONS every day. That kind of proficiently is not found in the casual trader. That is where they come to the rescue with their weekly publication of a Trade Alert. This service gives clear, actionable trade ideas to help traders get started quickly.

Each Trade Alert includes three recommendations: two covered call Options and one cash-secured put. The alerts are published every Saturday and are based on data from the stock market's closing on Friday. The trade ideas are designed to be used on the following Monday when the market reopens. These suggestions focus on weekly expiration Options, which are short-term trades.

The Trade Alert also includes three helpful charts:

1. S&P 500 OutLook Chart: A two-month trend forecast created using VISIONS.
2. Three-Month S&P 500 Chart: Shows key support and resistance levels for better decision-making.

3. VIX Chart: A tool that tracks market volatility to help you gauge the mood of the market.

These charts help you understand market trends and give you a clearer idea of what to expect for the coming week.

On Monday, Tommy shares additional details about how he manages these trades, including his own execution data and trade management strategies. This information helps traders learn how to handle trades effectively.

It's important to note that the Weekly Trade Alert is not a service where you simply copy trades. Instead, it serves as an educational tool on selling covered calls and short puts for income. It provides a way for you to look over the shoulder of a seasoned trader and see how it is done. There is no need to subscribe to VISIONS to profit from Ron's great software tool. Let Tommy and Ron do the research.

Show below is a slide from the Trade Alert. It shows how they track the trades, helping you see the results and how to manage the trades. Their success record is awesome. In 2024, they had a win rate of 93% with a total return of 24.40%.

Tracking Results for the month ending 12/27/24

WCC is a Weekly Covered Call   WNP is a Weekly Naked Put

It was a good month. We skipped issuing a trade alert one week. Only one position added to the Trade Management section that is still open.

SYMBOL	TRADE	Alert Date	Alert Close Price	EXPIRE	STRIKE	Expire Date Close	number of shares	premium	RESULT	profit/ loss	capital required	
MTCH	WCC	12/06/24	$32.93	12/13/24	$31.00	$31.45	300	$2.46	CA	$159.00	$9,141	1.74%
UAA	WCC	12/06/24	$10.12	01/03/25	$9.00		1000	$1.07	CE		$9,050	
NUGT	WNP	12/06/24	$41.24	12/13/24	$39.00	$40.51	300	$0.40	PE	$120.00	$11,700	1.03%
HPE	WCC	12/13/24	$21.83	12/20/24	$21.50	$21.61	500	$0.55	CA	$110.00	$10,640	1.03%
TZA	WCC	12/13/24	$11.30	12/20/24	$10.50	$12.84	1000	$0.96	CA	$160.00	$10,320	1.74%
BOIL	WNP	12/13/24	$44.05	12/20/24	$40.00	$50.36	300	$0.48	PE	$144.00	$12,000	1.20%
HPE	WCC	12/20/24	$21.61	12/27/24	$21.50	$21.65	500	$0.50	CA	$195.00	$10,556	1.85%
XLF	WCC	12/20/24	$48.51	12/27/24	$49.00	$48.75	200	$0.15	<	$78.00	$9,672	0.81%
BOIL	WNP	12/20/24	$50.36	12/27/24	$43.00	$51.00	300	$0.41	PE	$123.00	$12,900	0.95%
								For the week =>		$396.00	$33,127	1.20%
								For the month =>		$1,109.00	$33,127	3.35%

© Copyright 2024 MoneyTreeVISIONS, LLC

CFTC RULE 4.41 - Hypothetical or simulated performance results have certain limitations. Unlike an actual performance record, simulated results do not represent actual trading. Also, since the trades have not been executed, the results may have under- or over-compensated for the impact, if any, of certain market factors, such as lack of liquidity. Simulated trading programs in general are also subject to the fact that they are designed with the benefit of hindsight. No representation is being made that any account will or is likely to achieve profit or loss similar to those shown.

2. MTVAID (MoneyTreeVisions Artificial Intelligence Decisions)

As of publication, Ron and Tommy are working on a AI-driven email system that takes a snapshot of the market at 10:00 AM EST and generates a list of equities (stocks and ETFs) that have actionable entry points. This service is geared towards traders that have a buy-hold-sell approach. However, it is applicable to covered call traders that are looking for equities that have good entry points, and have monthly or weekly expirations for calls and puts. When launched, more information will be posted on the website.

3. Monthly User Meetings

Anyone can join monthly Zoom meetings to ask questions, share experiences, and learn from Ron and Tommy. These sessions are an excellent way to deepen one's understanding of VISIONS and its strategies.

4. Support and Education

Ron and Tommy are available throughout your subscription to answer questions and provide assistance. The goal is to empower traders to use VISIONS effectively, confidently and profitably.

Learn More

For more information, visit www.moneytreevisions.com. The website offers a free 21-day trial and Options to subscribe to the full software or the weekly Trade Alerts. It also provides a way to contact Tommy for more details.

PowerOptions and Ernie Zerenner

During a 30 year career at Hewlett Packard, Ernie Zerenner forged a trail of achievement. He developed four patents, delivered six well-received papers, received an international award for his invention of the Fused Silica Column, and had an impressive list of industry firsts, including the first microprocessor-driven instrument in the analytical industry.

During his tenure, Ernie continued his lifelong fascination with the stock market, building a successful portfolio. When retirement loomed. Ernie felt it was necessary to switch his investing philosophy from seeking capital gains to creating income from assets owned, So be turned to covered calls, designed to generate consistent income.

Using a calculator and the financial pages, it took eight to ten hours to find good opportunities. In an attempt to cut that time frame, Ernie teamed with a colleague to design a program to scan the entire market and find the best covered calls. The time required to do the job dropped from eight hours to eight minutes. It was breakthrough technology that earned a patent, and was the basis for a web site called PowerOpt.com, which now not only supports Ernie's covered call investments, but thousands of subscriber / investors in, at last count, 57 countries all over the world

Michael Chupka has co-authored the most authoritative book on Protective Options Strategies – Married Puts and Collar Spreads. He is from Delaware where his father was a Ph.D. in Chemistry and his mother a registered nurse. His major fields of study at the University of Missouri Rolla were geology, micro-paleontology, and English Literature. So both scientific studies and service have been the major part of his life.

With such a background in scientific methods and service, and over twenty years and many tens of thousands of PowerOptions customers later, Mr. Chupka has established himself as Head of the PowerOptions Support Team and a recognized Options strategy educator in the industry. Michael has written dozens of educational articles and produced webinars and videos for PowerOptions. He has also co-authored another book, Naked Puts – Power Strategies for Consistent Profits.

PowerOpt.com is still the largest subscription program of the Power Financial Group, the trading company Ernie established in 1997. Today, he continues to innovate and seek ways to help investors grow through Options trading.

If you want great free resources to learn more about stock Option trading, Power Options is there to teach and guide you. The Learning Center consists of: webinars, tutorials, tips, lessons, coaching sessions, publications, statistics, and a glossary. They are continually adding to and improving the Learning Center; bringing you the best Options education materials - and it's 100% free.

Beyond the great free resources, you can sign up for a monthly subscription to one of the most powerful Options screening and analysing tools ever developed. The Power Options Screener contains literally thousands of pages of data that traders can access in seconds

You can select from over 23 different Options strategies, and either fill in your criteria for selection based on your personal trading profile, or review Options suggestions and their recommendations and the current market conditions.

All of your stock's fundamental and technical analysis is done for you so that you can select from the very best Options choices to trade whether you are looking for the safest or the most profitable, or a combination of both.

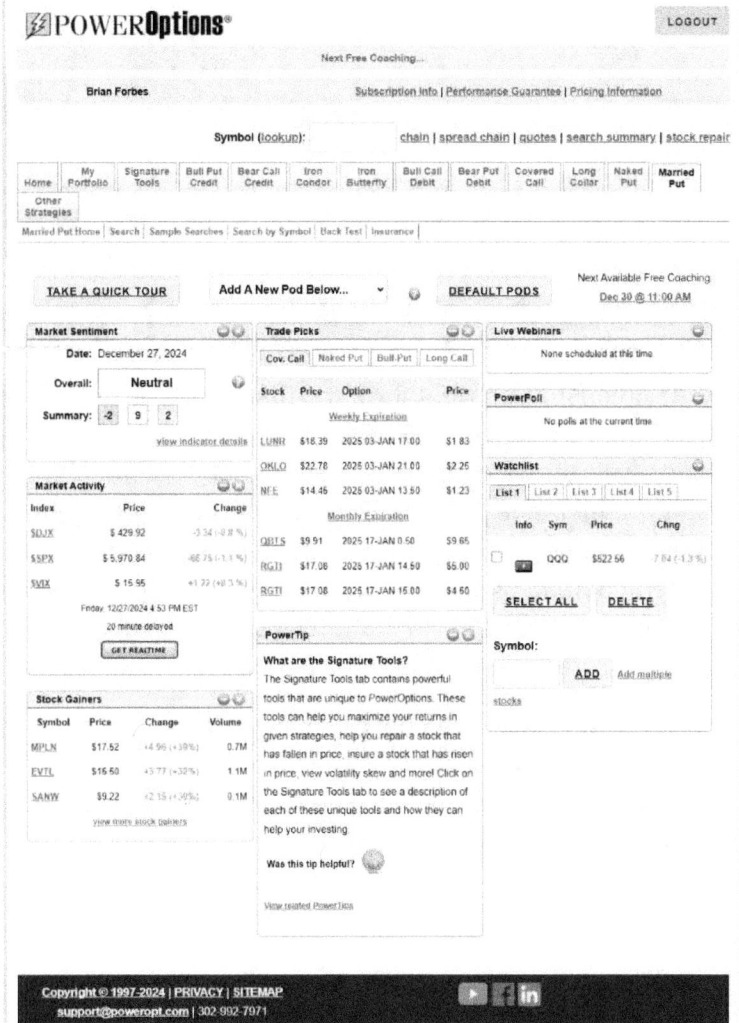

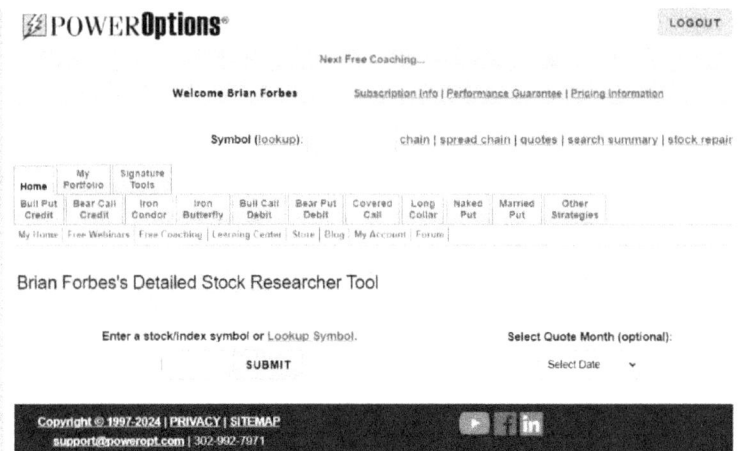

In the screenshot above, this is the first thing you see when you log on as a subscriber. You can enter a stock's symbol, or click on one of the tabs according to your personal Option strategy preference. I already have my most used stock Options strategies arranged on the tabs above, from the Bull Put Credit Spread on the far left, to the Married Put on the far right. If you click on the Other Strategies tab you will be taken to the next screenshot below.

The next screenshot is the next level down when you click on the Other Strategies tab. Here you have your choice of popular stock Options strategies which you can place on the tabs for quick access. Below you can see how I placed mine.

Here is an example of using the Power Options screener to find the best weekly Covered Calls.

As a subscriber I do receive the Morning Update PriceWatch Alerts in my E – Mail every morning. But I also can come to the screener and click on the Covered Call tab on my dashboard. From there I can click on Monthly Picks of the Day, or even Weekly Picks of the Day among other selections.

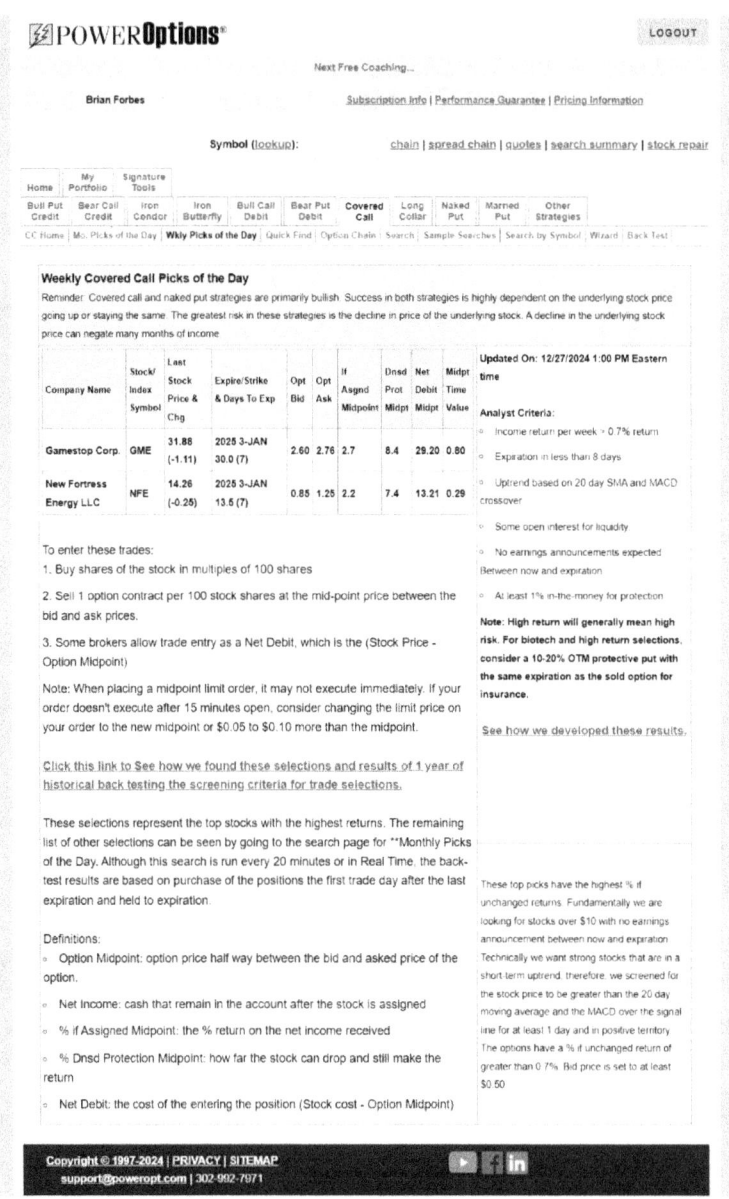

The page explains everything I need to know about the stocks chosen; the date of expiration; the strike price and premium I should expect to receive as well as their criteria for selecting these particular stocks and Call Options. But maybe I would like to choose a different strike price. So I can look at the Option Chain for the January 03, 2025 Weekly Gamestop (GME NYSE) Options.

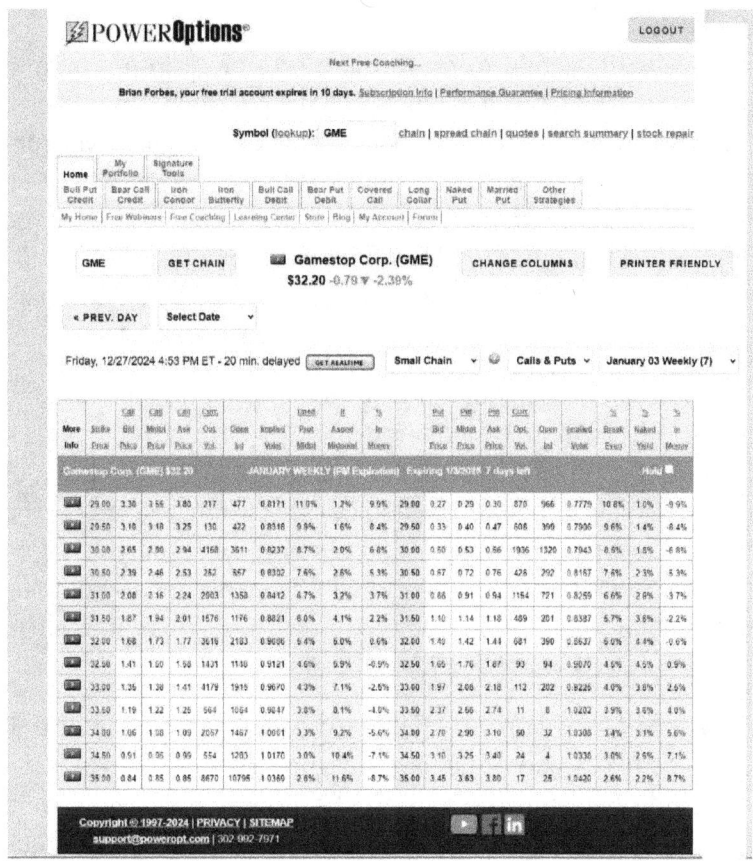

In the Option above, the blue shaded areas are the ITM (In The Money) Options available. The Weekly Picks of the Day suggested the 30 strike ITM (In The Money) Call for which I should receive about $2.80 ($2.80 x 100 shares = $280.00) in premium. This means I am willing to have my shares of GME sold for $30.00 per share if the stock price is above $30 at expiration at the end of next week. Since I will be buying GME shares at $32.20 (the price has gone up during after-hours trading since the original closing price of $31.88) I am willing to take a loss of $2.20 per share and still I would net a profit of $60.00 from the premium I received on the deal ($2.80 - $2.20 = $.60 per share).

If however I wished to make more of a profit in premium, I could sell the 31 strike which is paying a premium of $2.16 ($2.16 x 100 shares = $216.00). The loss I might have from agreeing to have my stock shares sold for $31.00 per share when I bought them for $32.20 is $1.20 per share ($1.20 x 100 shares = $120.00). So, subtracting the stock loss of $120.00 from the premium I received of $216.00 would still net me a profit of $96.00.

Then I could sell the 32 strike which is ITM (In The Money by $.20. The premium I am offered is $1.73 ($1.73 x 100 shares = $173.00). If the stock settles above $32.00 per share at expiration I would lose the $.20 per share from the loss of the stock but still have the $173.00, so my net profit would be $153.00. ($173.00 - $20.00 = $153.00). In this case I would be trying for a higher profit, but very little downside protection in case the stock value declines by expiration.

If I wanted to sell an OTM (Out of The Money) Call I could sell the 33 strike which would pay me a premium of $1.38 ($1.38 x 100 = $138.00) and in addition, if the stock price is over $33.00 per share at expiration, I would receive the profit of the stock of $.80 per share so I would net $218.00 ($138.00 + $80.00 = $218.00).

If for some reason I decided that I really want to keep the stock, but still want some reasonable premium, I could sell the OTM (Out of The Money) 37.50 strike which would pay me a premium of $.53 per share ($.53 x 100 = $53.00). $53.00 doesn't seem like a lot of profit to make on a Covered Call, but if you are an investor who has had at least 100 shares of stock sitting in your portfolio for a very long time and are concerned about long term capital gains in case your stock is sold, you might want to make some money on the stock that has been in your possession for a long time, and at the same time you want to make sure that the Call Option is not assigned and your stock is not sold. So you would sell a much higher OTM (Out of The Money) strike trying to make sure that your stock isn't sold and you would at least be happy with some reasonable premium for the week, knowing that you can keep selling Covered Calls week after week indefinitely.

I have a friend who inherited more than 500 shares of General Electric (GE NYSE) that had been in her family for generations. She found she could make extra income each week by selling several Covered Calls each week on the stock at far OTM (Out of The Money) strikes, which has made her a lot of extra income without risking the sale of the stock. Of course, she does watch the market once or twice a day to make sure that in the event GE stock increases to much too rapidly, she can buy back her Covered Call Options at any time before expiration.

In the above examples I have shown the choices you have as an investor. Some of you might want better downside protection in case the stock price falls during the week, in which case the better choice is to sell ITM (In The Money) Covered Call Options. Some of you may be willing to take the risk on the stock price staying where it is or increasing, in which case you might sacrifice the downside protection and opt for greater profit from the premium and the increase in the stock value at expiration.

The question is whether I want more premium or more downside protection in case the stock price drops before expiration. Of course no matter which strike price I choose, if the stock price drops below my strike price, then I receive the full premium and still keep my stock so that I can either wait for the price to come back up and sell it, or sell another Covered Call Option the next week after this expires.

With the other Weekly Pick of the Day, New Fortress Energy (NFE NASDAQ) suggested I sell the 13.5 ITM (In The Money) strike of the January 03, 2025 Call Options for a premium of $1.23 ($1.23 x 100 shares = $123.00). If I purchase the stock at the present price of $14.45 per share, and the stock closes at expiration above $13.50 per share, I would lose $.95 per share. My net profit from selling the 13.50 strike would be $28.00 ($123.00 - $95.00 = $28.00)

If you wanted a trade that is more profitable you might want to sell the 14 strike which would give you a premium of $.88 per share ($.88 x 100 = $88.00). If the stock price of NFE closes above $14.00 per share at expiration, you would lose $.45 per share on the stock so your net profit would be $43.00 ($88.00 - $45.00 = $43.00).

If you still want more profit from the trade, you could sell the 15 strike which would pay you a premium of $.40 per share ($.40 x 100 = $40.00). If the stock price is above $15.00 per share at expiration, you would receive the $40.00 premium as well as the profit from the stock price increase of $55.00 for a total of $$95.00.

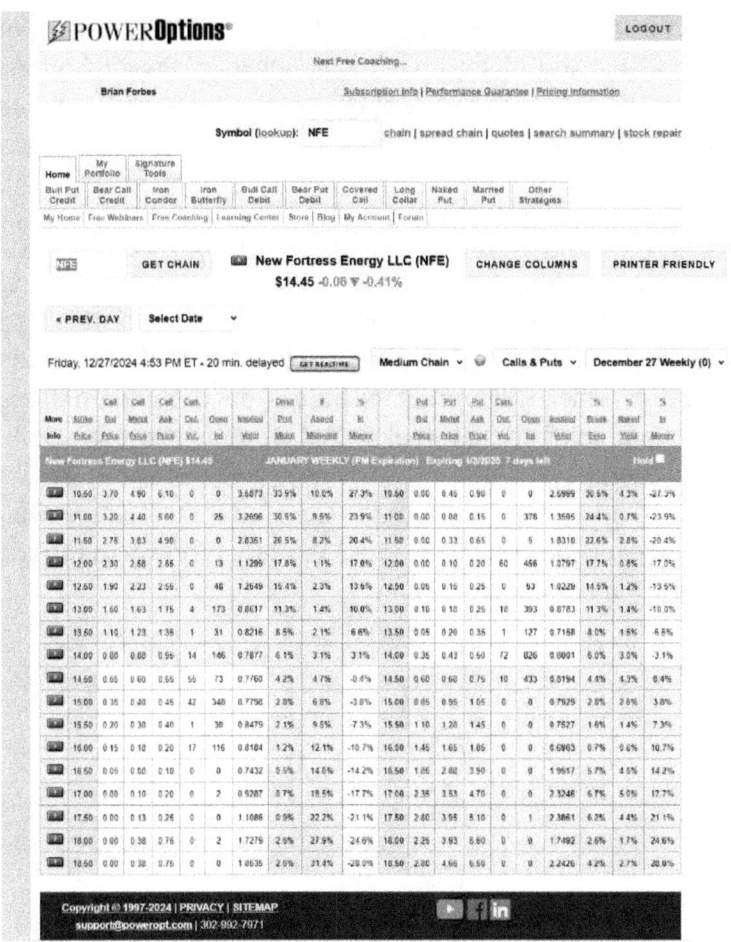

I regularly trade both weekly Covered Call Options and Cash-secured Put Options, but what I really like are called the Married Put Collar trades. A Married Put is a strategy where you buy the 100 shares of stock as you would for a Covered Call, but you then buy a long-term Put Option (from a month to 6 months seems to be ideal) to protect your stock from going down in price. In the event that your stock price goes down, the value of the Put Option will increase. Once I have both the 100 shares of stock and the Protective Long Put Option, I can sell weekly Covered Call Options to make more income and to cover the cost of the Long Protective Put Option. This sort of set-up is the specialty of Power Options Group. They have a number of books; seminars, and courses showing you how to easily profit from selling Options while bulletproofing your trades so you don't lose money.

In this example I'm going to show you how I selected a trade idea from the Power Options Screener. My trade is a Collar starting with a Married Put. I will buy 100 shares of a stock and then buy a Protective Put Option going out about 6 months expiration which will protect the stock from dropping in price. Then I am going to sell weekly Call Options (Covered Call), which over the next 6 months will pay for the Long Put Option and then bring in profits from the Covered Calls. Here is what I see when I click on the Married Put tab. It brings me to the Married Put Home Page.

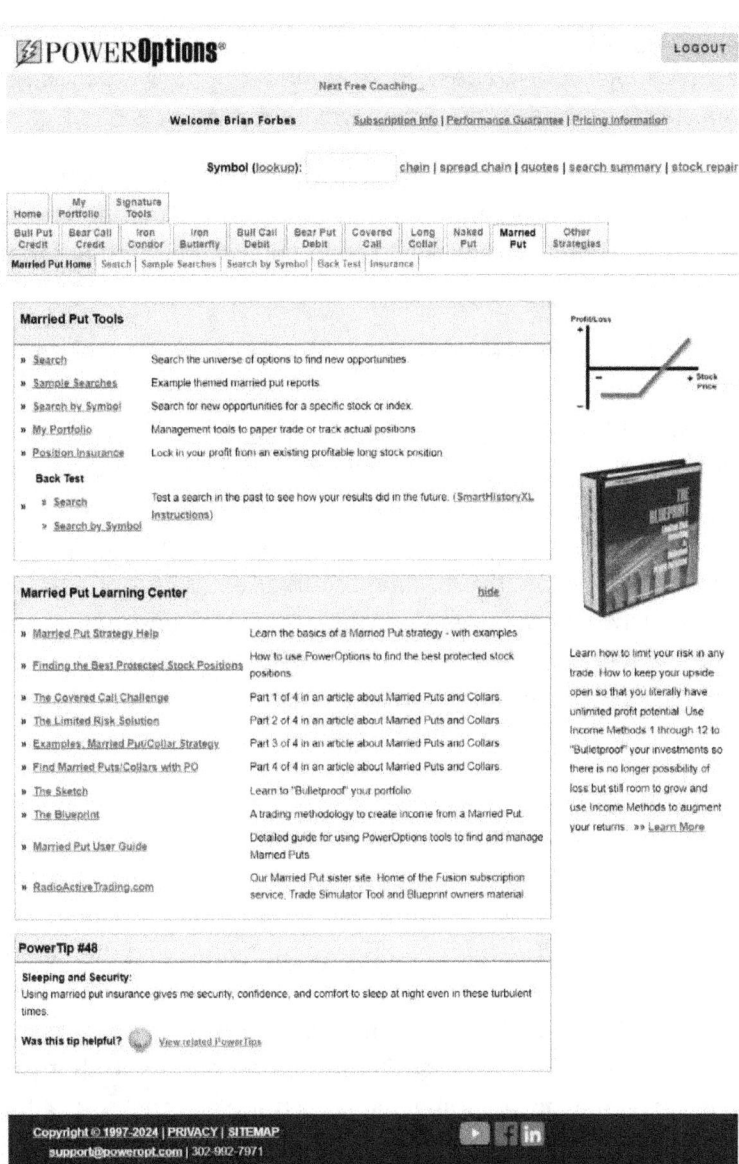

As you can see the Married Put Homepage is divided into three sections. The Married Put Tools, the Married Put Learning Center and then a tip pertaining to the Married Put Option strategy. If I were exploring Options strategies and didn't know anything about this strategy, the Learning Center is filled with articles, sample trades, instructions on how to place a Married Put trade, and texts on why this strategy is used.

In the Tools section are the tabs to search the universe of trades, other sample trades and even a back testing tool to show you how this strategy has worked on a particular stock historically.

When I click on Search in the Married Put Tools section, search results come up with stocks according to either the search criteria that I have set, or according to the default preferences. In this case the default is called the Radioactive sort by EPSG, which stands for Earnings Per. Share Growth (a calculation of how a company's earnings change from year to year). The Radioactive trading techniques are proprietary to Power Options and were created by Kurt Frankenburg and Ernie Zerenner as special techniques to protect stock positions with Married Puts and then maximize profits with added other Options.

In this example the stocks are listed by company name and then going across from the left to right the columns are the stock's symbol; the latest price of the stock; the optimum suggested Put Option for the strategy (remember we ideally go out 6 months.); The midpoint between the Ask and the Bid for the Option (this is the price we hope to pay for the Option); the Option's Ask Price (the price that Sellers of this Option to you are hoping to get); the Net Debit is price per share that you should be paying including the stock price and the cost of the Put Option; the Maximum Risk Percentage (in case your trade doesn't work out this is the most you could lose as a percentage of the total trade); The Maximum Risk (the actual maximum dollar figure you could be at risk for in the trade); the % EPSG (the percent that the company has increased in earnings from the previous year).

The Screener lists the top stocks found based on the search criteria. Below the list of stocks is the section for the Search parameters. There is a box that shows you the current search name (in this case the default is named, Radioactive Sort by ESPG) and there is a complete description of the this search and how it works. Then there are blue tabs which allow you to clear current filters and create your own search criteria and name and save your search.

The rest of the page allows you to see in detail what the specific parameters of the search is, and also allows you to input your own specific criteria and filters for searches in the categories of the Options themselves, the stock's Technical details; the stock's Fundamental details, and Lists.

To the right of the page you can specify how you want the results to be sorted and you can review all of the filters of the results by individual criteria categories of Options, Technicals; Fundamentals, and Lists.

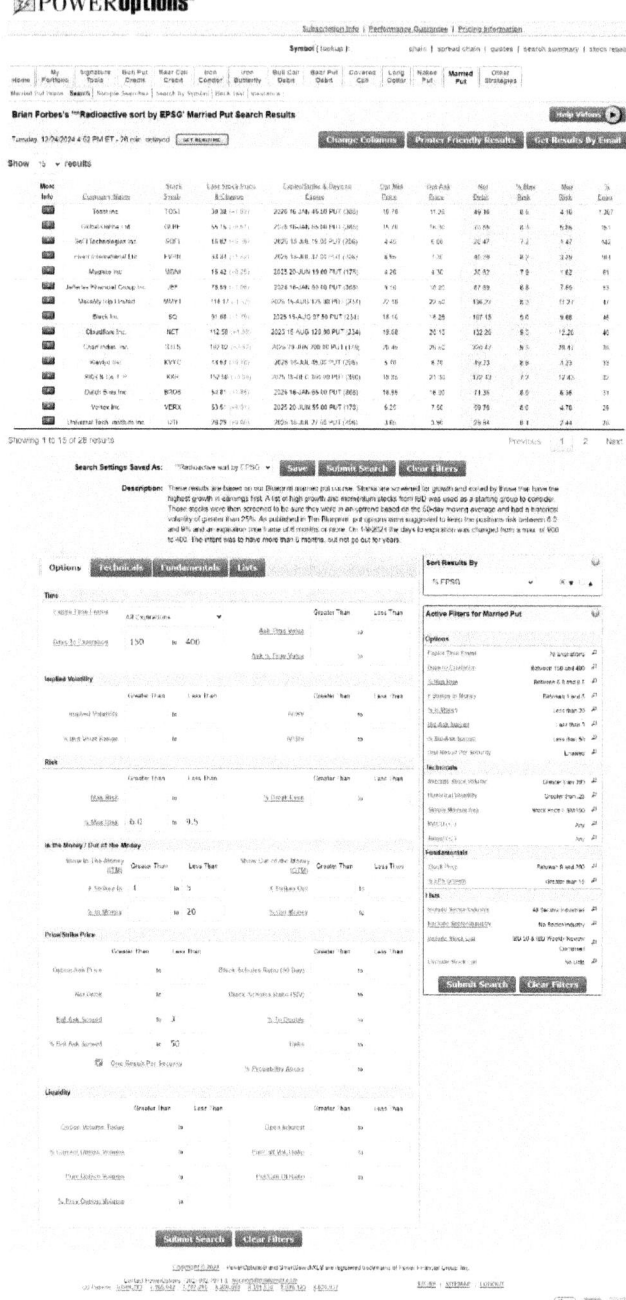

Based on the list of best fit choices, I decided to try a trade with the company TOAST (TOST NYSE), so to the left of the stock name in the search results, there is a little blue button when I press it and click on Search by Symbol, I get a full page of results of available Put Options for TOAST that expire in June of 2025.

At this point I can select an ITM (In The Money) Put Option based on the price I want to pay, or based on the maximum risk of the overall trade. Ideally I would want both a low price but a reasonable risk amount and I want a strike price for the Put Option that has enough room for the stock itself to increase in price.

For this trade, I decided to buy the 43 strike, giving the stock which is currently trading at $38.13 per share some room to increase in value. The price I am paying for the Put Option is 8.30 (8.30 x 100 shares = $830.00), and my maximum risk is 3.43, or $343.00. The total invested with stock and the Put Option is $46.43 per share.

POWER**Options**®

Next Free Coaching...

Brian Forbes

Subscription Info | Performance Guarantee | Pricing Information

Symbol (lookup): chain | spread chain | quotes | search summary | stock repair

Home	My Portfolio	Signature Tools							
Bull Put Credit	Bear Call Credit	Iron Condor	Iron Butterfly	Bull Call Debit	Bear Put Debit	Covered Call	Long Collar	Naked Put	**Married Put**	Other Strategies

Married Put Home | Search | Sample Searches | **Search by Symbol** | Back Test | Insurance

Brian Forbes's Search By Symbol Tool for Married Put Research

Tuesday, 12/24/2024 4:52 PM ET - 20 min. delayed [GET REALTIME]   CHANGE COLUMNS   PRINTER FRIENDLY RESULTS

Toast Inc. (TOST) $ 38.38 ($ +1.09) +2.9 %

Stock Symbol Lookup Symbol	Put Expiration	Filters	
TOST	Jun 20 2025 (177)	All Results	SUBMIT

Show 25 results   Search:

More Info	Expire/Strike & Days to Expire	Opt Mid Price	Opt Ask Price	Net Debit	% Max Risk	Max Risk	% Epsq
	2025 20-JUN 60.00 PUT (178)	21.50	22.15	59.88	-0.2	-0.12	1,267
	2025 20-JUN 65.00 PUT (178)	26.83	27.25	65.21	0.3	0.21	1,267
	2025 20-JUN 55.00 PUT (178)	17.38	17.60	55.76	1.4	0.76	1,267
	2025 20-JUN 50.00 PUT (178)	13.15	13.35	51.53	3.0	1.53	1,267
	2025 20-JUN 49.00 PUT (178)	12.38	12.60	50.76	3.5	1.76	1,267
	2025 20-JUN 48.00 PUT (178)	11.55	11.75	49.93	3.9	1.93	1,267
	2025 20-JUN 47.00 PUT (178)	10.80	11.00	49.18	4.4	2.18	1,267
	2025 20-JUN 46.00 PUT (178)	10.50	11.15	48.88	5.9	2.88	1,267
	2025 20-JUN 44.00 PUT (178)	8.53	8.60	46.91	6.2	2.91	1,267
	2025 20-JUN 45.00 PUT (178)	9.65	10.15	48.03	6.3	3.03	1,267
	2025 20-JUN 43.00 PUT (178)	8.00	8.20	46.38	7.3	3.38	1,267
	2025 20-JUN 41.00 PUT (178)	6.60	6.70	44.96	8.8	3.96	1,267
	2025 20-JUN 42.00 PUT (178)	7.75	8.35	46.13	9.0	4.13	1,267
	2025 20-JUN 40.00 PUT (178)	6.03	6.10	44.41	9.9	4.41	1,267
	2025 20-JUN 39.00 PUT (178)	5.43	5.50	43.81	11.0	4.81	1,267
	2025 20-JUN 38.00 PUT (178)	4.90	4.95	43.28	12.2	5.28	1,267
	2025 20-JUN 37.00 PUT (178)	4.40	4.45	42.78	13.5	5.78	1,267
	2025 20-JUN 36.00 PUT (178)	3.95	4.00	42.33	15.0	6.33	1,267
	2025 20-JUN 35.00 PUT (178)	3.50	3.55	41.88	16.4	6.88	1,267
	2025 20-JUN 34.00 PUT (178)	3.10	3.15	41.48	18.0	7.48	1,267
	2025 20-JUN 33.00 PUT (178)	2.72	2.76	41.10	19.7	8.10	1,267
	2025 20-JUN 32.00 PUT (178)	2.40	2.61	40.78	21.5	8.78	1,267
	2025 20-JUN 31.00 PUT (178)	2.04	2.24	40.42	23.3	9.42	1,267
	2025 20-JUN 30.00 PUT (178)	1.43	1.96	39.81	24.6	9.81	1,267
	2025 20-JUN 29.00 PUT (178)	1.62	1.76	40.00	27.5	11.00	1,267

Showing 1 to 25 of 28 results   Previous 1 2 Next

Copyright © 1997-2024 | PRIVACY | SITEMAP
support@poweropt.com | 302-092-7971

After selecting the Stock and the Option I want to buy, Power Options will even show me the 5 step set-up for this trade and give me an idea of the results in different scenarios.

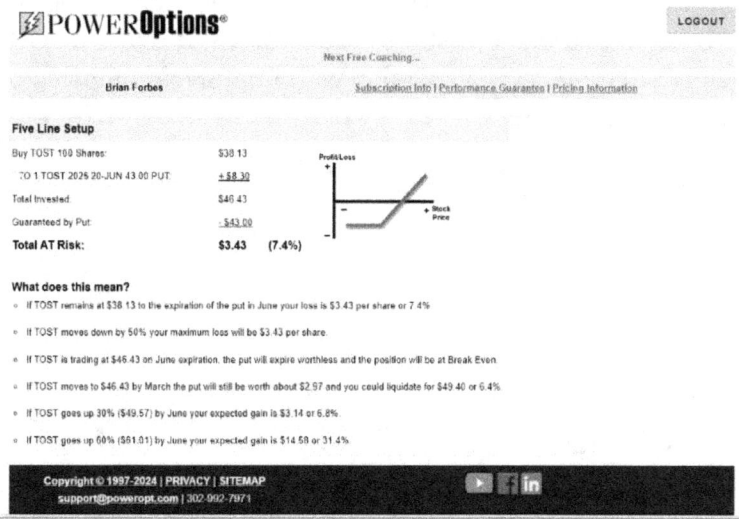

Now that I own 100 shares of TOAST and I have purchased the June 2025 expiration Put Option with a Strike Price of 43.00, I can start selling weekly Call Options (because I own the stock remember it's called a Covered Call) which will pay for the Put Option I just bought, and bring in additional weekly income from selling the Call Option premiums.

Here is the Option chain for TOAST for the next weekly Call Option available to sell. Notice that the current stock price of TOAST is $38.38. I have a choice of selling an ITM (In The Money) Call Option; an ATM (At The Money) Call Option, or an OTM (Out of The Money) Call Option. Normally I would say that any of these strategies may have an advantage, but I this case I have already purchased a protective Put Option on the shares of stock, so there is no reason to sell an ITM (In The Money) Call Option. The whole purpose of selling ITM Call Options is to protect from a drop in the stock price before expiration. But I already have downside protection from the Put Option I purchased. In this case an ATM (At The Money) Call Option doesn't make a lot of sense because there is limited profit, and again, I don't need the downside protection. So with this strategy I am more free to sell an OTM (Out of The Money) Call Option without the fear of losing on the value of the stock.

Let's look at the Option chain for the January 03, 2025 weekly Call Option for TOAST.

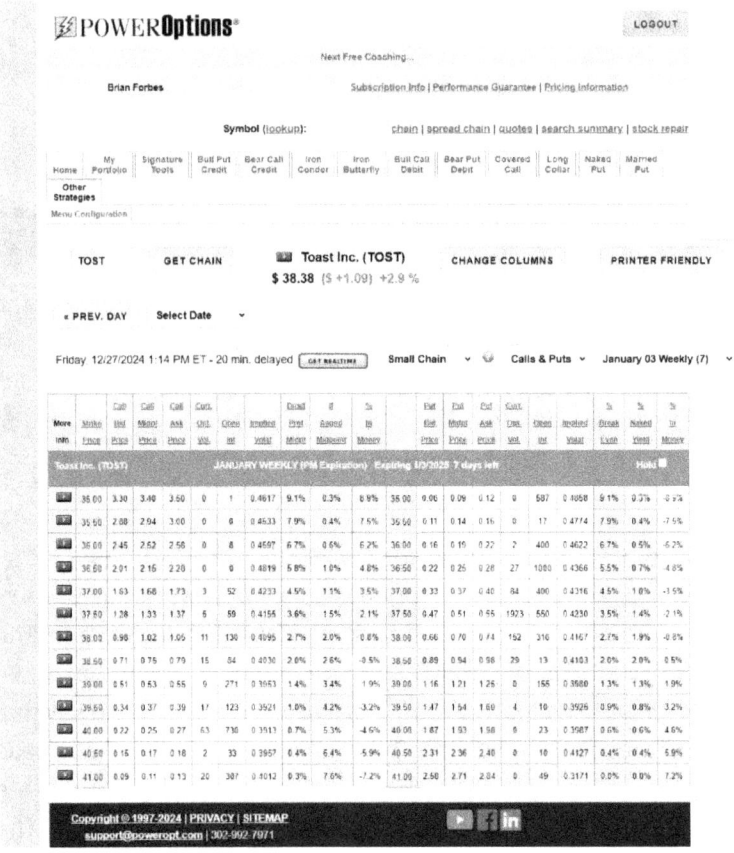

To make it easier to see action at a glance, most Option chains will shade all of the rows that are ITM (In The Money). Above the blue shaded areas are ITM (In The Money). Since the stock is now selling for $38.38, the 37.50 Call is ITM (In The Money), the $38 Call would be considered the ATM (At The Money) Call, but the $38.50 Call is OTM (Out of The Money).

Here are my choices.

1. If I sell the $38.00 Call I receive $1.02 in premium ($1.02 x 100 shares = $102.00), but since I bought the shares for $38.38 I would lose $38.00 when the $38.00 Call Option is assigned, so I would net $64.00 ($102.00 - $38.00 = $64.00), unless upon expiration the stock prices goes down below $38.00, in which case I would keep the entire premium of $102.00 and I would still own the stock so I could wait for the stock to increase again in value and in the meantime, continue the following week to sell another Covered Call Option.
2. If I sell the $38.50 Call Option I would receive a premium of $.75 ($.75 x 100 shares = $75.00) and if the price of the stock increases more than $38.50 by expiration I would also receive an additional $12 in profit from the increase in the stock from $38.38 to $38.50 before the stock is assigned. That's a potential profit of $87.00 ($75.00 + $12.00 = $87.00). Of course, again if the stock price doesn't increase past $38.50 upon expiration, then I keep the $75.00 in premium and I still own the stock.
3. If I sell the $39.00 Call Option I would make a premium of $.53 ($.53 x 100 = $53.00). If the price of the stock go up more than $39.00 I would receive the $53,00 premium plus the profit of the stock price increase of $.62 ($.62 x 100 shares = $62.00), so the total profit if the stock is assigned would be $115.00. If the stock does not increase beyond $39.00 by expiration then I

would have a net profit of $53.00 and still own the stock.

You can visit PowerOptions at www.poweropt.com and they offer a completely free 14 Day Free Trial with no credit card required, which means really "completely free". Along with the massive search pages on different stocks, indexes, ETF's and equities, you can browse their products, subscription information, information about them, free webinars and Options investment courses.

Again,

the best thing about PowerOptions is their personal service. If you call you will always get a member of their gracious support team, often Ernie Zerenner, Michael Chupka or Greg Zerenner themselves and they don't charge to speak with them about anything that will help you become a more successful trader.

For more information, you can check them out at

https://www.poweropt.com/bforbes/

0-DTE with the S&P 500 Index

I am including a technique of trading devised by my friend Ernie Varitimos (the name is Greek, so if you ever call him, be sure to say "Yasoo").

Ernie has been a coach and trusted advisor to hundreds of traders and executives over the past 25 years. His background was heavily focused on financial technology (fintech), has run an experimental hedge fund, and managed 9 figure portfolios.

As the former chief technologist of a fortune 50 company, Ernie pioneered agile business processes, and directed the development of financial systems for exchanges and many of the major financial institutions on Wall Street.

Ernie was a quantitative scientist developing Options and futures-based algorithmic strategies used to produce asymmetric returns for clients.

All his work experience has culminated in the creation of his 0-DTE (zero days to expiration) service, which focuses on teaching traders 0DTE Options strategies and methods to help them advance as professional traders.

His strategy is called 0-DTE stands for zero days to expiration. Yes, it is a day trade and I always caution investors against day trading. Outside of this particular trading strategy, I would say, don't ever day trade. Every day trader I have ever met, and there have been a lot, has lost everything in no time.

The General Premise of 0-DTE

Trading on the last day of expiration allows us to take advantage of the exponential decay of premium. As time moves toward the expiration of the Options contract, our ability to take in premium/profit increases dramatically, which is a huge edge!

Options on S&P Futures have five expirations, every day of the week, Monday through Friday. That's five opportunities every week to take advantage of this edge. Most Options only have one opportunity per week, or one opportunity per month.

What are 0DTE Options?

0DTE refers to Zero Days to Expiration: the last day of expiration of an Options contract. Selling and buying Options at zero days to expiration offers uniquely attractive trading opportunities. And although you may not understand the mechanics of time decay, all you have to know is that if you are selling Options, then you want time decay to increase quickly because it is more likely that you will be able to keep more of the premium you collect.

Although Ernie Varitimos's unique 0-DTE strategies are more complex than the other strategies in this book, I've included him and his techniques for several reasons. His technique of trading produces what he refers to as largely asymmetric trades. That is, these trades have very little risk and potentially huge rewards. I know because I have been trading with him successfully for a long time.

Also these trades can be done for relatively little investment, so they're great for small accounts. And because the strategy is 0-DTE, or zero days to expiration, traders can place their trades, ideally within an hour of the stock market opening at 9:30am (EST). and if they achieve profits, they will happen in anywhere from a few minutes to several hours of the same day. If your trades are profitable you can take off the rest of the week, or come back again the next day to try another trade.

For those who aren't early risers or want another opportunity through the same trading day, 0-DTE Options can be entered at various times of the trading day.

Because you are only trading the S&P 500 Index (SPX or the XSP mini Options) it is set up differently than other stock Options where you enter into weekly contracts or monthly contracts.

When I first started trading with Ernie, the S&P Index (SPX) only traded on Mondays, Wednesdays, and Fridays. But in the last couple of years, the Chicago Board of Options Exchange (CBOE) added Tuesdays and Thursdays to the SPX trading days. Now, you can enter a completely new trade every day or any day.

Trading the S&P Index (SPX and XSP mini Options) has major advantages over other stocks for a trade like this.

1. The SPX is cash settled at the end of the day and there are no stock assignments.
2. The S&P 500 presents more stability in the market. Because it is an index of the top 500 companies in America, a whopping 80% of the market is represented. In the event one stock in the Index goes down it doesn't have a great effect on the rest of the Index's value. Therefore there is more stability and less volatility.

3. Because the SPX represents the top performers in the Country, there tends to be decent movement on a daily basis and therefore presents greater opportunities for profit on a short timed trade like the 0DTE. Because of the type of Option strategy that Ernie uses, traders can take advantage of the very expensive prices of the SPX while not having to invest much. This equates to low investment for potentially very high gains. The XSP mini Options contracts cost half the price and deliver half the gains or losses, but for those on a budget they can be a great alternative to be able to place more trades for less money. Although the prices for Ernie's Option strategies are pretty affordable even with small accounts.
4. The SPX has high liquidity which is important to enter and exit trades quickly and at the prices you want.
5. For those concerned about capital gains taxes, any gains made from trading the SPX are not taxed as long term capital gains. They are subject to the tax 60/40 rule which means that anything traded on the SPX will have lower capital gains taxes.

What's really great about 0-DTE Option plays, are that the risks to rewards on the trades are Asymmetrical like the Credit Spreads, but in reverse. This means that the risk is very low and the rewards can be very high. Not all trades are profitable and you might find that the majority are losses, but they are small losses in comparison to the potentially large wins. And you can usually control your losses, so the cost of the trade can usually be recovered, at least in part throughout the trading day. So if you learn this strategy and keep with it, you can definitely be very profitable. You also have a chance of getting out of most bad trades with at least part of your original investment if not all.

What is an Asymmetric Strategy?

An asymmetric strategy is one where the risk you take in a trade differs greatly from the potential profit you can earn. He calls this the risk to reward ratio.

Most Options strategies like credit or debit spreads are asymmetric in a difficult to manage direction, where the risk is larger than the reward. That simply isn't a good approach to risk management. Statistically while using spreads may bring moderate profits, over time you will have a losing trade that can completely wipe out all of the profit from your previous trades.

Ernie's 0-DTE strategy takes these negative ratios and inverts them so that the reward is much larger than the risk. This makes all the difference in the world to the trader by increasing the chances for a positive outcome, reducing their anxiety and elevating their level of confidence with superior performance. Yes, as I've said before, you may have some losing trades, but when a winning trade comes along the reward for the small risk associated with the trade will more than make-up for previous losses.

Ernie's concept is relatively simple.

1. All trades are made with the S&P Index (SPX and the mini ES). The S&P tracks the S and P 500 index which is not only a stable index but is the benchmark of the entire market sentiment. So instead of trading any one stock Ernie only trades the SPX and the ES mini.
2. Since there is no single stock, there is no need for fundamental analysis and instead of using most technical indicators, Ernie uses a tool the Wall Street corporate investors and institutional traders have always used called Volume Profile. Before the advent of computers and technical analysis an investor

would call their broker or have a ticker tape machine that would spit out the name of a stock, its current trading price, percentage of change up or down and the Volume sold. Whereas most technical indicators give a look back in time at a stock or index with price and time, the Volume Profile gives a live and running indication of the volume of stocks sold at different price levels. Why is this important? Because the largest institutional traders are the ones who influence the market movements. And if you can see at what exact price points they are buying as well as the volume that they are buying, you can have a good indication of where the markets might go.
3. Ernie only uses one type of Option for his 0-dte trades called an OTM (Out of The Money) Long Butterfly Spread. The Butterfly, or Long Fly as it is also called, is basically a Debit Spread with a Credit Spread on top of it sharing a common short leg.
4. He is out of the trade or several trades the same day, often well before the close of the trading day.

Ernie's system trades Options on the 0-DTE — the expiration date — in order to collect or profit from this rapidly decaying premium. And this combined with an asymmetric strategy that provides small risk with large potential returns.

Why 0-DTE?

The other reason to trade 0-DTE Options is the strategy's incredible versatility in varying market conditions.

The last day of expiration is a special case that presents a significant edge, allowing traders to take a small risk for potentially large profits while spending a very short time in the market.

While you could trade 0-DTE Options with any asset type, Ernie's 0-DTE strategy chooses Options on the S&P 500 for specific reasons that give us an incredible edge.

The strategy is to open a position (trade) before expiration, hold it until you've collected the desired premium (assuming the price is within the profit zone of your strategy), then exit the position, or allow it to expire to collect the maximum amount of profit.

0-DTE uses Volume Profile to help determine where price movement may go.

Volume Profile is no ordinary tool—it's the key to unlocking the secrets of the market's memory. Like scars etched in the fabric of time, trading events leave lasting impressions, guiding future price movements. With Volume Profile, we can visually represent trading volume distributed across different price levels, revealing significant liquidity and free price movement areas.

Market memory is the idea that market behavior tends to repeat over time. In the context of volume profiles, analysing long-term volume profiles can help identify specific market structures. These structures represent areas of difference in market liquidity and are crucial for understanding future price movements.

Volume Profile is an advanced indicator that shows how trades are distributed by price so given a candlestick or a bar chart with the price scale on the vertical axis, each tick of the scale will contain a horizontal bar showing the number of trades that occurred at that price

The horizontal bars will show which prices or range of prices were valued by the market and which prices were not valued.

The horizontal bars look to be grouped into what looks like a map tilted 90° showing a profile of hills and valleys.

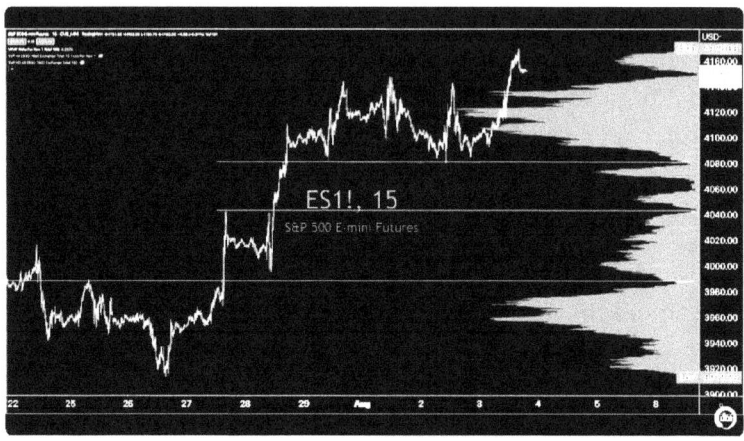

The hills are called high-value nodes, or HVN and the valleys are called volume wells.

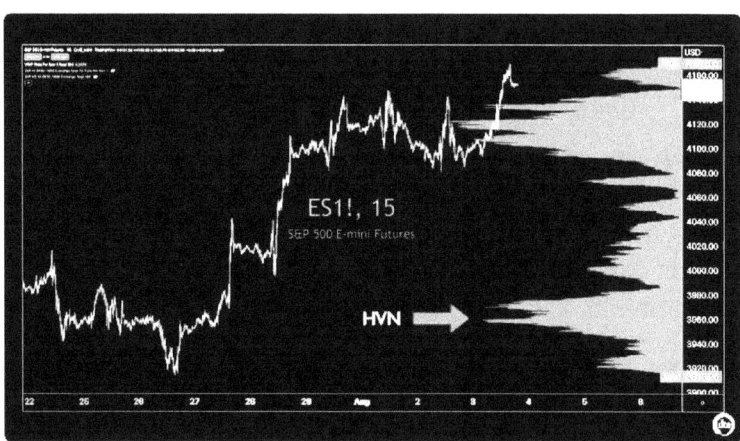

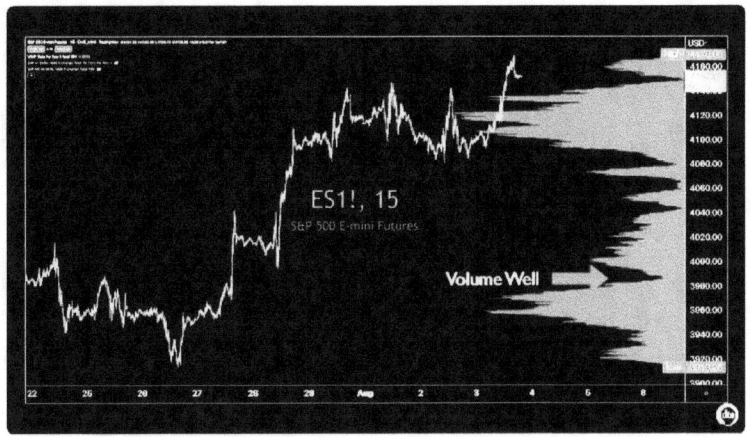

The bigger the HVN the more the market valued those prices.

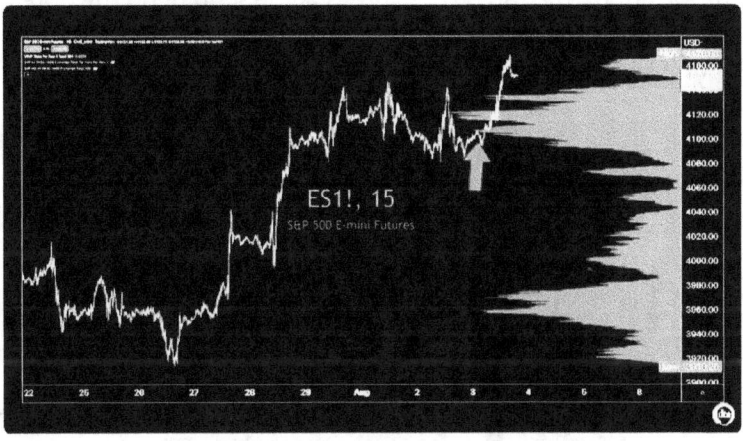

Volume wells are the opposite of HVN's, and they look completely valueless due to the apparent lack of interest by the market.

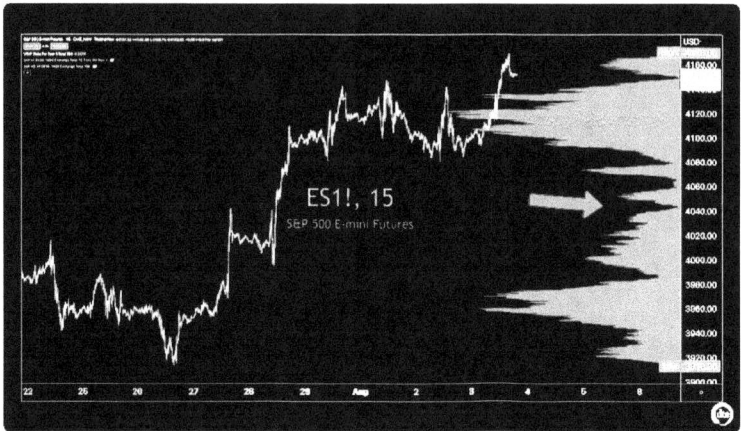

Now, both HVN's and volume wells have extremes which are important to the trader. The HVN's highest point on the note is called the point of control or POC. It doesn't really control anything that's just the name.

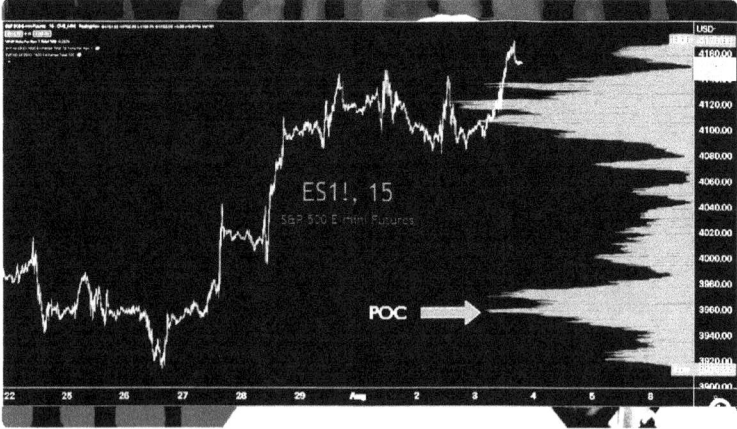

The lowest point on the volume well is called the Low Value Node, or the LVN. Sometimes there can be more than one LVN where certain prices seem to be ignored by the market all of these low points are significant to the trader.

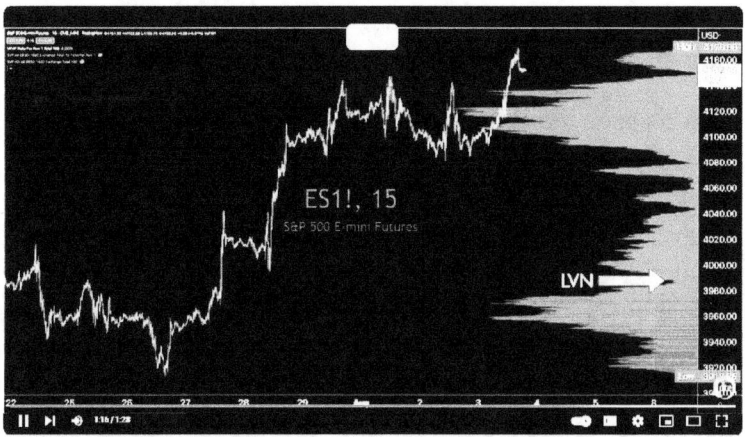

High Volume nodes are contiguous price levels that have accumulated significantly more volume than others. They indicate a volume concentration over a range of prices and provide information about market structure. Low-Volume Nodes, on the other hand, are areas between High Volume Nodes with curiously low volume levels. Traders should look for distinct levels within low-volume nodes called Low Volume Levels (LVLs).

By drawing lines at levels representing abrupt changes in volume, such as the edges of volume nodes and LVLs, traders can uncover market structure on long-term charts. This information helps predict future price movements and build trading strategies based on market structure. Price often finds support or resistance when encountering these lines.

When the price moves from a long-term volume node to a low-volume node, it transitions from an area of high liquidity to a place of low liquidity. This transition can accelerate price movement as the price seeks out new levels of liquidity or value. If the price encounters an LVL before reaching another volume node, it may temporarily pause or get rejected and return to the volume node. Understanding these price reactions helps identify trading opportunities and manage risk.

You can liken the movement of Price from a High Volume Node through a Volume Well to get to the next High Volume Node as if you were driving from Los Angeles to Las Vegas through the Mojave desert. You can think of the cities along the way of Los Angeles; Victorville; Barstow; Baker; Primm and then Las Vegas. Traveling in between these towns, both small and large, you have to travel for some time in the desert. While you are in the cities you might hang around for a little while, stop for gas or a snack or a rest stop, but once you are on your way you'll probably be traveling as fast as you can to get to the next city, where you might slow down again and even stop for a short time.

Price traveling up and down on the SPX is very similar. The High Volume Nodes and hills attract prices. As the Price starts to move, it tends to move very quickly as it is attracted to the next High Volume Node. So, on the chart we want to accentuate the Nodes and set lines to show us the Points Of Control of the High Value Nodes, as well as the lines that define the hills from the wells.

All of these lines are created from the bigger and more inclusive profile going back at least a year. Because of that concept we spoke of before, which is Market Memory. The Volume Profile is extended way out so that it accentuates the size of the nodes and the valleys here because it's important so that you can very clearly see where the edges of the abrupt changes in volume. Those are the inflection points in the market and those are the points that you have to identify.

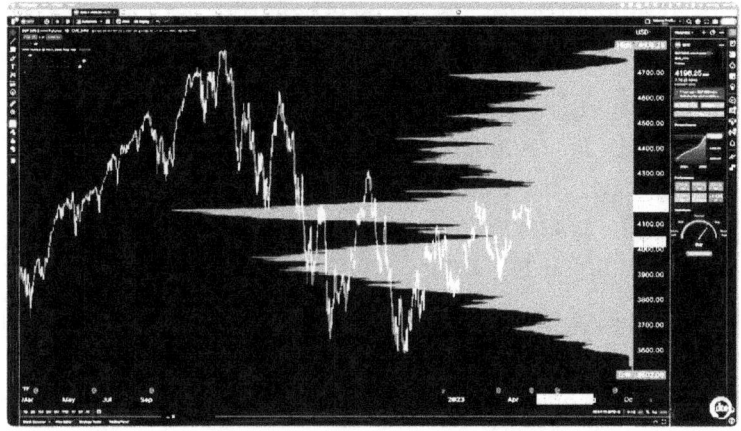

When you zoom in you can see those lines see where those abrupt changes are and that's what's going to be providing your real-time, support and resistance, and your liquid and illiquid zones and also give you a great insight to the potential behavior of price as it traverses.

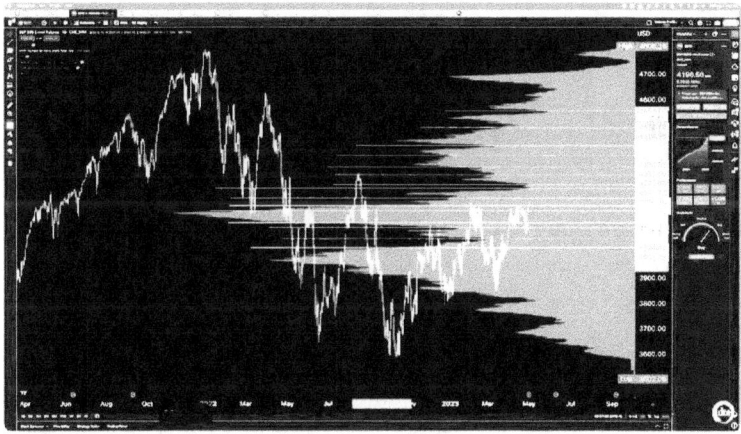

That allows you to create scenarios in your trading, so you can come up with a number of different scenarios a Bullish, a Bearish and maybe one that is sort of consolidating or whatever and the lines that we're going to draw are going to directly impact how you're going to set up your trades so that's the power of Volume Profile.

So, the first thing you do is set up your profile correctly and extend it far enough out that it's accentuated and exaggerated. This way, you can really see where the Nodes are, the lines of distinction between them, and exactly where Volume changes toward the Wells.

Understanding market memory and utilizing volume profiles can significantly improve your technical analysis skills and trading strategies. By identifying market structure and analysing price reactions at volume nodes and LVLs, you gain a deeper understanding of market behavior and make more informed trading decisions. Following a well-defined routine, we can optimize our decision-making process, adapt to market changes, and stay ahead of the game.

Options Premium Collection Strategies

Ernie's 0-DTE uses premium collection strategies, which are multi-leg strategies. The preferred strategy is the Long Butterfly also known as a Long Fly.

This OTM (Out of The Money) Butterfly is a uniquely designed Options strategy that is central to your quest to become a consistently profitable trader. It includes considerations for entering a trade and how to manage the risk-to-reward ratio based on market conditions and personal risk tolerance.

The OTM (Out of The Money) Long Butterfly strategy, also known as the "Classic Fly," is a specialized Options strategy involving the simultaneous execution of three different Options contracts. All components of this strategy are placed OTM (Out of The Money), providing you with a highly tailored trading approach.

The Classic Fly consists of two short Options contracts at the same strike price, flanked by two long Options contracts. One of these long contracts is placed below the shorts and the other above, at an equidistant width from the short contracts.

This highly adaptable strategy allows us to take advantage of market volatility and directional movements while also maintaining a high level of risk control.

The construction of the OTM (Out of The Money) Long Butterfly strategy is guided by what we refer to as the '10% debit rule'. According to this rule, the debit (or cost) of our butterfly trade should not exceed 10% of the width of the spread. For instance, if we have a butterfly spread that is 30 points wide, we should aim to enter the trade for a debit of $3 or less, which is 10% of the spread's width.

This approach enables us to achieve our desired minimum risk-to-reward ratio of 1:9. We aim for a potential profit of $9 for every dollar risked.

A 30-wide Call Butterfly placed far OTM (Out of The Money) such that the debit is below 10% of the width of the fly.

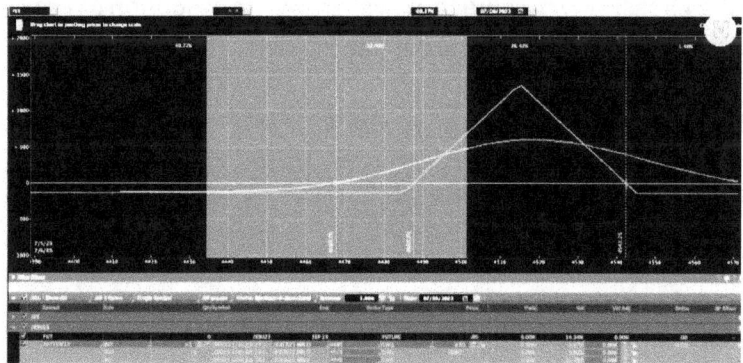

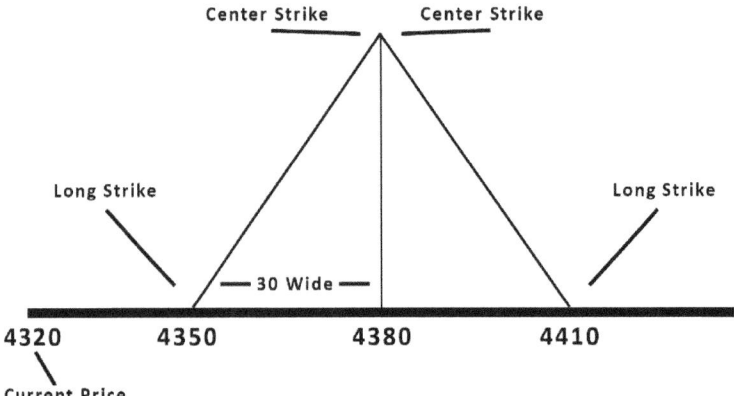

In the above drawing a 30 wide OTM (Out of The Money) Call Butterfly is set between 4350 and 4410. The width of 30 is measured from the point of the first Long Strike at 4320 to the Center Strike of 4380. If the actual price of the SPX increases, you would start to see your greatest profit under the Profit Tent. Once the SPX Price has entered the Profit Tent at 4350, your profit will increase up to the Center Strike. After the Center Strike, you will continue to see profit, but at a lower amount until the SPX moves out of the tent.

The Classic Fly is a directional strategy; its execution depends on our market outlook. If bullish, we employ call Options and position the butterfly spread above the current market price. Conversely, if our stance is bearish, we use put Options and place the spread below the market price.

Adhering to the Classic Fly principles aligns with our foundational trading philosophies, prioritizing capital preservation, asymmetric reward, a process-driven approach, and an appreciation for randomness. This strategy's unique risk/reward structure ensures that we can pursue substantial gains while strictly limiting potential losses.

Ernie's strategy does not seek to predict exact price movements with the Classic Fly. Instead, he teaches you to use your understanding of market volatility and your expertise in risk management to make a series of well-informed decisions to achieve consistent profitability over time.

Trade Entry

Each morning, we begin by determining the market trend using a simple moving average (SMA). If the price is above the SMA, we consider the trend bullish and prepare to enter a long call butterfly. If the price is below the SMA, we see the trend as bearish and look to enter a long put butterfly. Once the trend is clear, we wait for a countertrend move (a pullback or bounce) into a key market structure level derived from the volume profile. When the market shows signs of resuming the trend from that level, we open our butterfly trade, keeping risk low and aligning the structure with the day's dominant trend.

Risk-to-Reward

The OTM (Out of The Money) Butterfly strategy allows us to explore different risk-to-reward ratios and trade widths at entry, allowing us to find the most capital-efficient trade for the day. For example, a risk-to-reward ratio as high as 1:18 might be achievable in certain market conditions.

Profit Management

Profit management is central to the OTM (Out of The Money) Butterfly strategy. This is where we make our hold or fold decisions, optimizing the maximum profit opportunity for the given trading day.

The profit management framework is three-dimensional and operates based on 'when,' 'where,' and 'what':

- **When:** This refers to the time of the trading day. Our decision-making process shifts as we move through the morning session, afternoon session, and near the close. Each phase of the trading day presents its unique opportunities and challenges.

- **Where:** This aspect looks at the price's position relative to the real-time profit and loss (P&L) and the at-expiration P&L of the strategy. We analyze whether the price is at break-even points or if it has entered into Zone 1, 2, or 3 of the Butterfly spread.

- **What:** The third dimension pertains to the underlying market structure and price action. Understanding these nuances can provide vital information about the market's potential direction, enabling us to react accordingly.

Remember, you're not attempting to predict market moves but to manage the probabilities. Given the context of the three dimensions, your aim is to exit the strategy when and where you believe your maximum profit-making opportunity is for that trading day. This dynamic approach to profit management leverages your asymmetric risk-to-reward to work in our favor.

Real-World Example

The market is highly volatile today. Your experience tells you that wider butterflies perform better in such conditions. So, you enter a trade with a wider butterfly spread, maintaining a debit that is around 10% of the Fly's width. As a result, you have initiated a trade with a risk-to-reward ratio of 1:12, still preserving your original risk.

Ernie's 0-DTE uses an Inversion of Risk strategy. That means the asymmetric risk is in our favor, not against like other strategies. Risk is managed through the benefit of low cost of the strategy. This way you can spend your efforts managing profits, not managing risk.

Your win rate will be higher and your return on capital is an order of magnitude higher. That means you never sweat a trade, there's zero anxiety. And probably most significantly, you get world-class support and coaching from Ernie personally.

Attitude is Everything

Trading this 0-DTE strategy promotes zero anxiety and high confidence in traders who follow it. Nothing is more important to a trader's mental state than their ability to maintain discipline.

The service is focused on coaching and mentoring so that each and every member is given the attention they need to become successful. Ernie knows you're there to learn the strategy and the mindset, so he enables that.

His alerts demonstrate the strategy, not the central feature of the service, even though his alerts provide far greater and more consistent profit opportunities than the other services.

Strategy Performance

- Win Rate- 45-55%, varies by volatility regime
- Returns- Avg > 150-200% of risk taken
- Risk per trade - $50-$350
- Break down of returns:
    - 75% of returns are 25-250% of risk capital
    - 20% of returns are 250-450% of risk capital

- 10% of returns are > 450% of risk capital, max return was 1500%
- Breakdown of losses, 45-55% of trades result in a loss
  - 100% result in max loss. Ernie does not manage losses.

What is also great about Ernie's 0DTE service is its complete transparency

All trades are posted in Discord, prior to the admin taking a position in the reference account.

After the position is entered, a screenshot of the admin's trading account is posted in Discord.

After it is filled, screenshots are posted, showing the fill event and the current Profit and Loss.

Support Services in a trading program make all of the difference to becoming a successful trader and Ernie Varitimos provides all support personally.

Mentoring and Coaching

Every person is entitled to personalized attention. If the question or need is general in nature, it's preferable to do it on one of our Discord channels.

But if you want a Zoom session or live stream on Discord, no problem, just ask. At the end of each week, he hosts a webinar on Sundays at 1 p.m. Eastern. Every member is invited.

At the end of each month, he conducts a Retrospective of the previous month's trades and execution of his trading 0 DTE Options campaign plan. This is held via live stream, on the last Sunday of the month at 1 p.m. Eastern time. you will be notified in advance by email and an @everyone announcement in the Discord.

For further information you can find hundreds of videos that Ernie has posted about the 0-DTE Program.

Any questions about his 0-DTE Program? Feel free to contact Ernie, send an email, or give him a call.

https://go.0-dte.com/application/?n=forbes

How to Deal with the Day Trading Rule With 0-DTE

In 2001 the Financial Industry Regulatory Authority created the Pattern Day Trading Rule to protect novice investors and Trading Brokers from major losses in securities.

The PDT Rule simply says that if your account has below $25,000 you are restricted from Day Trading. Day Trading occurs when you open an order and then close it again in a single trading day. In other words, if you buy a Stock or Option and you sell the same Stock or Option in the same trading day it is considered a Day Trade.

You are allowed to buy a Stock or Option at the very end of a trading day and then sell it as soon as the market opens the next day. The Day Trading Rule only applies to buying and selling the same Stock or Option in the very same day.

So the question is, how to you trade 0-DTE if you have a small account (in this case a small account is any amount under $25,000)? Ernie Varitimos has a way to trade his 0-DTE strategies without breaking the PDT Rule. This is called a Box Order. Basically you open the trade by buying a Long Butterfly and when it gets to a point during the day when you want to lock in your profits for the day, you create a second completely opposite order that essentially zeroes out both orders.

In the example in the last section on the 0-DTE Strategy I presented an example of a trade on the SPX (S&P 500 Index).

In this example, the S&P 500 was currently trading at 4320. Ernie then placed a 30 wide, Long Call Butterfly with the first long leg at 4350, then the short legs at 4380 and the second long leg at 4410. The Fly would start to profit above 4350 and would reach maximum profit at 4380. If the price goes above 4380 the trade is still profitable, but the profit declines again until the price gets to 4410, after which there would be no profit in the trade unless the price of the SPX comes back down into the profit tent again before the end of the trading day.

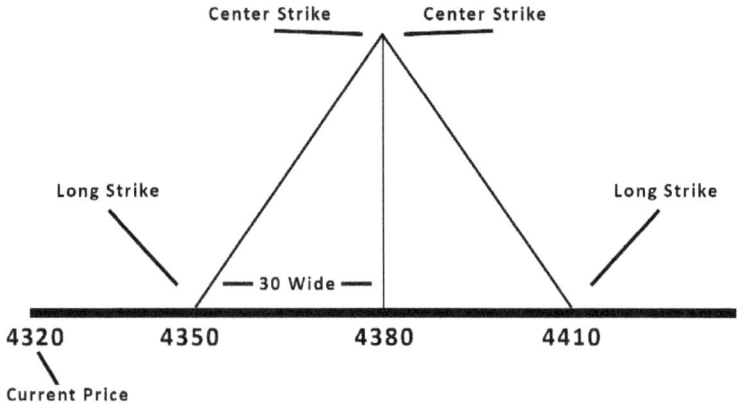

So in this example, let's assume that you have reached the maximum profit at the Center Strike of 4380 and you want to lock your profit in and get out of the trade. Normally you would close the trade by selling your long strikes and buying back your short strikes. But doing this would constitute day trading since you are closing the exact same positions you opened the same day.

There are two ways to avoid the PDT Rule.

1. You can try to place the order for a Butterfly or a Batman (Iron Butterfly) at the end of the previous trading day. The problem here is that the SPX may make stronger moves in after hour trading and pre market trading the next day so that when the Stock Market officially opens for you the next morning, the current SPX may be in a different direction.
2. Instead of placing a closing order for your Butterfly you can create a new opposite order which will avoid the PDT Rule. To do this you would create opposite legs. The Long Legs would become Short Legs and the Short Legs would become Long Legs in the Spread and it would be ordered as a Put if your original Fly was a Call. Or if your original Fly was a Put, then the new order would be a Call.

In this above example let see how the original order was placed and how you could create a Box order to lock in your profit and get out of the trade without breaking any of the Day Trading Rules.

Originally here was the order you would have placed on this trade

Buy 1 of the 4350 Call Options
Sell 2 of the 4380 Call Options
Buy 1 of the 4410 Call Options

This is the Long Butterfly that you see in the illustration above.

Normally, to close this trade you would sell to close as follows

Sell 1 of the 4350 Call Options
Buy 2 of the 4380 Call Options
Sell 1 of the 4410 Call Options

In the closing order above you are simply closing out all of the Legs that you originally ordered which would constitute as a Day Trade if you did this in the same trading day.

To avoid the PDT Rule you could box this trade and you would create a new completely opposite order as follows.

Sell 1 of the 4410 Put Options
Buy 2 of the 4380 Put Options
Sell 1 of the 4350 Put Options

Ernie has a great explanation of this on his 0-DTE YouTube channel https://youtube.com/@0dte

How To Defeat the Pattern Day Trade Rule with SPX and 0-DTE

https://youtube.com/watch?v=QeteriBXJKI&t=11s

-

Small Accounts

The truth is that the more money you have, the more money you can make. And this presents a challenge for people with small accounts. There are numerous strategies in the stock Option world that can build up small accounts very quickly but many are higher risk and this book specifically focuses on safe trading.

But the subject of how to invest with small accounts is such an important one, that I do have another book called, Small Trading Stock Options Profitably with Small Accounts. As with the Level 2 Trading book, you can either wait for the revision this year or find a copy through a used book seller.

It doesn't mean that if you have a small account you can't start trading successfully and build up your account in a relatively short amount of time. There are a couple of really safe, low-risk methods of using Option to do this. One of which I have already discussed and that's Ernie Varitimos's 0-DTE Program. The Butterfly Spreads that he teaches you to place can be entered for as little as $25.00, although most higher probability spreads are in the neighborhood of $150 to $200.

Another I'll show you are Iron Condors using the SPY which is an ETF (Exchange-Traded Fund) connected to the S&P 500. While Ernie Varitimos uses the SPX which is the actual S&P 500 Index, the Iron Condor strategy I am going to show you uses the SPY. It does have some risk, but if managed properly you can build up your account.

First, let me explain the differences between the SPX and the SPY and why they are perfect for different strategies. Today, as I write this the Standard and Poor's 500 Index, or the SPX is 5,817.20. Because it's an Index you can't actually buy or sell individual shares, which is good in a way because your Options trades can't be assigned if they go against you. But it's bad in that it is expensive. I don't know many active traders who could afford a share and since Options require 100 shares the SPX would be unaffordable to most individual traders. Luckily though you can afford to trade some Option strategies against the SPX so the 0-DTE works well for this.

The SPY which is the symbol for the SPDR S&P 500 ETF Trust or sometimes called the Spider or Spyder for short.

The SPDR stands for the Standard and Poor's Depositary Receipt, which Thompson Reuters Practical Law describes as a negotiable instrument certifying that a stated number of securities have been deposited with the depositary (usually a bank) issuing the certificate.

The SPDR , or SPY as it is known as the symbol on the NYSE (New York Stock Exchange) is an Exchange Traded Fund which is similar to a Mutual Fund except that ETF's can be traded throughout the day on a stock exchange. The SPDR tracks the S&P 500 Index but the shares can be traded close to one tenth of the price. So, in this case, as of today, the SPX (S&P Index) is trading at 5,871.21 and the SPY (SPDR S&P 500 Trust ETF) is trading at $587.00. While this is still expensive for a stock, the lower price point makes it perfect for some Options strategies.

Another great plus with the SPY is that like the SPX, contracts are traded every day, Monday through Friday. So, you could place a new trade each day if you want to, accumulating profits throughout the week.

Option Spreads are good for conserving capital because although you are buying shares of SPY, you are also selling shares, so the profit is capped but also the maximum loss.

Remember that an Options Spread has multiple legs. The leg closest to the actual stock price always has a higher price because there is a greater probability that the stock price will move to the first leg than the farther second leg. The farther you go away from the actual stock price, the less the probability and the less expensive.

Knowing this, if the closest leg to the actual stock price is where you buy Options and then the father leg is where you sell the Options, it will cost you money to get into the trade. This is because the price of the closer leg is greater so you will be paying more for the Options, than you receive for the further out sale of the Options. This is a Debit Spread.

However if your closest leg to the actual stock price is where you sell the Options and the further point is where you buy them back, then it becomes a Credit Spreads and you will be paid upfront premium as soon as you open the trade. This is because the closest leg is more expensive and the money you bring in from selling the Option is greater than the money you will pay to buy the Options back.

So, for the SPY let's take a look at today's chart to see if we can sell an Iron Condor. An Iron Condor is a Call Credit Spread on top of the current stock price and a Put Credit Spread underneath the current stock price.

The SPY trade Price right now is 587.00. If you go to the Options Chain for today you want to go up close enough from the 587.00 to sell a Call Credit Spread for a decent enough premium but at the same time you want to have your spread far enough away to keep the stock price from coming into your spread. So, let's try to sell the 590 and then buy back Option at 591. This Credit Spread would give you an upfront premium payment of $.18 or $18.00 per contract.

Now we can sell a Put Credit Spread below the current price. Let's say we're going to sell the 583 and we'll try to by the Options back at 582. For this Put Credit Spread you'll receive a premium credit of $.13 or $13.00 per contract.

The total premium you receive on this Iron Condor trade is $18.00 + $13.00 = $31.00 and your maximum loss could be $69.00 ($100.00 - $31.00 upfront premium).

Most Spread traders sell a number of Options contracts at a time so it would be normal to sell 5 contracts of each Spread or even 10 contracts of each Spread.

If you sold 5 contracts the total premium you receive on this Iron Condor trade is $90.00 ($18.00 x 5) + $65.00 ($13.00 x 5) = $155.00 and your maximum loss could be $345.00 ($500.00 - $155.00 upfront premium).

If you sold 10 contracts the total premium you receive on this Iron Condor trade is $180.00 ($18.00 x 10) + $130.00 ($13.00 x 10) = $310.00 and your maximum loss could be $690.00 ($1,000.00 - $310.00 upfront premium).

As long at the stock price of the SPY stays between 591 and 583 you have a profit of $310.00 for the day. And again, since the SPY trades a new series of contracts each trading day, if you are careful you could build up your small account quickly.

Credit Spreads and Iron Condors can be traded on 1,000's of different stocks and ETF's but the SPY is a favorite because of high liquidity and because of the low volatility of the fund. This makes the Iron Condor a highly successful strategy for account building.

Again, please remember my warning about closing out short contracts (contracts you sell) by the end of the expiration day. At the end of the trading day your protective contracts (the ones you buy) expire, while the contracts you sell can still be exercised, putting you in a potentially dangerous position if the stock price makes a sharp move after hours.

How To Find The Best Stocks To Trade

You can certainly use the resources I've listed in this book to place trades and most likely be very successful but happens if your favorite resource disappears? What happens if Ernie Zerenner goes back to work at Hewlett Packard to develop another fused Silica Column? What if Tommy Brown on Marco Island, Florida decides to take up golf and becomes a fanatic? What happens If Ernie Varitimos retires taking his wife and Rhodesian Ridgebacks to Santorini to eat flaming cheese and drink Ouzo on the edge of the Mediterranean all day?

It's always a good practice to learn how and be able to research and select your own stocks and Options. And it's much easier than you think.

There are online publications which have all of the information you need on a daily basis such as The Wall Street Journal; Investor's Business Daily; Barron's, and Market Watch. In addition, there are several free websites which help you search and scan thousands of stocks reliably to find filtered results for any strategy you would wish to use, whether it's just buying stocks to trade or hold, or the various Options strategies.

In time and with practice you can become proficient at selecting the best relevant stocks for your trades. In the meantime, I can help you narrow down the stock universe for you.

1. First, you have to make sure that the stock you are choosing is Optionable. There are thousands of stocks that allow you to sell Options but not all stocks are on board. Also some stocks sell only Monthly Expiration Options Contracts and some sell both the Monthly and the Weekly Contracts.

2. For the Option strategies in this book (Not the Credit or Debit Spreads) it would be best if you start by sticking to stocks within the S&P 500.

    The S&P 500 is a weighted index of the top capitalized public companies in the United States. This means that the stocks are highly liquid which is important if you want to get into a trade at your desired price quickly, and more importantly, you'll have a better chance to be able to get out of a trade quickly. Liquidity can also mean higher Implied Volatility for Options trading which is great if you are selling Options. There are earnings requirements for stocks in the S&P 500 including a positive sum of the most recent four consecutive quarters of trailing earnings and positive earnings for its most recent quarter. So, another important factor in selling Covered Calls with a stock that is in the S&P 500 is that in the event your stock price drops, the price should be able to recover in the market in a shorter period of time. I have a section following this chapter on stocks in the S&P 500.

3. You should choose a stock that sells for $20.00 per share or higher. Below $20.00, the stocks are often not stable and can be easily manipulated by the market. Also, stocks priced below $20.00 generally don't offer a lot of premium for the Options Contracts.

4. Market Capitalization should be at least 500 Million. Market Capitalization is the total value of a publicly traded company through it's out-standing shares. It helps investors determine the size and value of a company.

5. Annual Revenue of at least $250 million. While Revenue isn't a total indication of how well a company is doing, companies with very high Annual Revenue

tend to be more stable. But at the same time, high costs may impact profit, which is why Earnings information is also important to investors.

6. Earnings Per Share (EPS) for the next 5 years should be over 10%. Earnings Per Share is an important metric as it measures profitability of a company on a Per Share basis. This allows investors to help determine what their return on investment might be over time. So how does the market estimate projected earnings for the future? By polling the large collective of Stock Analysts.

7. Earnings Per Share (EPS) Quarter by Quarter should be Positive. In this case instead of looking at projected estimates of growth, the Earnings Per Share are calculated Quarter by Quarter for the last Quarter; year; several years or however long the investor wants to calculate.

8. Sales Quarter by Quarter should be Positive. Sales and Revenue can be analyzed Quarter by Quarter to make sure there is growth in sales and revenue.

9. Current Volume and Average Volume should be over 500 thousand. Volume traded is the number of shares traded within a trading day. So it is important to have decent volume when you enter a trade and it is good to know that the stock averages decent volume over a period of time.

10. Above the 20 Day; 50 Day, and 200 Day Simple Moving Averages (20 SMA; 50 SMA, and 200 SMA). Moving averages are simply the average stock price over a specified period of time. If a stock is above its 200 Day Simple Moving Average it means that its price is currently above a long-term price. If in addition, the Stock's price is also above its 50 Day or 20 Day Simple Moving Average it might indicate an uptrend which is

what you want to see if are trading Covered Call Options and Cash-Secure Puts.
11. Avoid the Company's Earning Date close to your contract's expiration. Earning dates can be very volatile. If you are trading Weekly Options, it's best to avoid trading on weeks with your company's earnings date. Some traders like the increased volatility that accompanies Earnings Dates, and some Options traders like the increased Implied Volatility around Earnings Dates, but trading too close to the Earnings Date can be dangerous.
12. Avoid Ex Dividend Dates. Some stocks pay stockholder dividends. There is a date before a dividend is paid out to investors by the company called the Ex Dividend Date. If you are selling Options on a company that pays dividends and your Option is In The Money (ITM) on an Ex Dividend Date you may get assigned early, as the buyer of your Option may want to own the stocks so they can get paid the dividend. The best rule of thumb is to make sure that if you are selling an Option on a company that pays dividends, don't have a contract open during the Ex Dividend date.

There are several websites that offer free information on stocks and companies, as well as scanners that will help you select the best companies and Options contracts to trade. The results shouldn't be used as your final trade choices. You still should examine the charts and the companies performance.

Free Websites with Stock and Option Scanners

Barchart.com

Barchart.com's basic services are completely free to use just by signing up for a free account. The free services available are all you really need to research basic Options trades.

When you get to the Barcharts.com Home Page you have a choice of reviewing main categories such as Major Market Overview including the S&P 500; NASDAQ 100; DOW Industrials; the U.S. Dollar' Treasury Notes (T-Notes); Crude Oil; Gold; Silver; Natural Gas, and even commodities including Wheat; Corn; Soybeans; Orange Juice; Coffee; Sugar, and Cocoa.

There are other categories such as Market Leaders; Most Popular EFT's; Unusual Option Activity, and the Top 100 Stocks

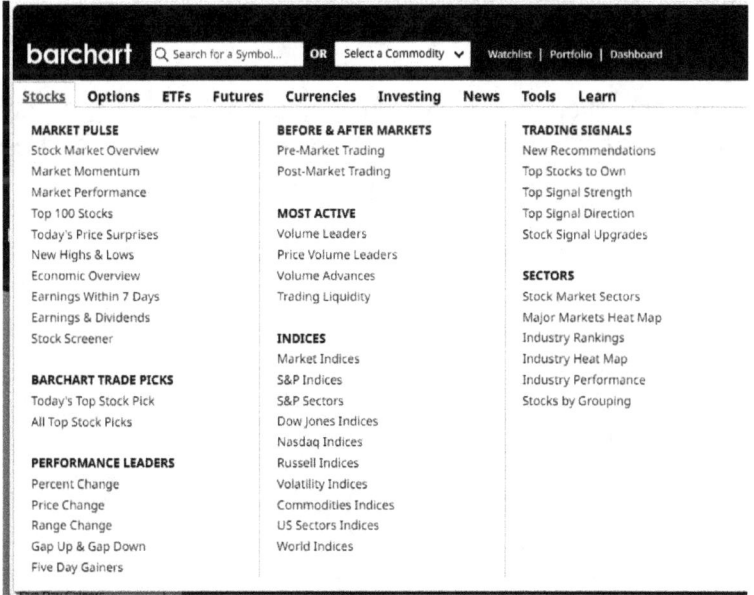

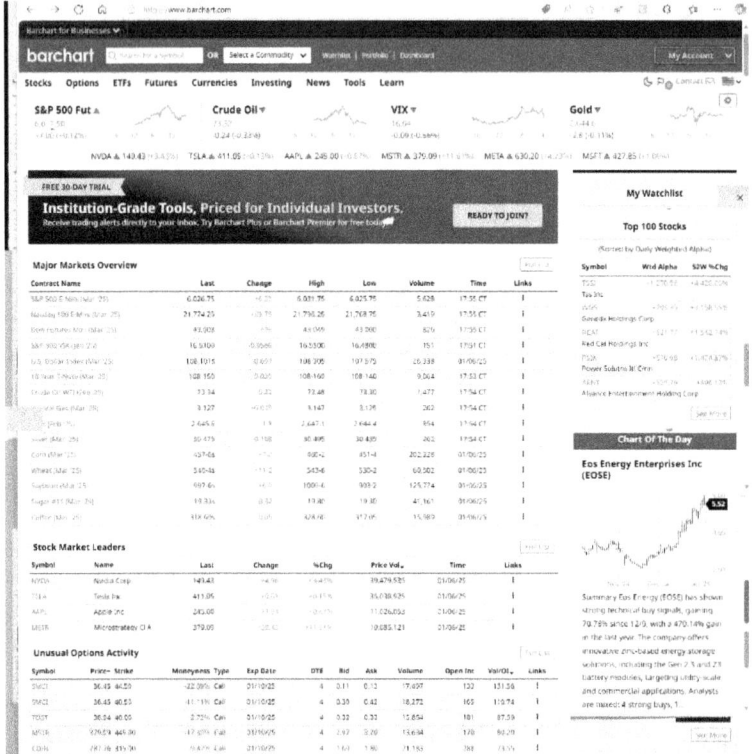

But if you click on Options on the horizontal menu you are taken to a complete list of the most popular Options strategies that barcharts.com provides information on.

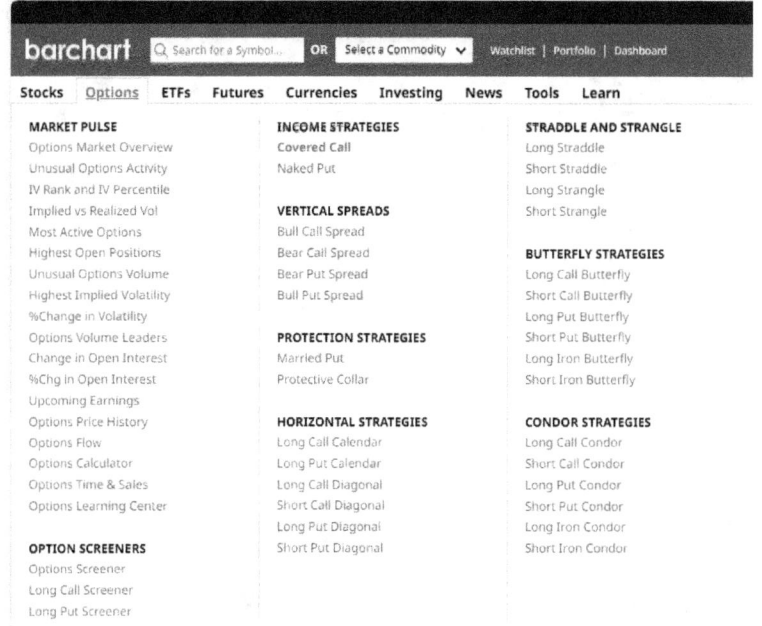

Selecting any one of the popular Options strategies will take you to a Screener for that Option.

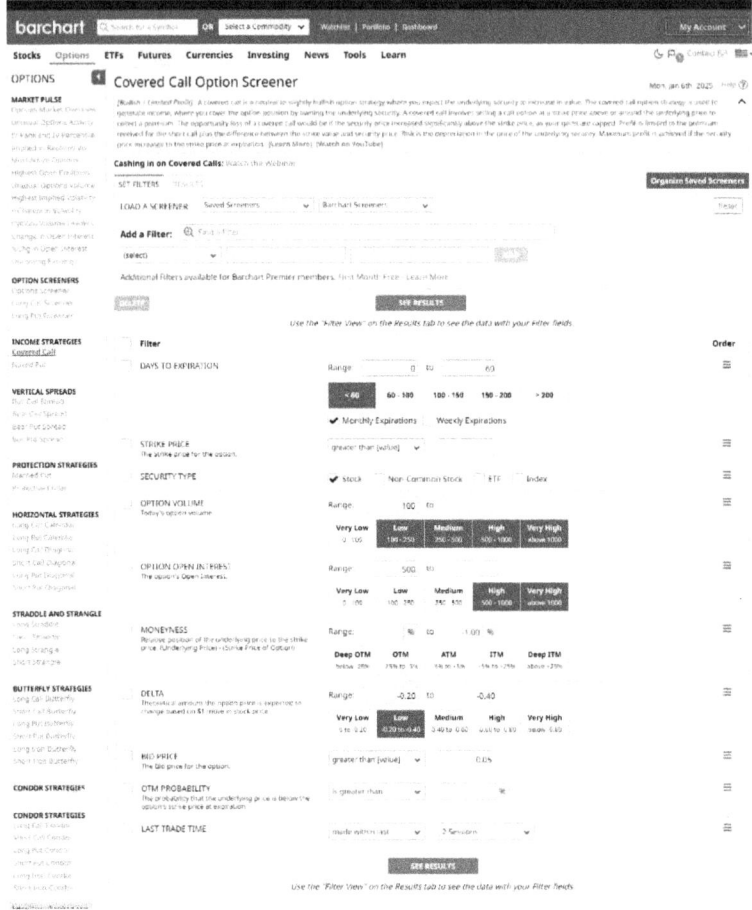

Above you see a screenshot of the Covered Call Screener. Once you fill in your filtering criteria you can save the screener.

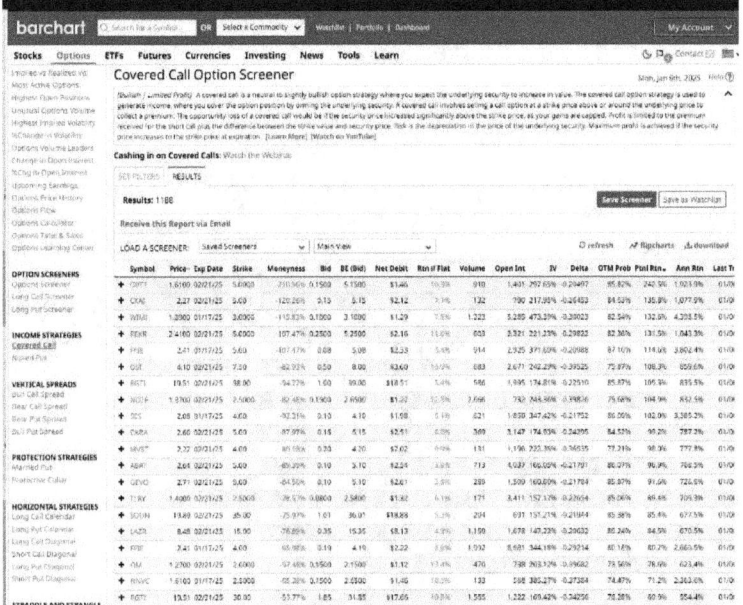

Results of the Screener are presented in a grid as seen above.

Scanning With Finviz

Finviz.com is another source for valuable information on stocks; ETF's; Indexes; Options and other equities.

Searching on Finviz.com is free and they have a very robust and thorough screener.

When you get to the finviz.com Homepage it can be a little overwhelming, but it is actually very well organized.

The first thing you notice are charts for the three top indexes, the Dow, NASDAQ and the S&P 500. Underneath are rows of the most active stocks of the day. And to the right is a heatmap. Red squares represent stocks with a loss and Green square represent stocks that are gaining. The square size is determined by the market cap size of the company.

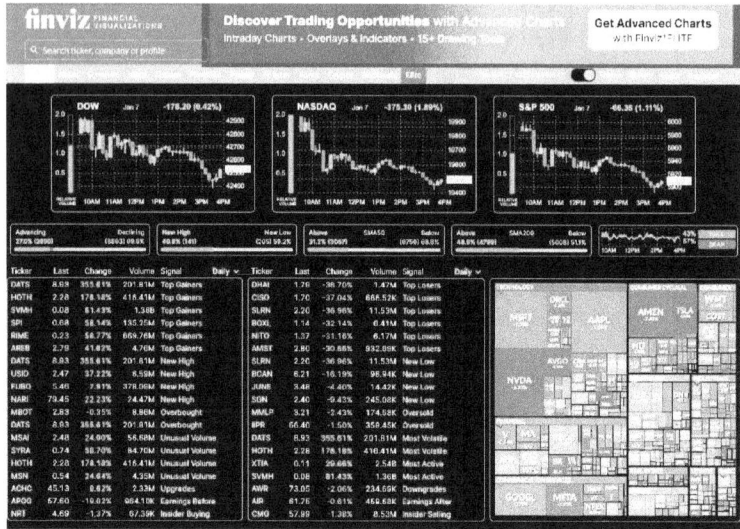

When you click on the Screener Tab on the menu row at the top, you get the Home Screener Page.

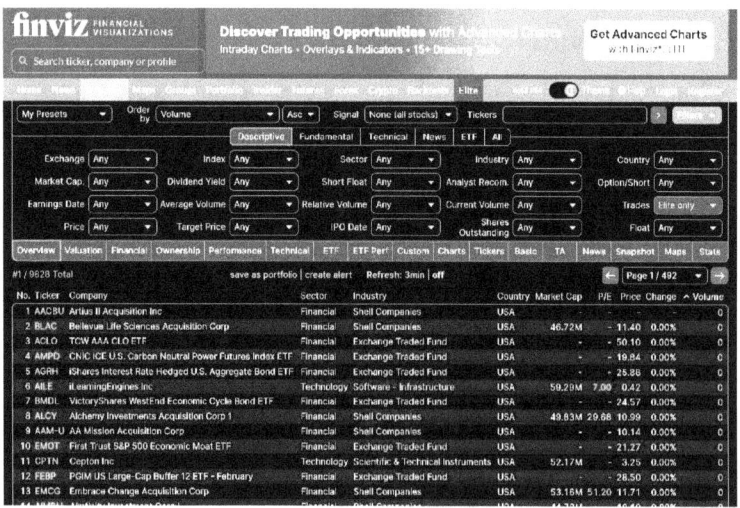

We haven't put any filters or given any criteria for a search yet so it shows a total of 9828 stocks listed. On the Home

Screener Page there are tabs for different types of filtering criteria including Descriptive; Fundamental and Technical. So, on Descriptive let's select a few filters.

We want our Market Cap to be over $100 million; The Price of the Stock to be over $20.00 per share; Average Volume to be over 500 thousand Shares; Current Volume to be over 500 thousand Shares; We want to search stocks on companies in the U.S.A., and we want to make sure these stocks are Optionable.

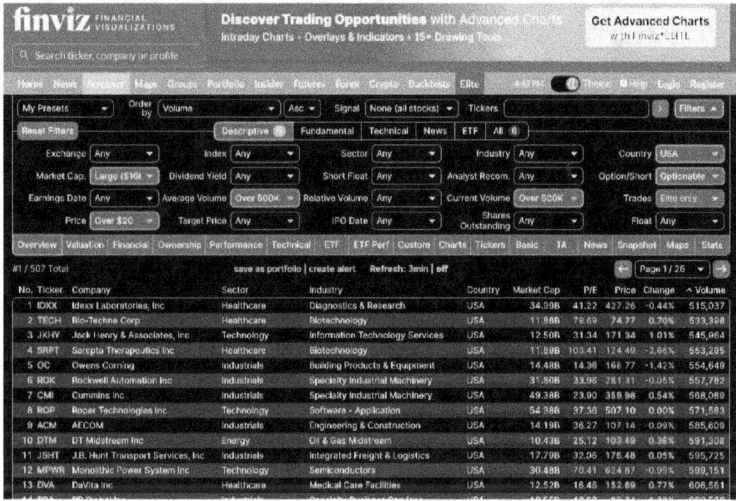

Just from these few filters, we have gone from a universe of 9828 stocks listed to 507 stocks. So if we go from the Descriptive Filters to the next tab of Fundamental we can narrow our selection down a bit further.

On the Fundamental screen we can select Earnings Per Share (EPS) growth over the next five years projected to be over 10%; the Earnings Per Share (EPS) growth this year to be Positive; Earnings Per Share (EPS) growth Quarter Over Quarter to be Over 10%; the Earnings Per Share (EPS) growth next year to be Positive, and the Sale growth Quarter Over Quarter to be over 10%. Now we have narrowed our universe of stocks from 507 down to 87 stocks.

We could possibly stop there and bring up the charts of all 87 stocks. In this example I didn't specify S&P 500 stocks which I could have done in the previous Descriptive Screen. But for now let's go to the Technical Tab.

Here I decided to ask for a Performance for the week of + 10%; above the 20 Day Simple Moving Average; above the 50 Day Simple Moving Average, and above the 200 Day Simple Moving Average. Maybe I'm asking for too much in this search but you can see that it narrowed down the universe of stocks that fit all of my criteria from 87 stocks to 2 stocks. Pulling up the chart of one of them I can get a feel for where this stock is going. Then I can look at the Options Chain to see of there is a Contract that will bring me the Premium I am looking for.

Another good site for basic across the board Stock and Equity Information is stockanalysis.com.

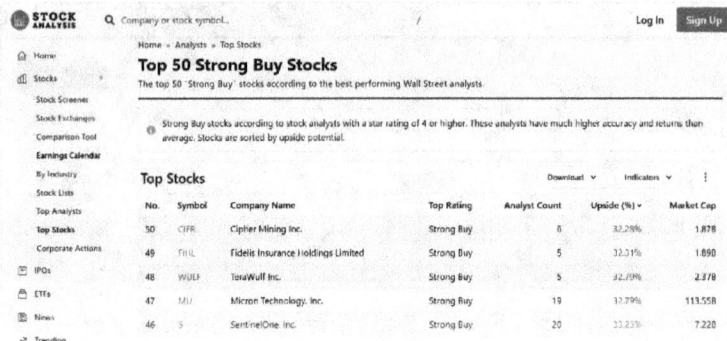

For a good take on up-to-date overall market analysis and compendium of financial news and especially news on individual companies, I like to start the morning with Yahoo Finance.

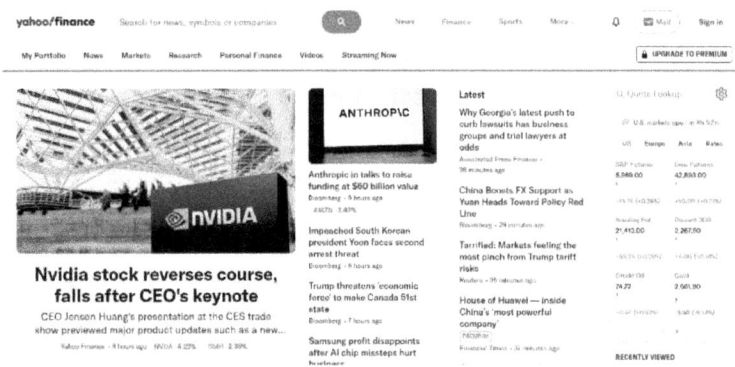

Subscription Sites

If you're going to become a regular trader, even part time, you should consider subscribing to at least the basic Stock Advisor Service from The Motley Fool. Two brothers, Tom and David Gardner started The Motley Fool in Alexandria Virginia in 1993 as a private financial investing company. In their own words, *"Our name derives from Elizabethan drama, where only the court jester (the "Fool") could tell the King the truth without getting his head lopped off. We're dedicated to educating, amusing, and enriching individuals in search of the truth."* And truth they tell. When it comes to financial markets and stock advice, their record is unbeatable. If you go to their site, www.fool.com you will find a lot of free advice and cutting-edge articles and research. The Motley Fool's Stock Advisor Service is extra and costs $99.00 per year, but it is so worth it!

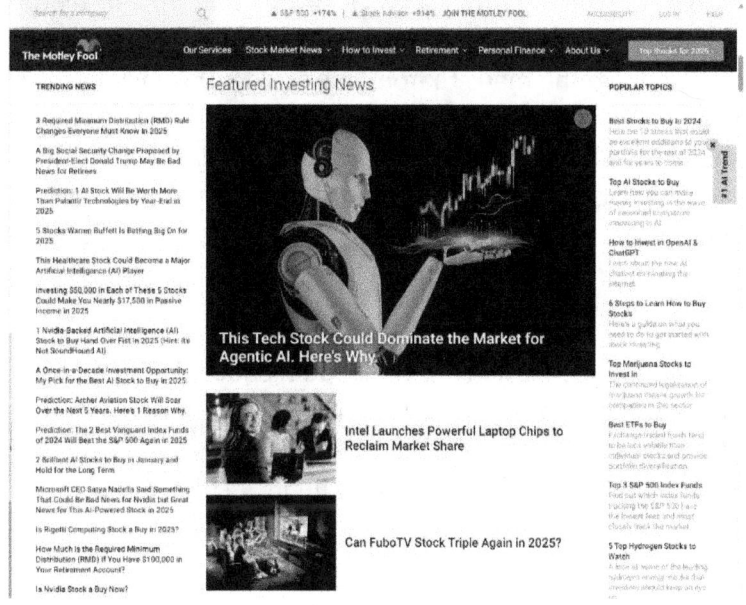

Platform News

If are using a platform such as TD Ameritrade's (Now Schwab) Think or Swim platform to trade then you have up to date news brought to you minute by minute about the market and individual companies. All you have to do is pull up a chart for any company and there is a tab marked News. Almost any article that has been published in financial publications will appear in chronological order for you to open.

Publications

Although there's nothing like picking up an actual newspaper, holding it in your hands over morning coffee and turning the pages, the great thing about having financial publications online is that they can be, and usually are updated within minutes throughout the trading day. Publications like The Wall Street Journal; MarketWatch; Barron's and The Investor's Business Daily provide a lot of insight into how the World at large affects the markets from day to day. They have a lot of insights on why the markets are behaving the way they from moment to moment and they closely examine the markets by exchange; by equity; by sector and by individual stocks. If you are going to be in the market even part time, a little bit of extra financial knowledge will definitely help make you a more profitable trader overall.

Normally subscriptions to these publications can be costly, but lately there have been a lot of incentives and special offers for those who look for them. For example I found this deal from Dow Jones, the Publisher of many financial publications.

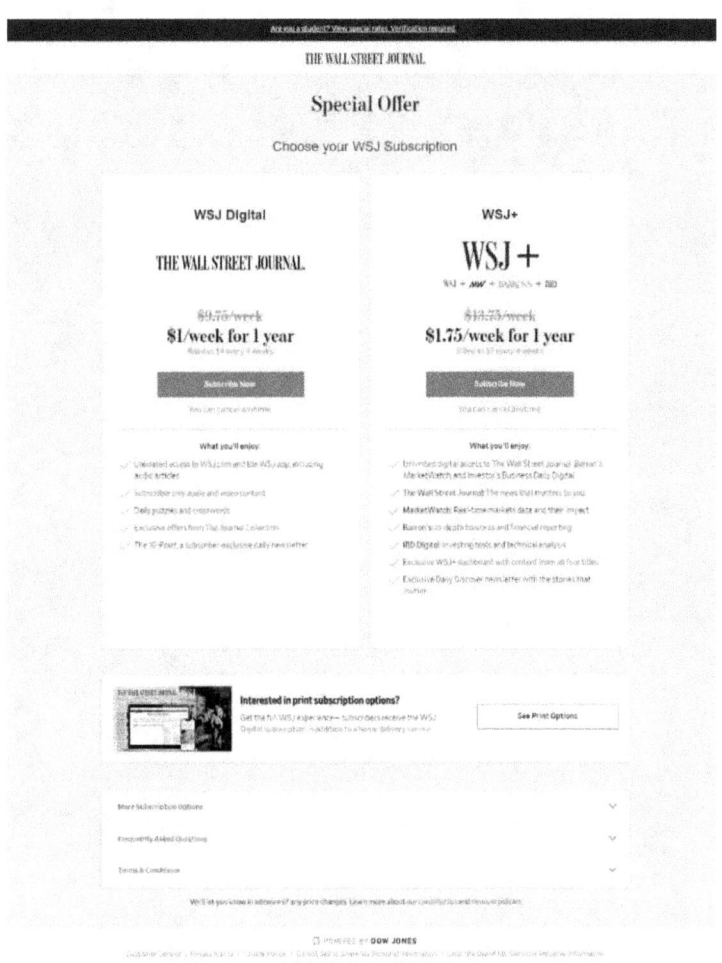

- So, for $7.00 per month I get subscriptions to The Wall Street Journal; MarketWatch; Barron's and The Investor's Business Daily. This price is good for one year and then the subscription becomes $54.99. You need to mark down the date you sign up to make sure you can cancel, and then call customer service to re-negotiate, which they should do. If you can't find this offer or think you can do better with them, their customer service number is 1-800-JOURNAL (1-800-568-7625) or Toll: 1-609-627-1351.

The Best Companies To Trade in the S&P 500

The Top Companies in the S&P 500 provide a great list of reliable candidates to trade Options. Any in the group of 500 are great companies, but I like to stick with those in the top 100 or so. I just pulled the top 25 with their current stock prices as of this writing for example. They are

    Apple (AAPL) 242.41
    Microsoft (MSFT) 423.74
    Amazon (AMZN) 223.13
    NVIDIA (NVDA) 141.90
    Alphabet (Google) Class A (GOOGL) 196.23
    Tesla (TSLA) 393.70
    Alphabet (Google) Class C (GOOG) 197.12
    Berkshire Hathaway (BRK.B) 453.91
    Meta (Facebook) Class A (META) 617.09
    UnitedHealth Group (UNH) 512.25
    Exxon Mobile (XOM) 109.38
    Eli Lilly (LLY) 773.51
    JPMorgan Chase (JPM) 244.73
    Johnson & Johnson (JNJ) 146.60
    Visa Class A (V) 312.76
    Proctor & Gamble (PG) 160.99
    Mastercard Class A (MA) 513.65
    Broad.com (AVGO) 230.90
    Home Depot (HD) 384.78
    Chevron Corporation (CVX) 149.99
    Merk (MRK) 101.32
    Abbvie (ABBV) 178.62
    Costco (COST) 917.69
    PepsiCo (PEP) 146.07
    Adobe (ADBE) 424.42

The great thing is that just because a stock might be at the top of the S&P 500, it doesn't mean it has to be an expensive stock. In the previous list of the Top 25, Costco is the most expensive stock at $917.69 per share. But the least expensive, Is Merk (MRK) currently going for $101.32

Even still when looking through the entire list of the S&P 500 the most expensive stock is NVR (NVR), a residential construction company currently at $7,971.17 per share and the least expensive stock in the S&P 500 is Amcor Plc (AMCR) a container and packaging company with a price currently at $9.52 per share.

The Best S&P 500 Company Stocks For Small Accounts

I've selected here a list of S&P 500 companies that currently have per share sales of at least $20.00 but no more than $70.00 for those who have smaller accounts and want to trade Covered Calls or Cash-Secured Puts.

Of course, stock prices change every day, many times throughout the day. So when you see the stock prices in the chart below, realize that these aren't current prices. But this will give you an idea of which stocks you might be able to trade.

Stockanalysis.com provides accurate information on 93,000+ stocks and funds, including all the companies in the S&P500 index. See stock prices, news, financials, forecasts, charts and more.

The following chart is courtesy of stockanalysis.com

No.	Symbol	Company Name	Market Cap	Stock Price
110	INTC	Intel Corporation	86.32B	20.02
233	KVUE	Kenvue Inc.	40.26B	21.00
433	KIM	Kimco Realty Corporation	14.94B	22.13
58	T	AT&T Inc.	161.13B	22.46
292	HPE	Hewlett Packard Enterprise C...	29.71B	22.59
489	APA	APA Corporation	8.81B	23.81
355	RF	Regions Financial Corporation	21.69B	23.87
277	CCL	Carnival Corporation & plc	31.30B	23.93
468	NCLH	Norwegian Cruise Line Holdin...	11.12B	25.29
494	MOS	The Mosaic Company	8.10B	25.49
383	CTRA	Coterra Energy Inc.	19.51B	26.49
447	CAG	Conagra Brands, Inc.	12.84B	26.90
410	GEN	Gen Digital Inc.	16.59B	26.93
60	PFE	Pfizer Inc.	154.31B	27.23
423	NWSA	News Corporation	15.71B	27.66
474	IPG	The Interpublic Group of Com...	10.37B	27.83
370	WY	Weyerhaeuser Company	20.26B	27.89
162	KMI	Kinder Morgan, Inc.	61.99B	27.91
325	HAL	Halliburton Company	24.64B	28.04
284	VICI	VICI Properties Inc.	30.73B	29.16
430	BAX	Baxter International Inc.	15.09B	29.55
254	KHC	The Kraft Heinz Company	36.25B	29.98

No.	Symbol	Company Name	Market Cap	Stock Price
409	HRL	Hormel Foods Corporation	16.64B	30.31
420	NWS	News Corporation	16.13B	30.47
226	KDP	Keurig Dr Pepper Inc.	41.87B	30.87
372	CNP	CenterPoint Energy, Inc.	20.13B	30.89
385	INVH	Invitation Homes Inc.	19.17B	31.19
337	PPL	PPL Corporation	23.54B	31.91
163	CSX	CSX Corporation	61.94B	32.12
501	BWA	BorgWarner Inc.	7.07B	32.31
380	LUV	Southwest Airlines Co.	19.65B	32.76
502	CZR	Caesars Entertainment, Inc.	7.02B	33.04
493	MTCH	Match Group, Inc.	8.32B	33.15
478	MGM	MGM Resorts International	9.91B	33.29
274	HPQ	HP Inc.	31.79B	33.90
341	DVN	Devon Energy Corporation	22.99B	35.00
363	SMCI	Super Micro Computer, Inc.	20.79B	35.50
407	NI	NiSource Inc.	16.65B	35.68
403	BF.B	Brown-Forman Corporation	17.11B	36.20
480	LKQ	LKQ Corporation	9.53B	36.66
68	CMCSA	Comcast Corporation	142.33B	37.20
247	EXC	Exelon Corporation	37.90B	37.72
449	JNPR	Juniper Networks, Inc.	12.65B	38.20
216	NEM	Newmont Corporation	43.43B	38.44
176	FCX	Freeport-McMoRan Inc.	55.70B	38.77
56	VZ	Verizon Communications Inc.	165.21B	39.25
344	FE	FirstEnergy Corp.	22.65B	39.30

No.	Symbol	Company Name	Market Cap	Stock Price
177	SLB	Schlumberger Limited	55.60B	39.38
308	DOW	Dow Inc.	27.84B	39.63
459	CPB	The Campbell's Company	12.02B	40.33
428	UDR	UDR, Inc.	15.41B	41.35
300	FITB	Fifth Third Bancorp	28.80B	42.96
218	BKR	Baker Hughes Company	43.03B	43.49
169	TFC	Truist Financial Corporation	58.48B	44.05
377	CFG	Citizens Financial Group, Inc.	19.77B	44.86
172	CVS	CVS Health Corporation	57.41B	45.62
349	ROL	Rollins, Inc.	22.23B	45.91
23	BAC	Bank of America Corporation	353.80B	46.11
352	FOX	Fox Corporation	22.06B	46.79
392	MRNA	Moderna, Inc.	18.09B	47.01
302	EQT	EQT Corporation	28.70B	48.10
228	GLW	Corning Incorporated	41.31B	48.25
134	USB	U.S. Bancorp	76.18B	48.84
345	FOXA	Fox Corporation	22.50B	49.26
256	LVS	Las Vegas Sands Corp.	36.02B	49.69
335	ADM	Archer-Daniels-Midland Com...	23.89B	49.93
503	FMC	FMC Corporation	6.35B	50.85
198	OXY	Occidental Petroleum Corpor...	48.37B	51.55
109	MO	Altria Group, Inc.	87.70B	51.75
191	MNST	Monster Beverage Corporation	50.53B	51.96
312	SW	Smurfit Westrock Plc	26.94B	51.98
204	O	Realty Income Corporation	46.11B	52.53

No.	Symbol	Company Name	Market Cap	Stock Price ^
172	GM	General Motors Company	57.53B	52.32
204	O	Realty Income Corporation	46.12B	52.54
388	IP	International Paper Company	18.62B	53.60
302	TSCO	Tractor Supply Company	28.76B	53.85
419	BALL	Ball Corporation	16.17B	54.20
205	D	Dominion Energy, Inc.	45.55B	54.23
465	TAP	Molson Coors Beverage Com...	11.43B	55.49
377	TSN	Tyson Foods, Inc.	19.80B	55.60
151	WMB	The Williams Companies, Inc.	67.80B	55.62
184	CPRT	Copart, Inc.	54.13B	56.18
363	ES	Eversource Energy	20.61B	56.26
495	HAS	Hasbro, Inc.	7.95B	57.01
236	CTVA	Corteva, Inc.	39.28B	57.15
329	VTR	Ventas, Inc.	24.19B	57.21
435	LNT	Alliant Energy Corporation	14.72B	57.36
84	BMY	Bristol-Myers Squibb Company	116.35B	57.37
353	WRB	W. R. Berkley Corporation	21.98B	57.69
125	CMG	Chipotle Mexican Grill, Inc.	79.25B	58.12
278	MCHP	Microchip Technology Incorp...	31.32B	58.33
127	MDLZ	Mondelez International, Inc.	78.28B	58.54
223	KR	The Kroger Co.	42.58B	58.85
32	CSCO	Cisco Systems, Inc.	234.53B	58.89
444	EVRG	Evergy, Inc.	13.93B	60.55
28	KO	The Coca-Cola Company	262.00B	60.82

No.	Symbol	Company Name	Market Cap	Stock Price
237	DAL	Delta Air Lines, Inc.	39.13B	61.04
261	GIS	General Mills, Inc.	33.77B	61.15
436	APTV	Aptiv PLC	14.54B	61.87
488	LW	Lamb Weston Holdings, Inc.	8.88B	62.23
274	CNC	Centene Corporation	31.69B	62.77
287	EBAY	eBay Inc.	30.34B	63.33
310	ON	ON Semiconductor Corporati...	27.06B	63.54
344	WDC	Western Digital Corporation	22.56B	65.26
248	XEL	Xcel Energy Inc.	37.64B	65.55
381	CMS	CMS Energy Corporation	19.65B	65.76
74	UBER	Uber Technologies, Inc.	139.81B	66.40
499	CE	Celanese Corporation	7.29B	66.71
318	SYF	Synchrony Financial	26.10B	67.04
425	TPR	Tapestry, Inc.	15.50B	67.63
315	EQR	Equity Residential	26.44B	67.64
477	AOS	A. O. Smith Corporation	9.94B	68.53
164	CARR	Carrier Global Corporation	61.60B	68.66
459	SOLV	Solventum Corporation	11.98B	69.37
66	NEE	NextEra Energy, Inc.	144.88B	70.46
447	REG	Regency Centers Corporation	12.83B	70.47
58	PLTR	Palantir Technologies Inc.	160.71B	70.55
451	BXP	BXP, Inc.	12.51B	70.91
467	DAY	Dayforce Inc.	11.22B	71.16

A Final Word

I've given you an introduction to a business or side business that you control yourself. With these methods of investing in Stock Options it's like owning your own virtual casino but better. You don't have the enormous construction costs or the overhead, and best of all, your odds for profit are much higher than any casino in Las Vegas.

Many people have read this book and have found it works for them. I'm grateful for this. It is my hope and desire that many more will learn how make profits from Stock Options.

If you decide to sign up for either PowerOptions, or 0-DTE, please use these links as, I will be able to keep in touch with you to assist you. If you use these links to sign up, I will also send you a free copy of my new edition of Trading Stock Options Profitably With Small Accounts coming out this Spring. And please feel free to visit my website at www.highprobabilityoptions.com.

Power options
 https://www.poweropt.com/bforbes/
0-DTE
https://go.0-dte.com/application/?n=forbes

Additional Resources

A word of caution – As you explore the following excellent resource videos on Youtube you will eventually be bombarded with very slick but often deceptive ads about Options Trading systems and AI Software that predicts the market for you.

No AI Software can or will ever be able to predict Stock Market Price Movement. This is a purely human experience and influence. If any of these systems worked even part time, we'd all be millionaires. Be wary of some of the expensive Youtube ads

Youtube Videos

+Ernie Varitimos and 0-DTE

    www.youtube.com/@0DTE

PowerOptions

    www.youtube.com/@PowerOptions

MoneyTreeVisions

    www.youtube.com/@moneytreevisions

SMB Capital

SMB Capital is a proprietary trading firm in New York and the video tutorials provided by SMB Founder Mike Bellafiore and Seth Freudberg, Head Trader of the Options Trading Desk are easy to understand and comprehensive. They have a very friendly, comforting style of communicating Options fundamentals

    www.youtube.com/@smbcapital

Project Finance

Chris Butler started his enthusiastic Options educational series on Youtube in 2016 and has since amassed over 380,00 subscribers and over 26,000,000 views. He is joined by financial content writer who has a lot of experience, having worked for thinkorswim, TD Ameritrade and Charles Schwab. His work has appeared in the Financial Times, the Chicago Sun-Times, and The Buffalo News.

    www.youtube.com/@projectfinance

More Advanced Options Information

Option Alpha

Option Alpha was founded by Kirk Du Plessis and has a vast array of videos on different aspects of Options and Option Trading

    www.youtube.com/@OptionAlpha

Tastytrade

Tastytrade is a financial company and trading platform just for Options. They also have a substantial video library on Youtube.

    www.youtube.com/@tastytrade_

Recommended Books

  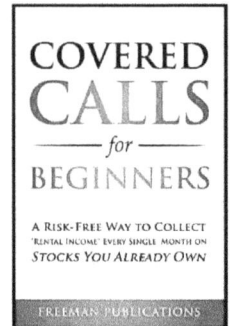

Protective Options Strategies: Married Puts and Collar Spreads by Ernie Zerenner and Michael Chupka

New Insights on Covered Call Writing by Richard Lehman and Lawrence G. McMillan

Covered Calls for Beginners by Freeman Publications

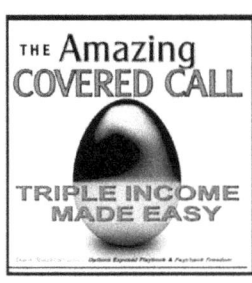  

The Amazing Covered Call by Don A. Singletary

Naked Puts: Power Strategies for Consistent Profits by Ernie Zerenner and Michael Chupka

The Wheel Strategy by Brad Finn

The Options Wheel Strategy by Freeman Publications

Options Trading Crash Course by Frank Richmond

Make Money Selling Options by Chuck McCleary

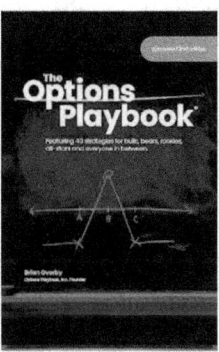

Options Trading Simplified For Beginners by Woodley Funtanilla

The Unlucky Investor's Guide To Trading Options by Julia Spina

The Options Playbook by Brian Overby

A number of years ago, I met Lee Finberg, and not only did we become good friends, but coincidentally, he had written what I consider to be the best book I've ever come across on trading low-risk Credit Spreads and Iron Condors.

Unfortunately, Lee passed away several years ago, but if you have the opportunity to get a copy of his book, it is well worth the investment. The book is expensive, but in 1 single trade after buying his book, I made more than twice what I had spent. www.safertrader.com   Another great book specifically on Iron Condors is Ernie Zerenner's book.

www.ingramcontent.com/pod-product-compliance
Lightning Source LLC
LaVergne TN
LVHW021232080526
838199LV00088B/4313